BATGIRL

BATMAN ADVENTURES

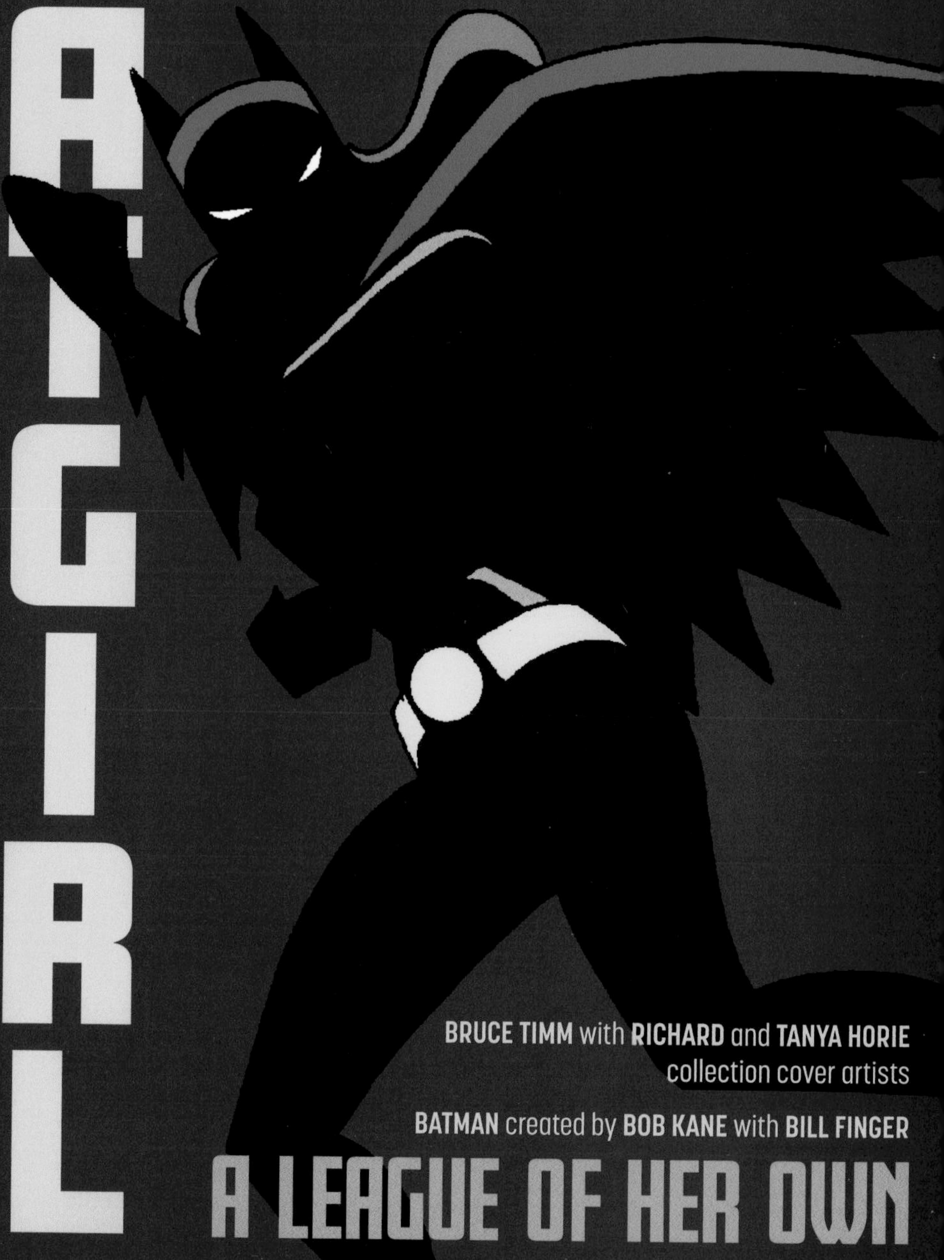

BRUCE TIMM with **RICHARD** and **TANYA HORIE**
collection cover artists

BATMAN created by **BOB KANE** with **BILL FINGER**

A LEAGUE OF HER OWN

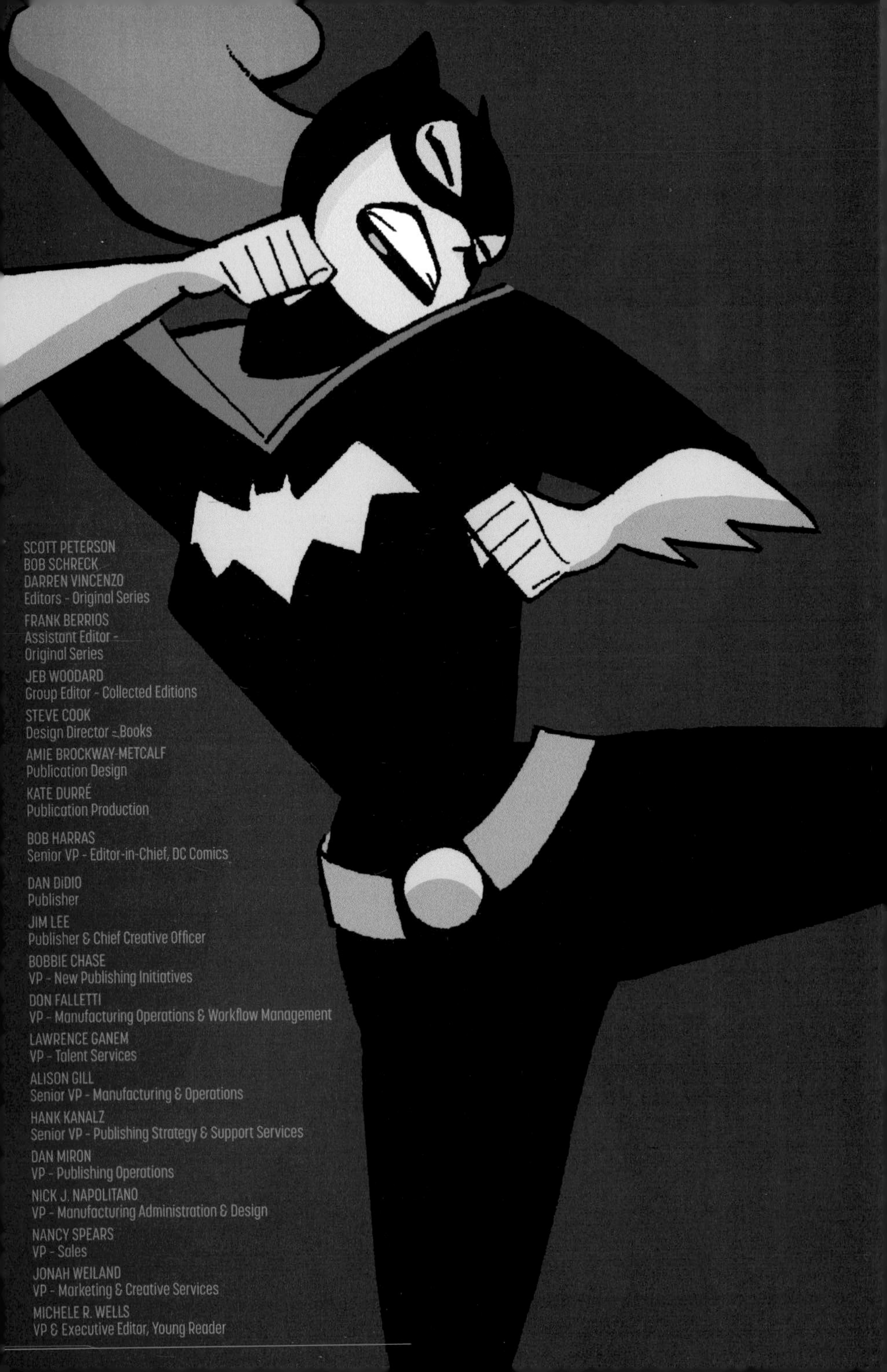

SCOTT PETERSON
BOB SCHRECK
DARREN VINCENZO
Editors - Original Series

FRANK BERRIOS
Assistant Editor - Original Series

JEB WOODARD
Group Editor - Collected Editions

STEVE COOK
Design Director - Books

AMIE BROCKWAY-METCALF
Publication Design

KATE DURRÉ
Publication Production

BOB HARRAS
Senior VP - Editor-in-Chief, DC Comics

DAN DiDIO
Publisher

JIM LEE
Publisher & Chief Creative Officer

BOBBIE CHASE
VP - New Publishing Initiatives

DON FALLETTI
VP - Manufacturing Operations & Workflow Management

LAWRENCE GANEM
VP - Talent Services

ALISON GILL
Senior VP - Manufacturing & Operations

HANK KANALZ
Senior VP - Publishing Strategy & Support Services

DAN MIRON
VP - Publishing Operations

NICK J. NAPOLITANO
VP - Manufacturing Administration & Design

NANCY SPEARS
VP - Sales

JONAH WEILAND
VP - Marketing & Creative Services

MICHELE R. WELLS
VP & Executive Editor, Young Reader

CONTENTS

ATMAN ADVENTURES: BATGIRL–A LEAGUE OF HER OWN

ublished by DC Comics. Compilation and all new material Copyright © 2020 DC Comics. All Rights
eserved. Originally published in single magazine form in *Batgirl Adventures* 1, *Batman: Gotham
dventures* 8-9, 22, 38. Copyright © 1998, 1999, 2000, 2001 DC Comics. All Rights Reserved. All
haracters, their distinctive likenesses, and related elements featured in this publication are trade-
arks of DC Comics. The stories, characters, and incidents featured in this publication are entirely
ctional. DC Comics does not read or accept unsolicited submissions of ideas, stories, or artwork.
C – a WarnerMedia Company.

C Comics, 2900 West Alameda Ave., Burbank, CA 91505
rinted by LSC Communications, Crawfordsville, IN, USA. 7/10/20. First Printing.
BN: 978-1-77950-671-9

brary of Congress Cataloging-in-Publication Data is available.

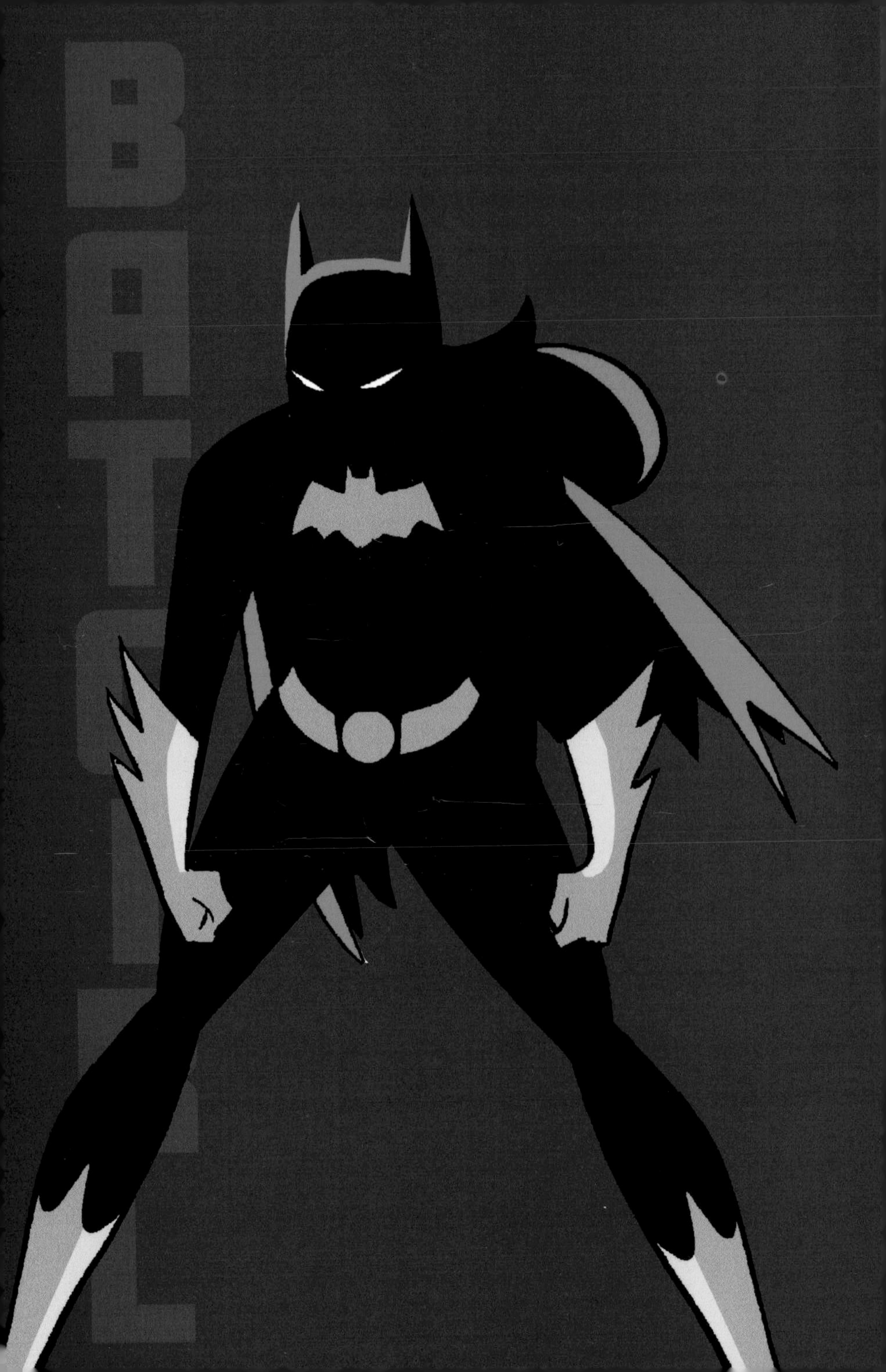

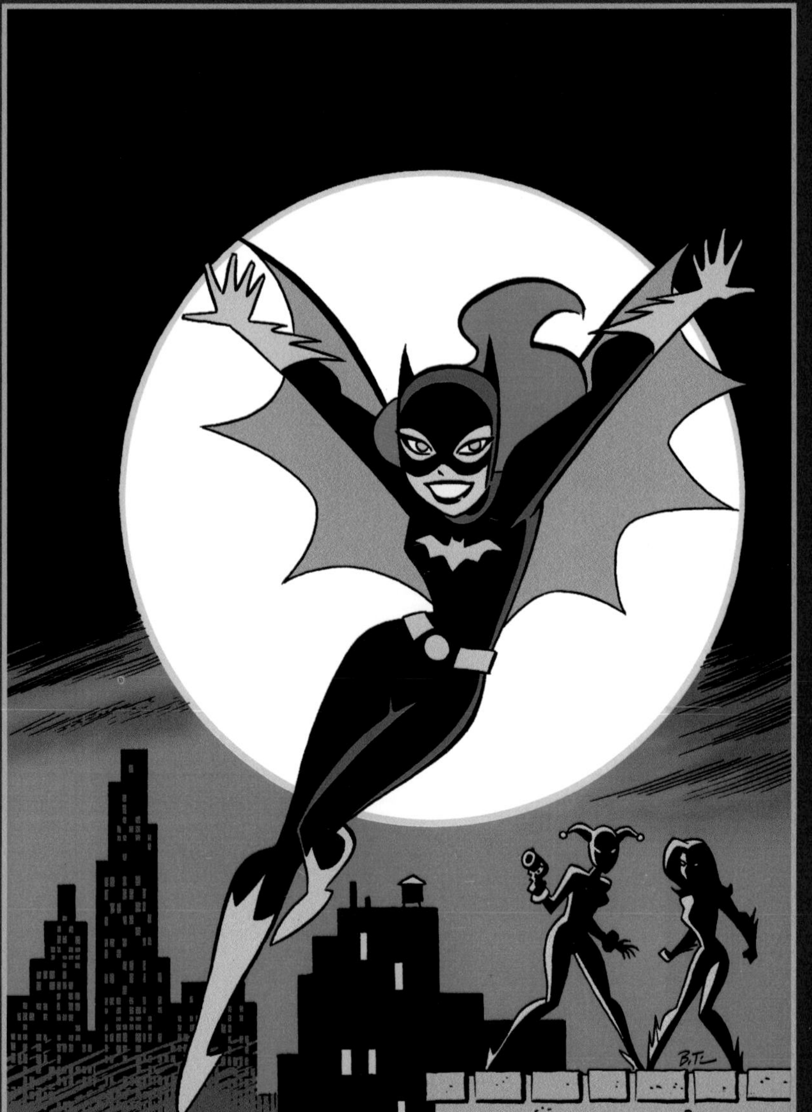
B.T.

CHAPTER 1: OY TO THE WORLD

BATGIRL

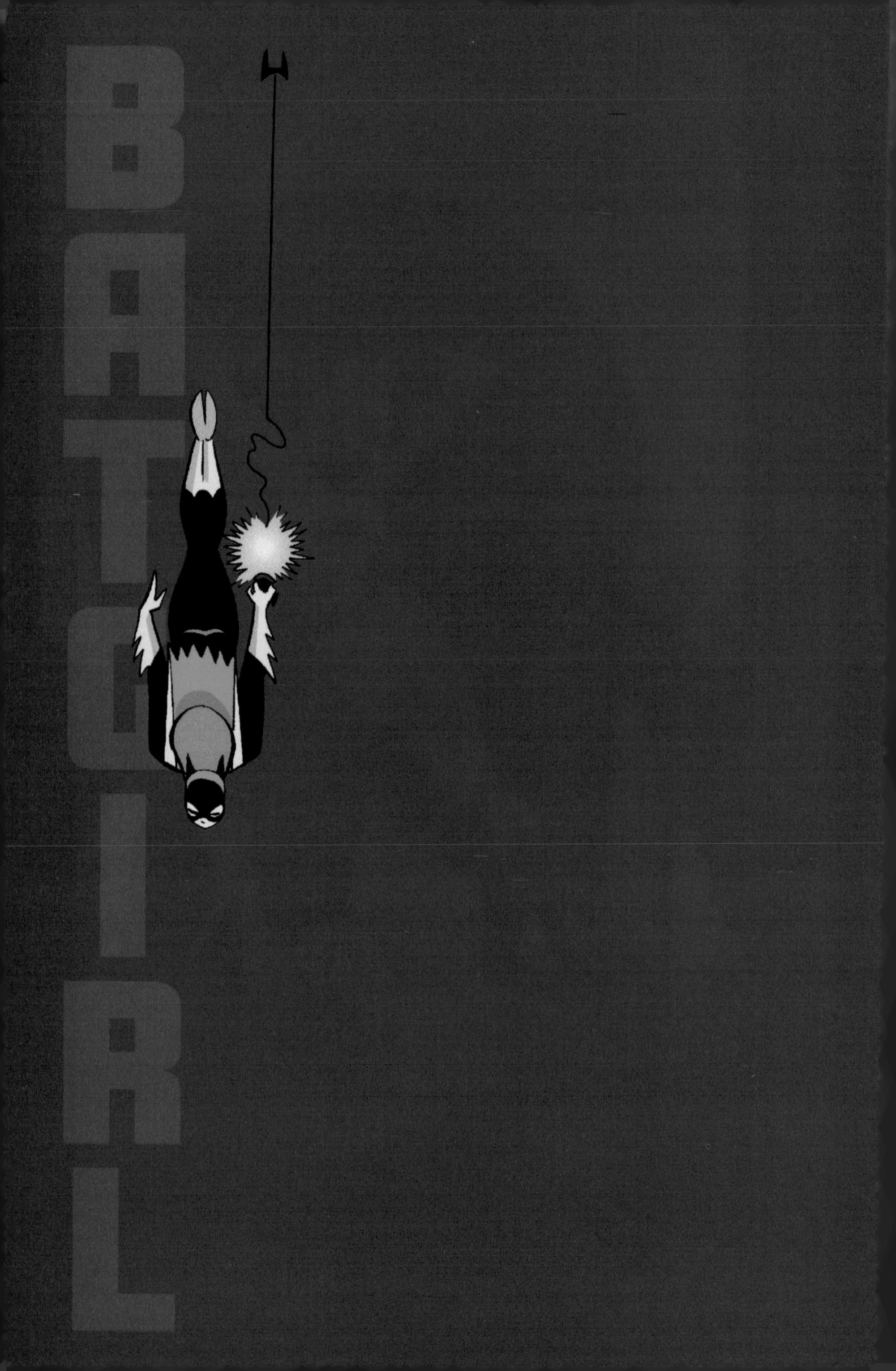
BATGIRL

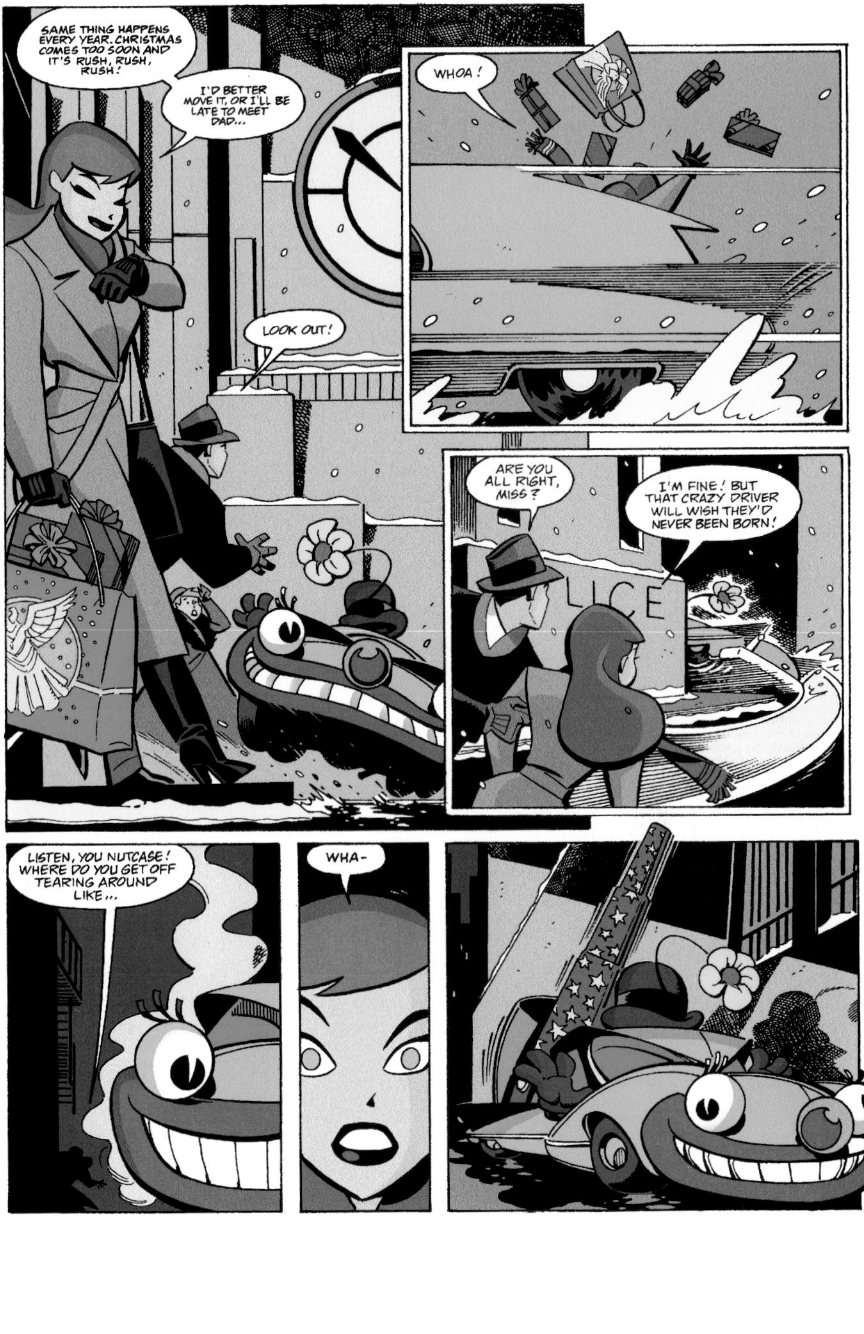
SAME THING HAPPENS EVERY YEAR. CHRISTMAS COMES TOO SOON AND IT'S RUSH, RUSH, RUSH!
I'D BETTER MOVE IT, OR I'LL BE LATE TO MEET DAD...
LOOK OUT!
WHOA!
ARE YOU ALL RIGHT, MISS?
I'M FINE! BUT THAT CRAZY DRIVER WILL WISH THEY'D NEVER BEEN BORN!
LICE
LISTEN, YOU NUTCASE! WHERE DO YOU GET OFF TEARING AROUND LIKE...
WHA-

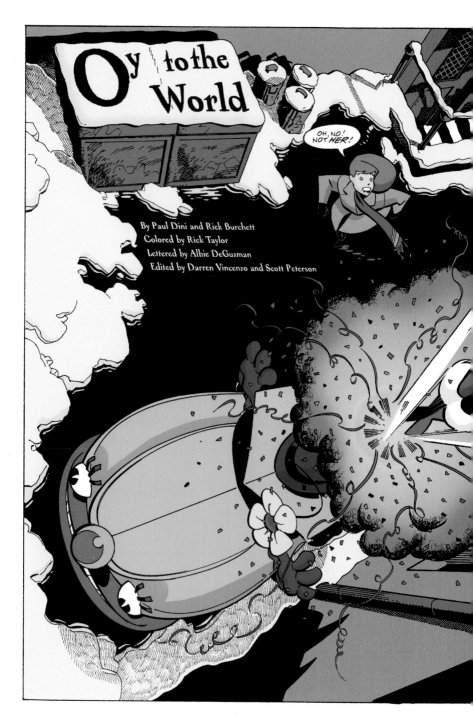

Oy to the World

OH, NO! NOT *HER!*

By Paul Dini and Rick Burchett
Colored by Rick Taylor
Lettered by Albie DeGuzman
Edited by Darren Vincenzo and Scott Peterson

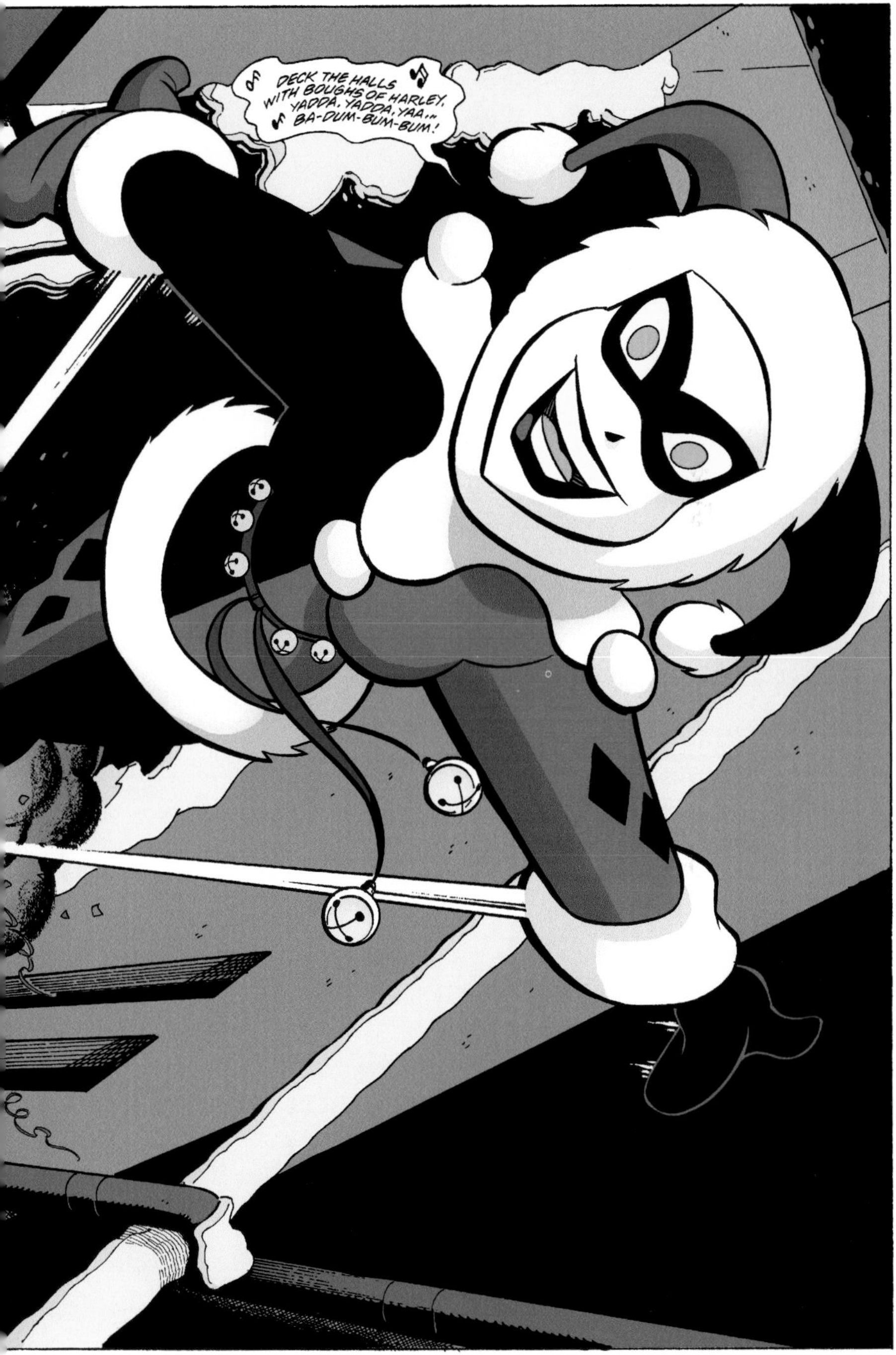
DECK THE HALLS WITH BOUGHS OF HARLEY, YADDA, YADDA, YAA... BA-DUM-BUM-BUM!

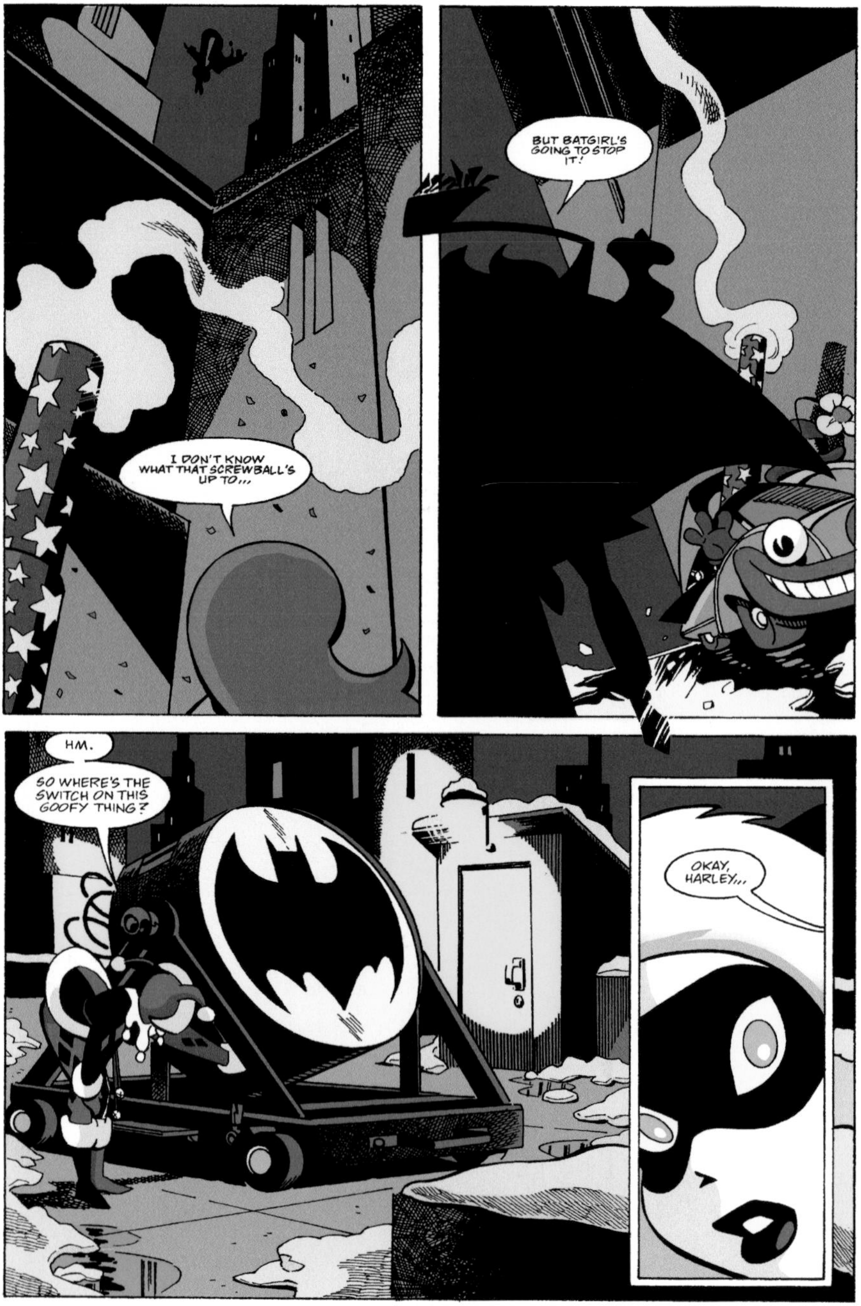
I DON'T KNOW WHAT THAT SCREWBALL'S UP TO...
BUT BATGIRL'S GOING TO STOP IT!
HM.
SO WHERE'S THE SWITCH ON THIS GOOFY THING?
OKAY, HARLEY...

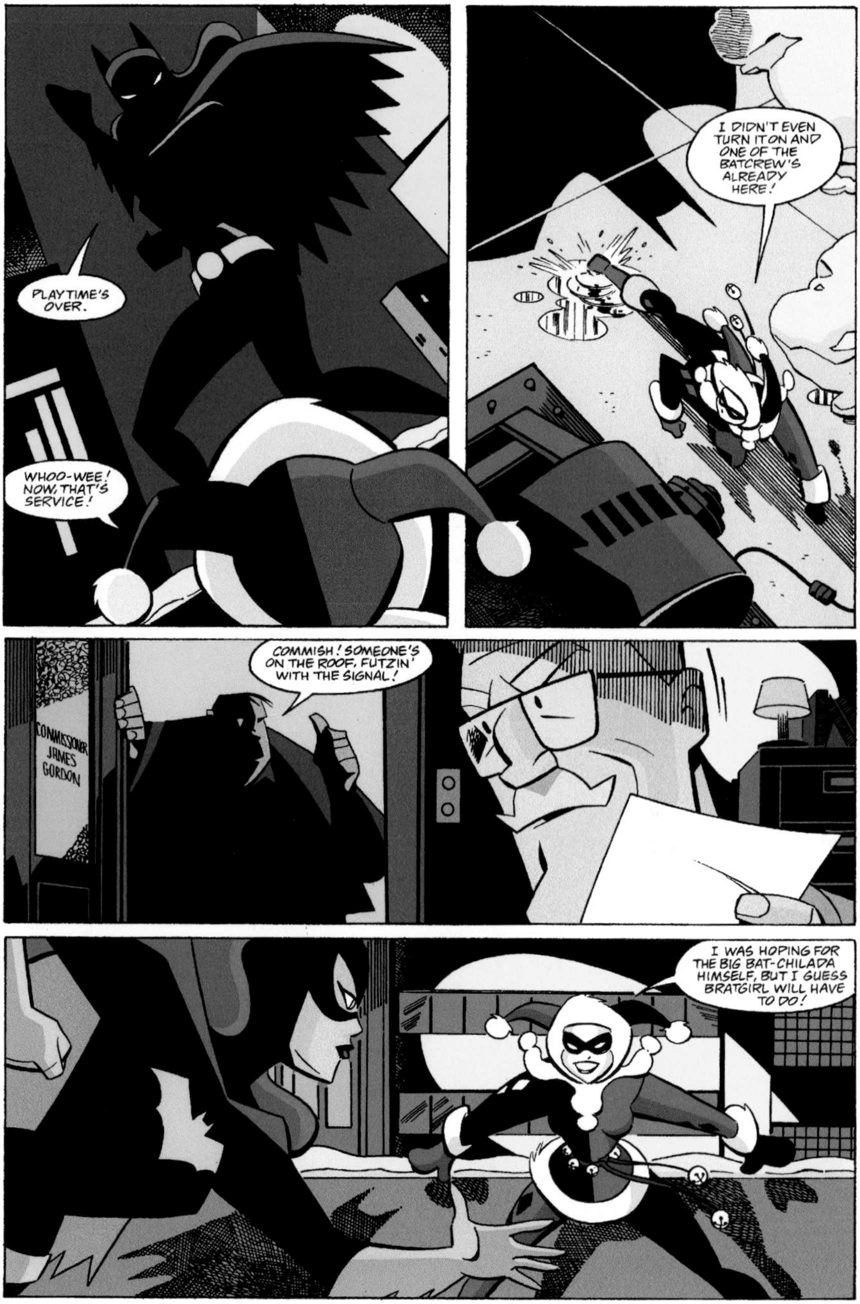
PLAYTIME'S OVER.
WHOO-WEE! NOW, THAT'S SERVICE!
I DIDN'T EVEN TURN IT ON AND ONE OF THE BATCREW'S ALREADY HERE!
COMMISSIONER JAMES GORDON
COMMISH! SOMEONE'S ON THE ROOF, FUTZIN' WITH THE SIGNAL!
I WAS HOPING FOR THE BIG BAT-CHILADA HIMSELF, BUT I GUESS BRATGIRL WILL HAVE TO DO!

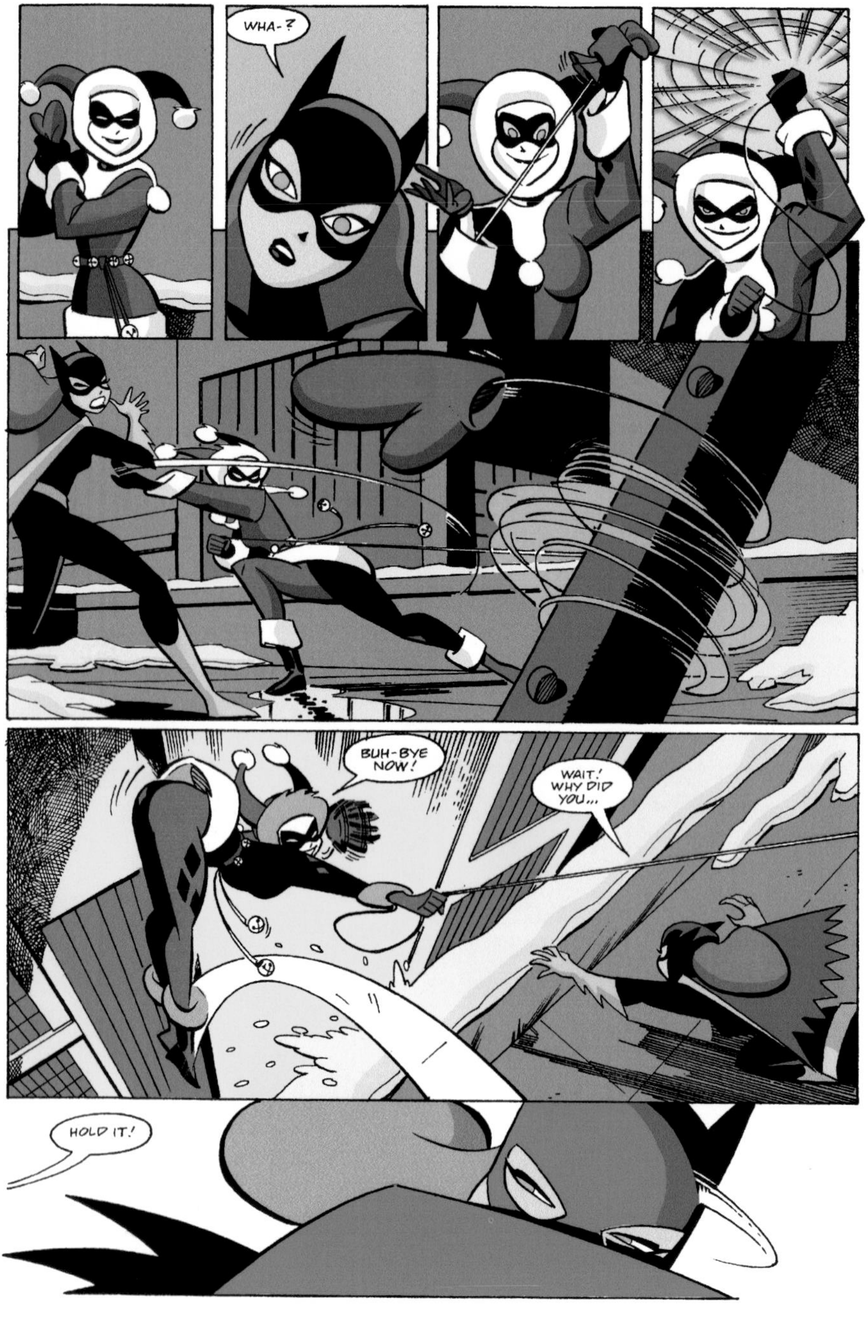
WHA-?
BUH-BYE NOW!
WAIT! WHY DID YOU...
HOLD IT!

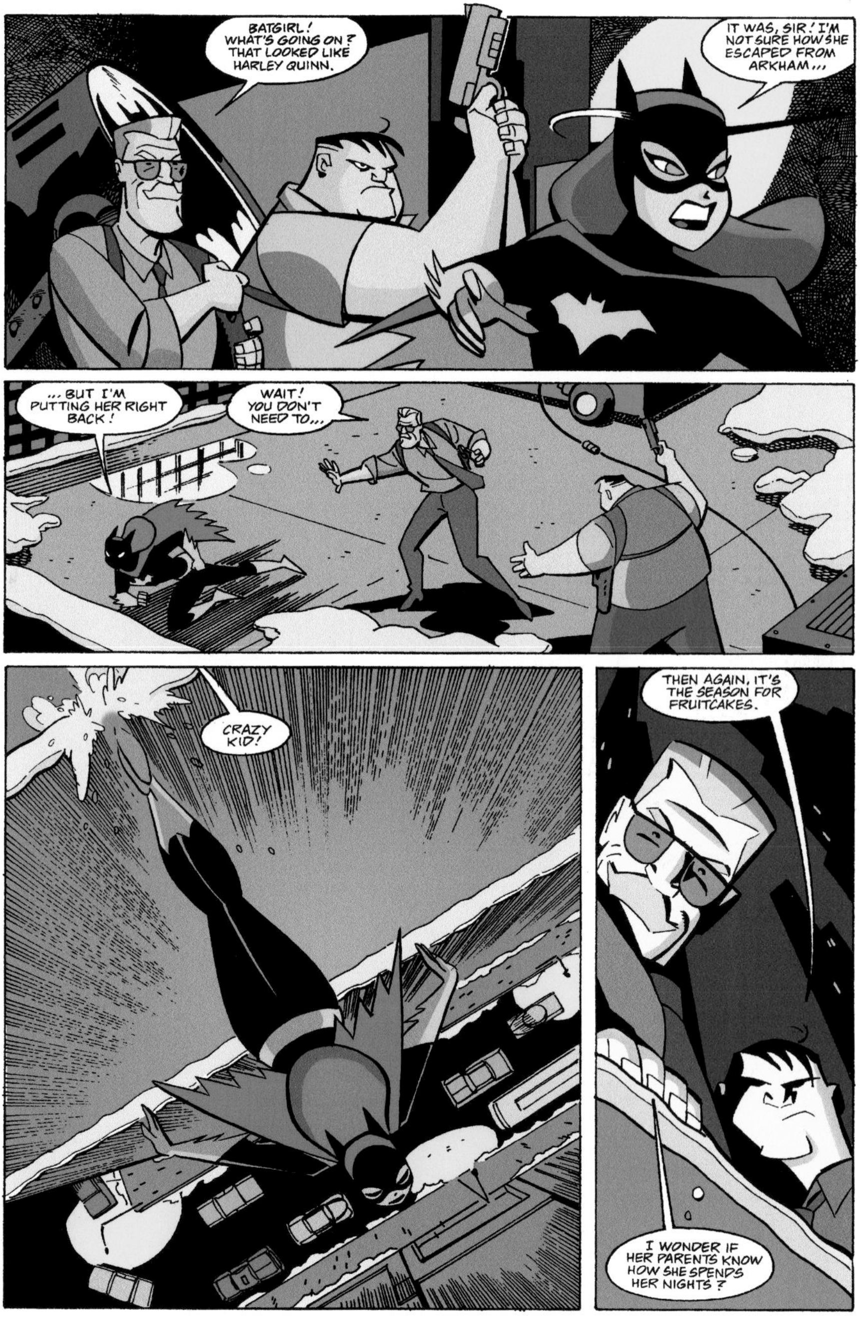
BATGIRL! WHAT'S GOING ON? THAT LOOKED LIKE HARLEY QUINN.
IT WAS, SIR! I'M NOT SURE HOW SHE ESCAPED FROM ARKHAM...
...BUT I'M PUTTING HER RIGHT BACK!
WAIT! YOU DON'T NEED TO...
CRAZY KID!
THEN AGAIN, IT'S THE SEASON FOR FRUITCAKES.
I WONDER IF HER PARENTS KNOW HOW SHE SPENDS HER NIGHTS?

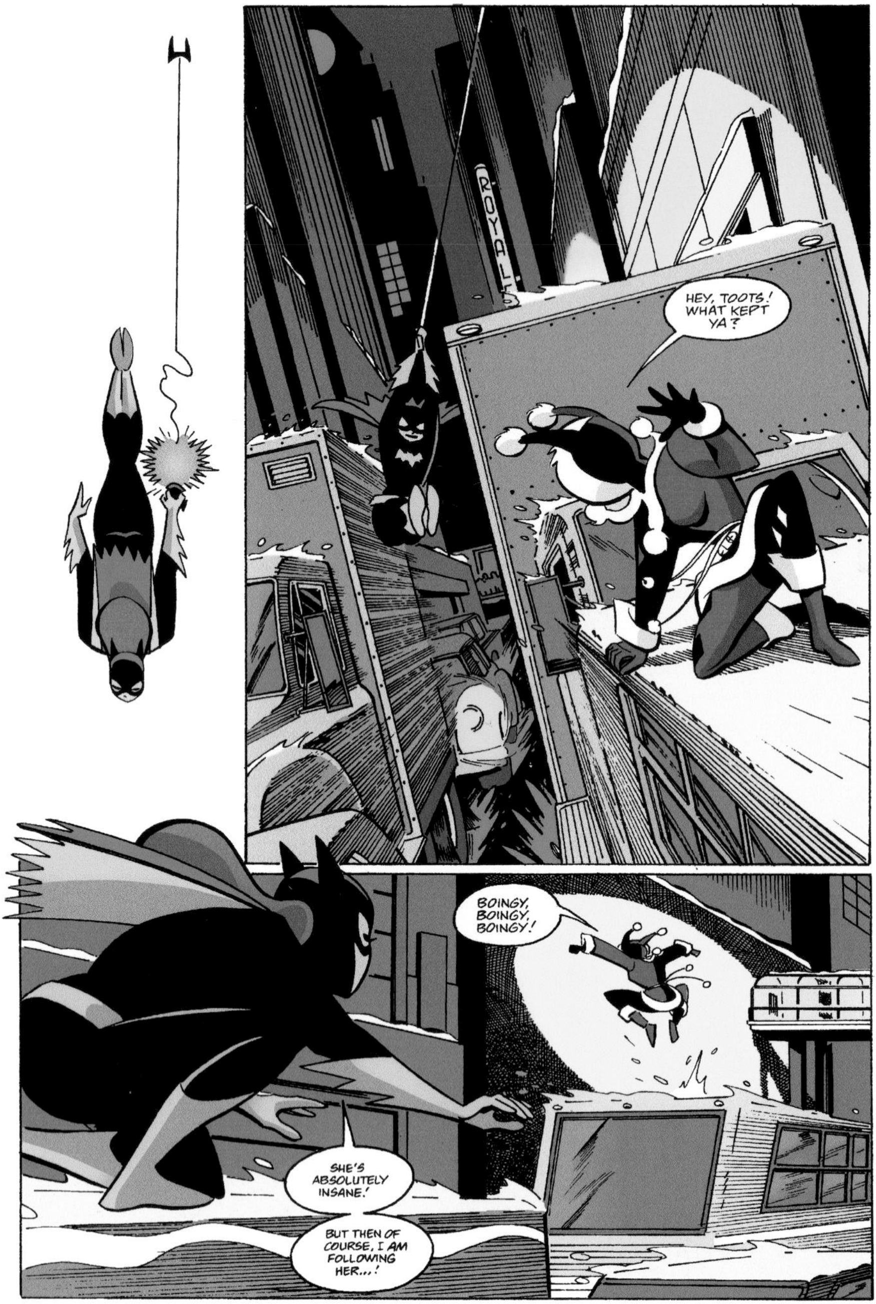
HEY, TOOTS! WHAT KEPT YA?
ROYALE
BOINGY, BOINGY, BOINGY!
SHE'S ABSOLUTELY INSANE!
BUT THEN OF COURSE, I AM FOLLOWING HER...!

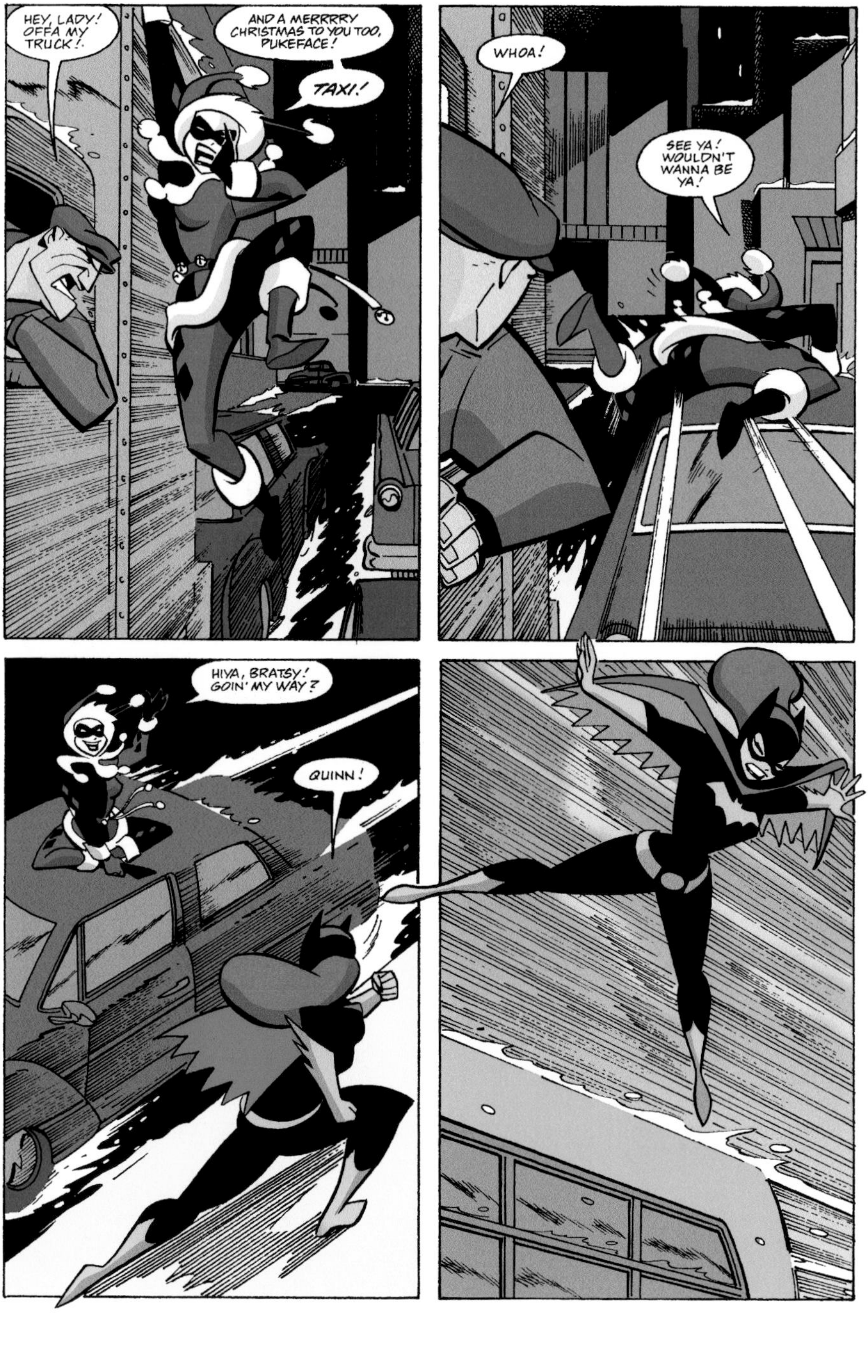
HEY, LADY! OFFA MY TRUCK!.
AND A MERRRRY CHRISTMAS TO YOU TOO, PUKEFACE!
TAXI!
WHOA!
SEE YA! WOULDN'T WANNA BE YA!
HIYA, BRATSY! GOIN' MY WAY?
QUINN!

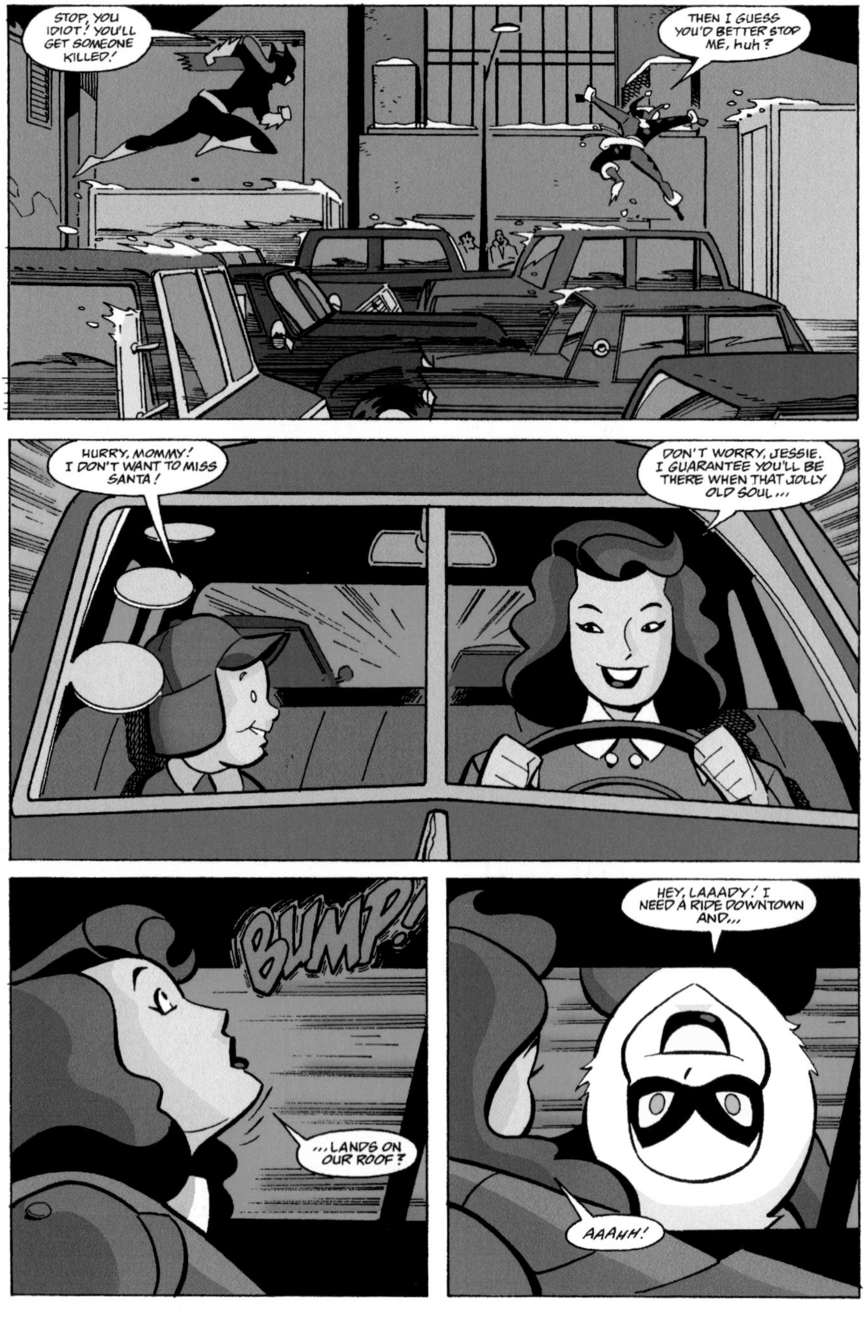
STOP, YOU IDIOT! YOU'LL GET SOMEONE KILLED!
THEN I GUESS YOU'D BETTER STOP ME, huh?
HURRY, MOMMY! I DON'T WANT TO MISS SANTA!
DON'T WORRY, JESSIE. I GUARANTEE YOU'LL BE THERE WHEN THAT JOLLY OLD SOUL...
BUMP!
...LANDS ON OUR ROOF?
HEY, LAAADY! I NEED A RIDE DOWNTOWN AND...
AAAHH!

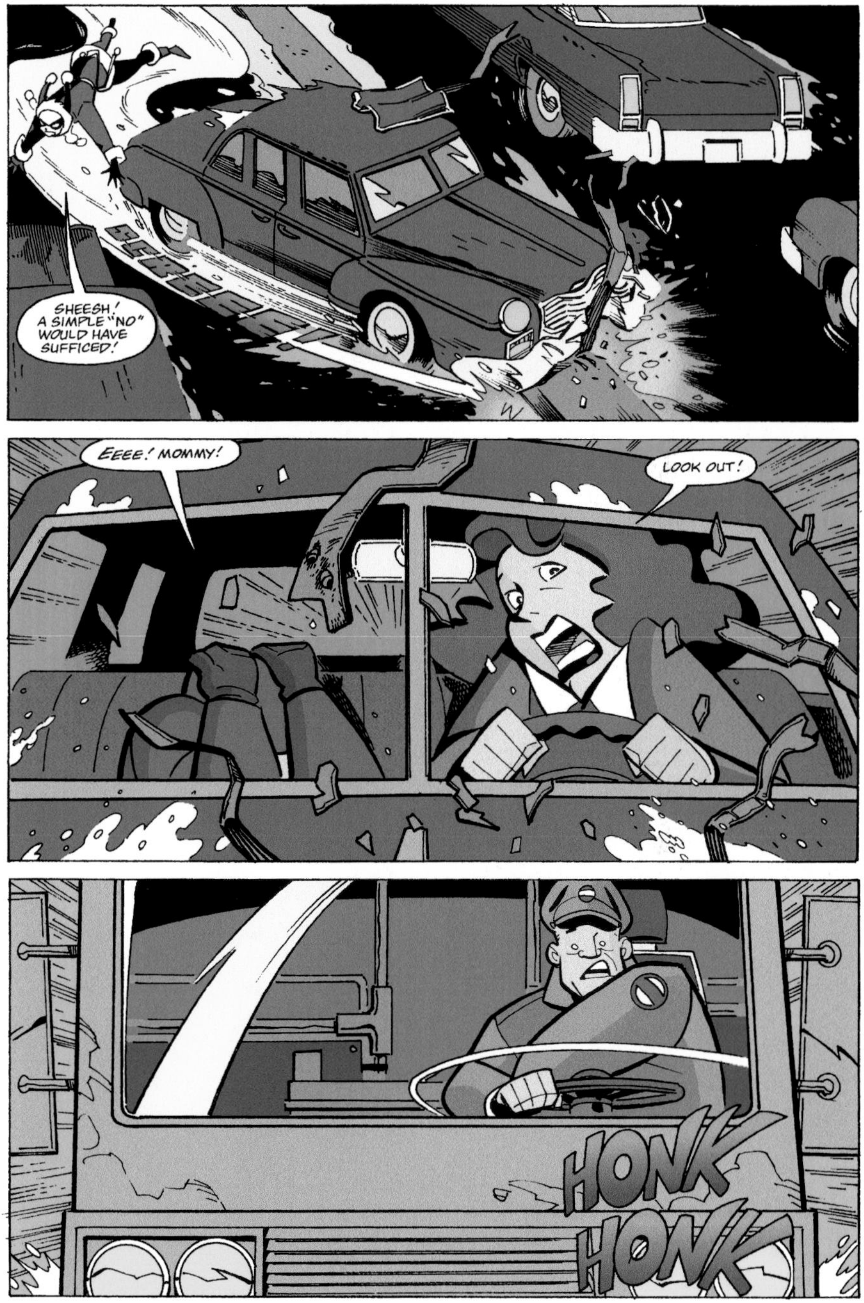
SHEESH! A SIMPLE "NO" WOULD HAVE SUFFICED!
EEEE! MOMMY!
LOOK OUT!
HONK
HONK

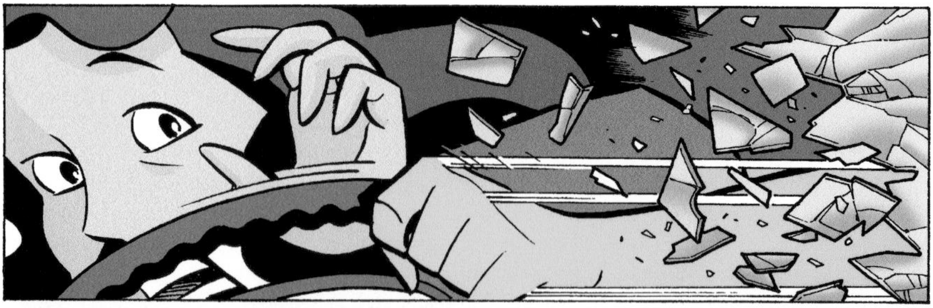

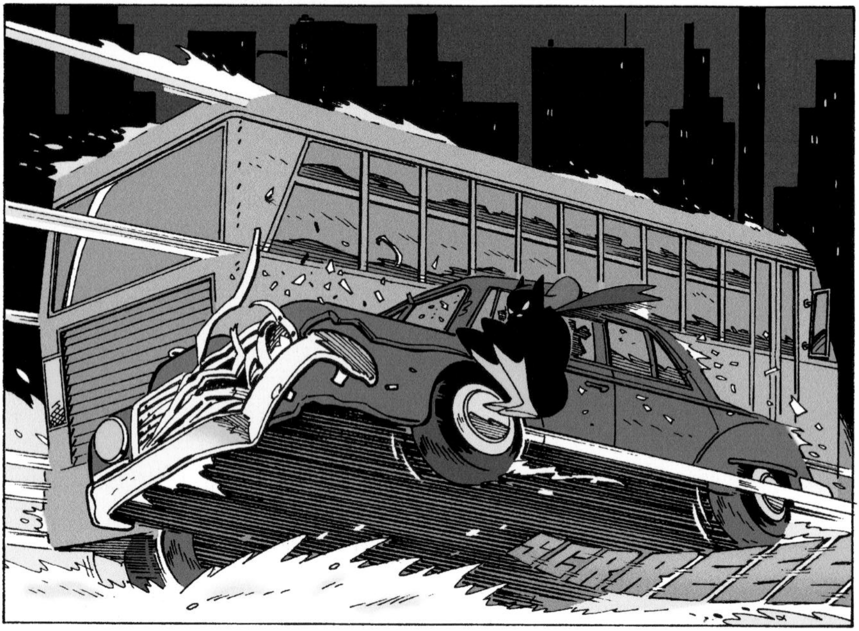

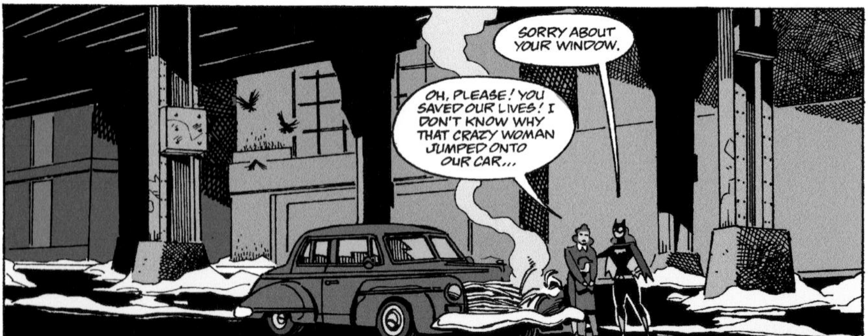
SORRY ABOUT YOUR WINDOW.
OH, PLEASE! YOU SAVED OUR LIVES! I DON'T KNOW WHY THAT CRAZY WOMAN JUMPED ONTO OUR CAR...

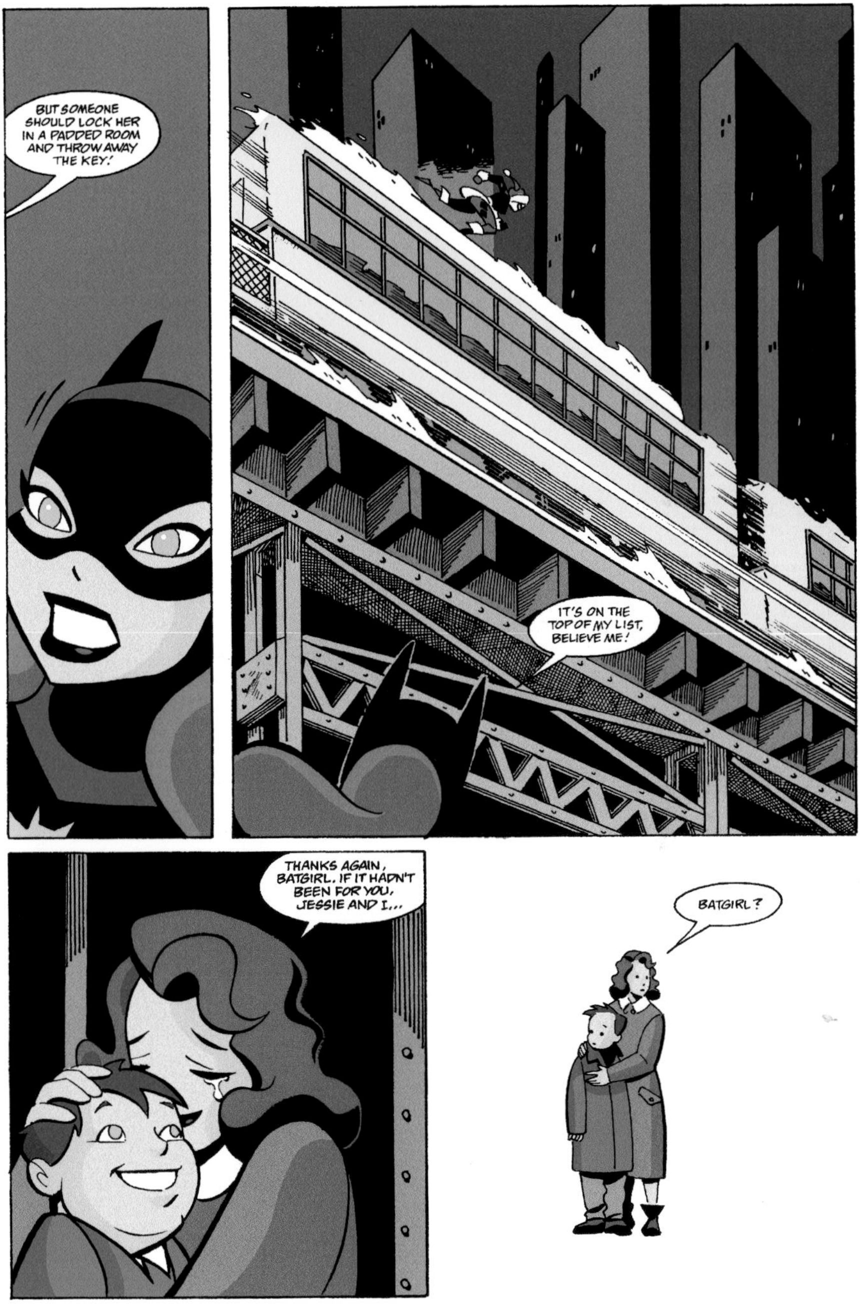
BUT SOMEONE SHOULD LOCK HER IN A PADDED ROOM AND THROW AWAY THE KEY!
IT'S ON THE TOP OF MY LIST, BELIEVE ME!
THANKS AGAIN, BATGIRL. IF IT HADN'T BEEN FOR YOU, JESSIE AND I...
BATGIRL?

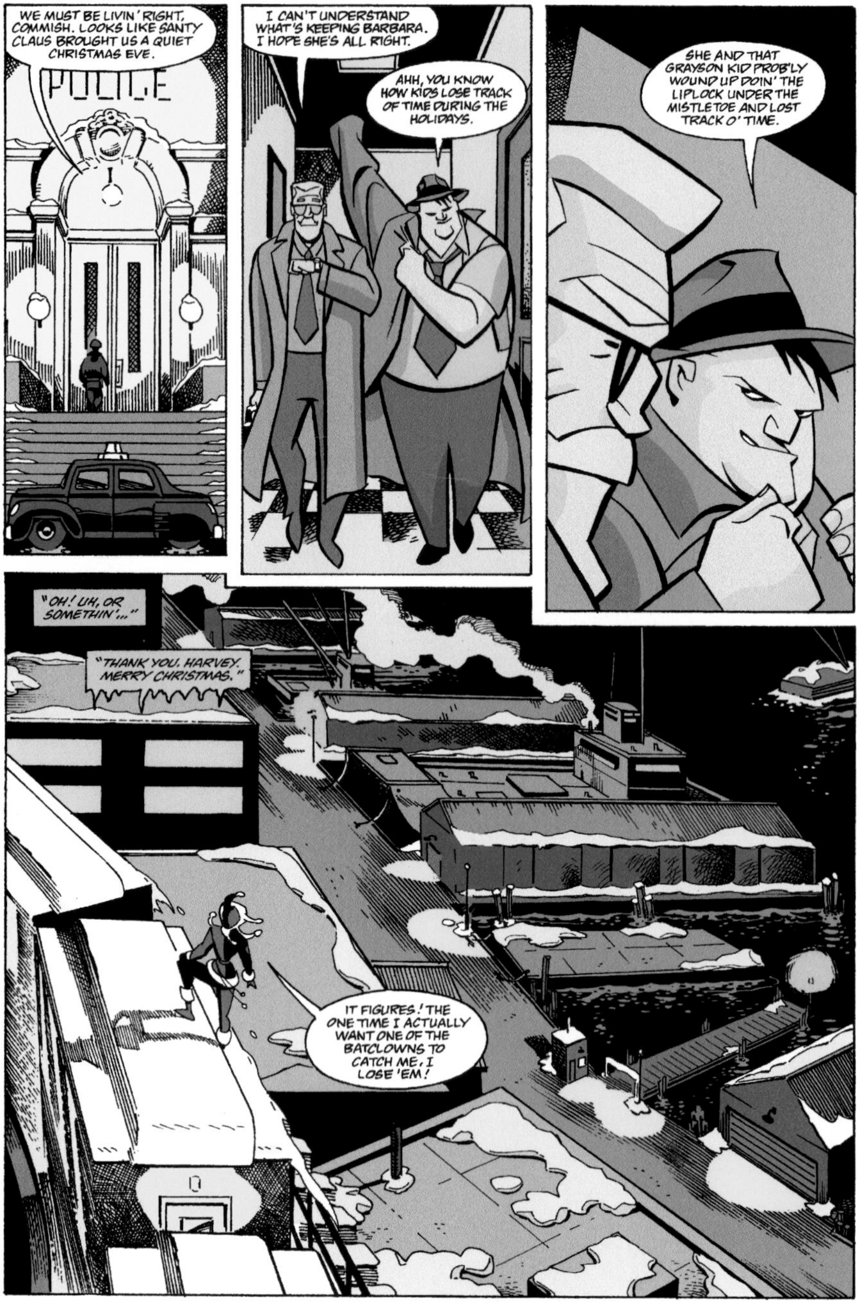
WE MUST BE LIVIN' RIGHT, COMMISH. LOOKS LIKE SANTY CLAUS BROUGHT US A QUIET CHRISTMAS EVE.
POLICE
I CAN'T UNDERSTAND WHAT'S KEEPING BARBARA. I HOPE SHE'S ALL RIGHT.
AHH, YOU KNOW HOW KIDS LOSE TRACK OF TIME DURING THE HOLIDAYS.
SHE AND THAT GRAYSON KID PROB'LY WOUND UP DOIN' THE LIPLOCK UNDER THE MISTLETOE AND LOST TRACK O' TIME.
"OH! UH, OR SOMETHIN'..."
"THANK YOU, HARVEY. MERRY CHRISTMAS."
IT FIGURES! THE ONE TIME I ACTUALLY WANT ONE OF THE BATCLOWNS TO CATCH ME, I LOSE 'EM!

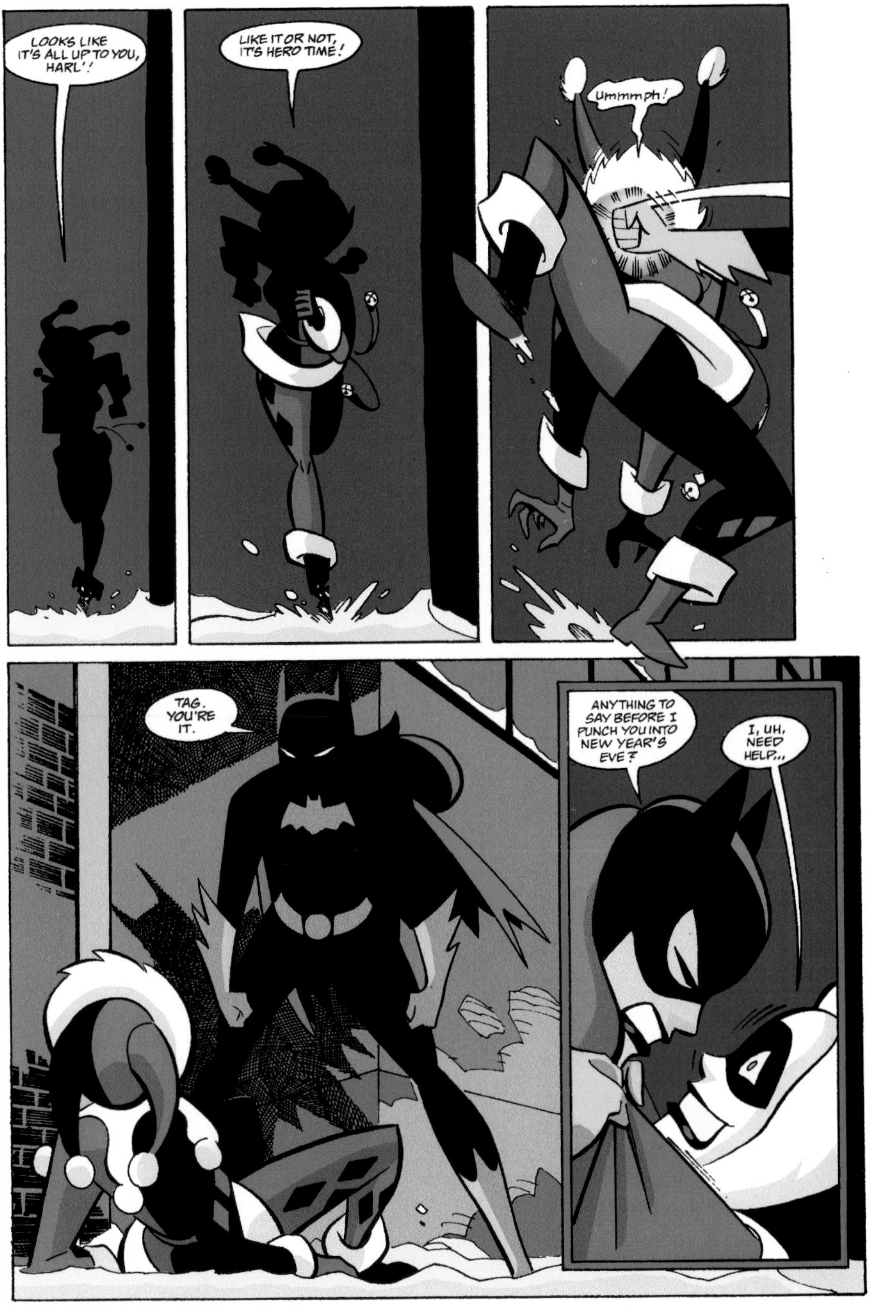

LOOKS LIKE IT'S ALL UP TO YOU, HARL'!
LIKE IT OR NOT, IT'S HERO TIME!
Ummmmph!
TAG. YOU'RE IT.
ANYTHING TO SAY BEFORE I PUNCH YOU INTO NEW YEAR'S EVE?
I, UH, NEED HELP...

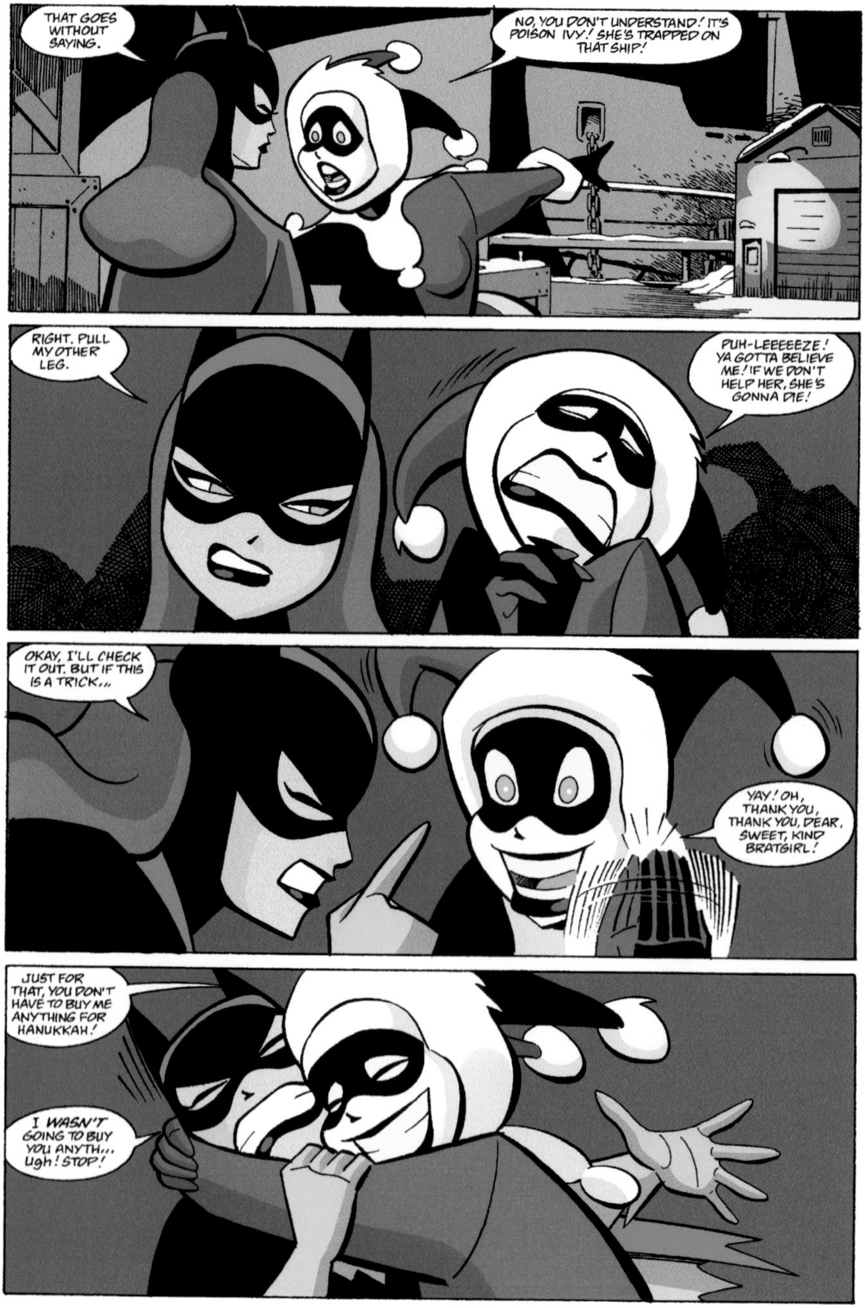
THAT GOES WITHOUT SAYING.
NO, YOU DON'T UNDERSTAND! IT'S POISON IVY! SHE'S TRAPPED ON THAT SHIP!
RIGHT. PULL MY OTHER LEG.
PUH-LEEEEEZE! YA GOTTA BELIEVE ME! IF WE DON'T HELP HER, SHE'S GONNA DIE!
OKAY, I'LL CHECK IT OUT. BUT IF THIS IS A TRICK...
YAY! OH, THANK YOU, THANK YOU, DEAR, SWEET, KIND BRATGIRL!
JUST FOR THAT, YOU DON'T HAVE TO BUY ME ANYTHING FOR HANUKKAH!
I WASN'T GOING TO BUY YOU ANYTH... Ugh! STOP!

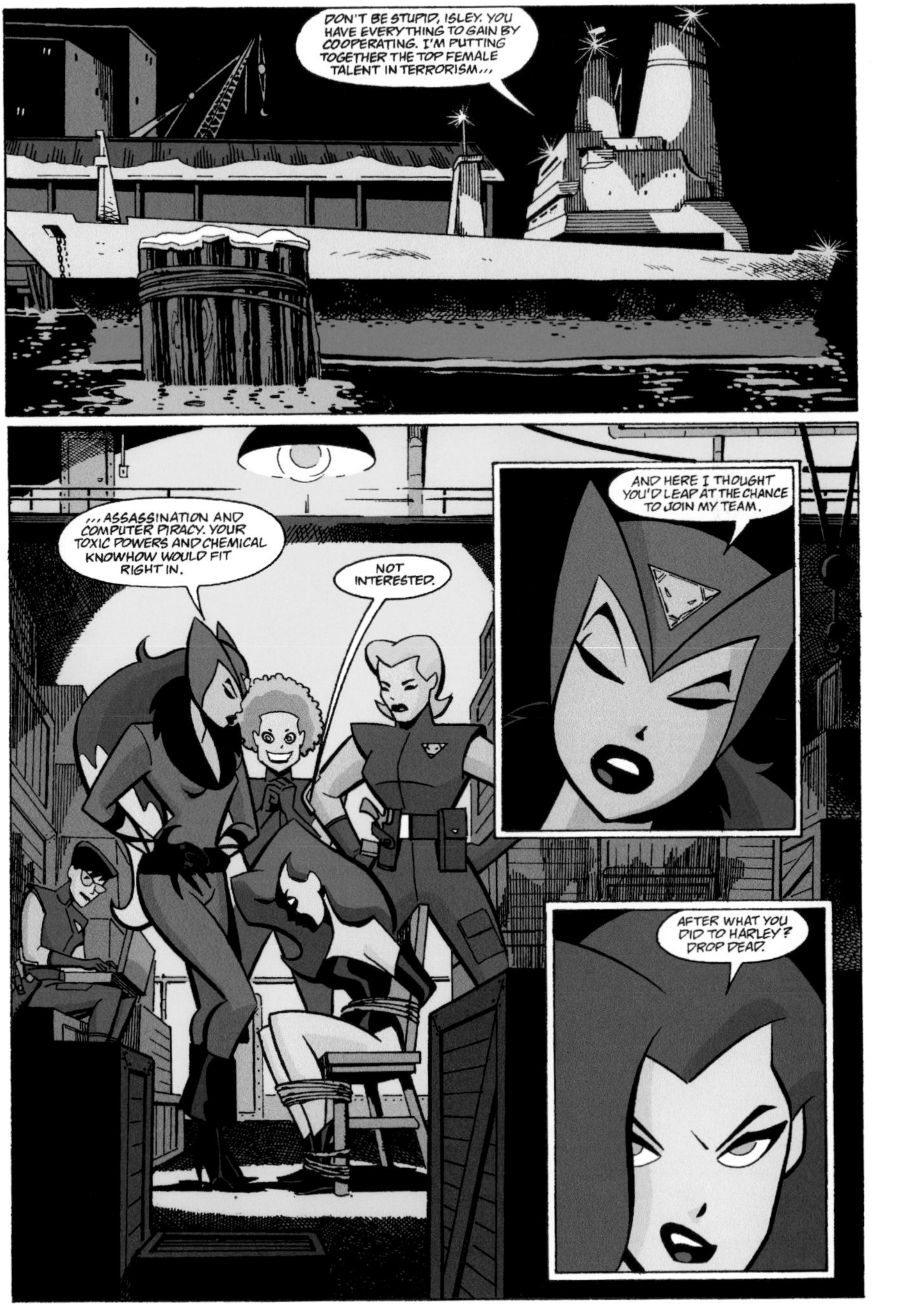
DON'T BE STUPID, ISLEY. YOU HAVE EVERYTHING TO GAIN BY COOPERATING. I'M PUTTING TOGETHER THE TOP FEMALE TALENT IN TERRORISM...
...ASSASSINATION AND COMPUTER PIRACY. YOUR TOXIC POWERS AND CHEMICAL KNOWHOW WOULD FIT RIGHT IN.
NOT INTERESTED.
AND HERE I THOUGHT YOU'D LEAP AT THE CHANCE TO JOIN MY TEAM.
AFTER WHAT YOU DID TO HARLEY? DROP DEAD.

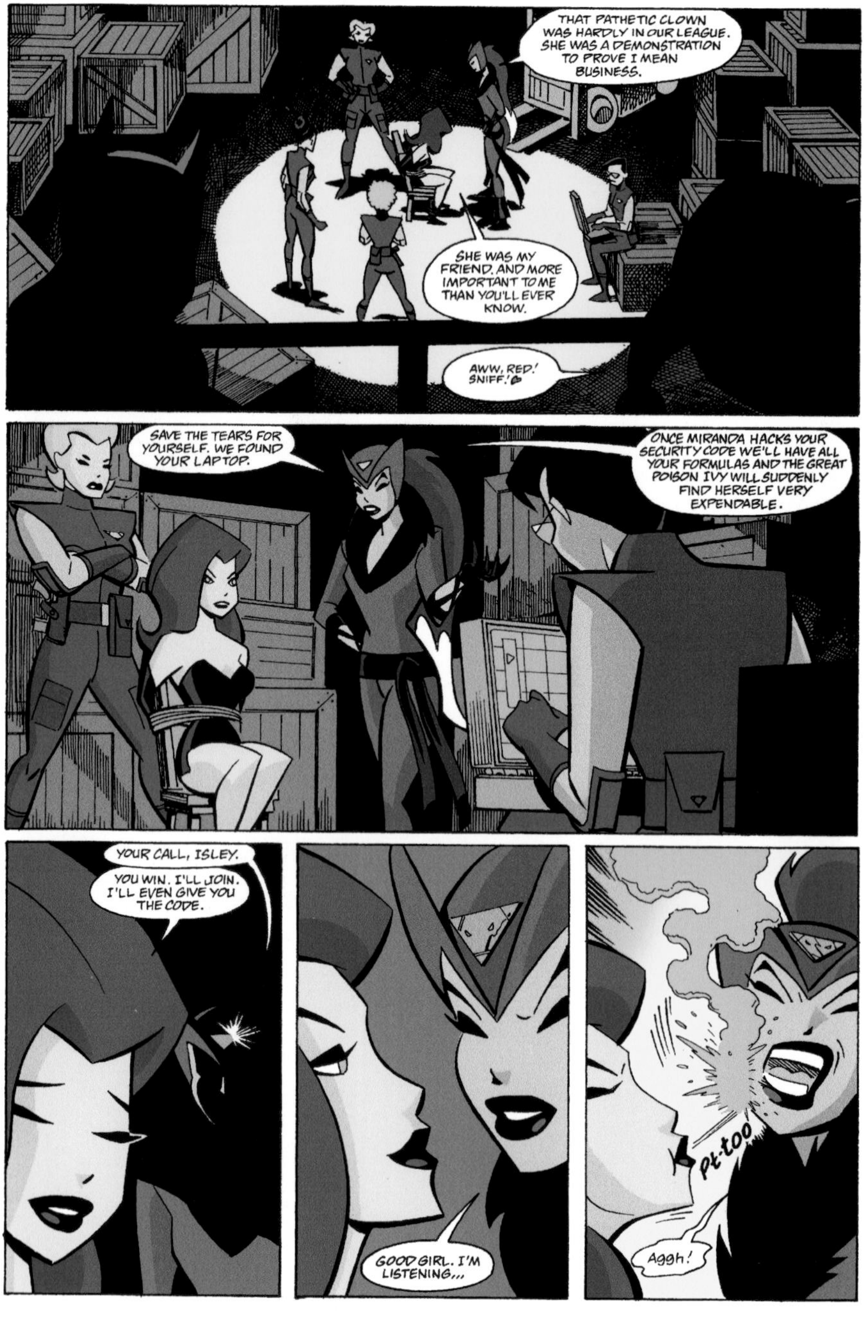
THAT PATHETIC CLOWN WAS HARDLY IN OUR LEAGUE. SHE WAS A DEMONSTRATION TO PROVE I MEAN BUSINESS.
SHE WAS MY FRIEND, AND MORE IMPORTANT TO ME THAN YOU'LL EVER KNOW.
AWW, RED! SNIFF!
SAVE THE TEARS FOR YOURSELF. WE FOUND YOUR LAPTOP.
ONCE MIRANDA HACKS YOUR SECURITY CODE WE'LL HAVE ALL YOUR FORMULAS AND THE GREAT POISON IVY WILL SUDDENLY FIND HERSELF VERY EXPENDABLE.
YOUR CALL, ISLEY.
YOU WIN. I'LL JOIN. I'LL EVEN GIVE YOU THE CODE.
GOOD GIRL. I'M LISTENING...
Pt-too
Aggh!

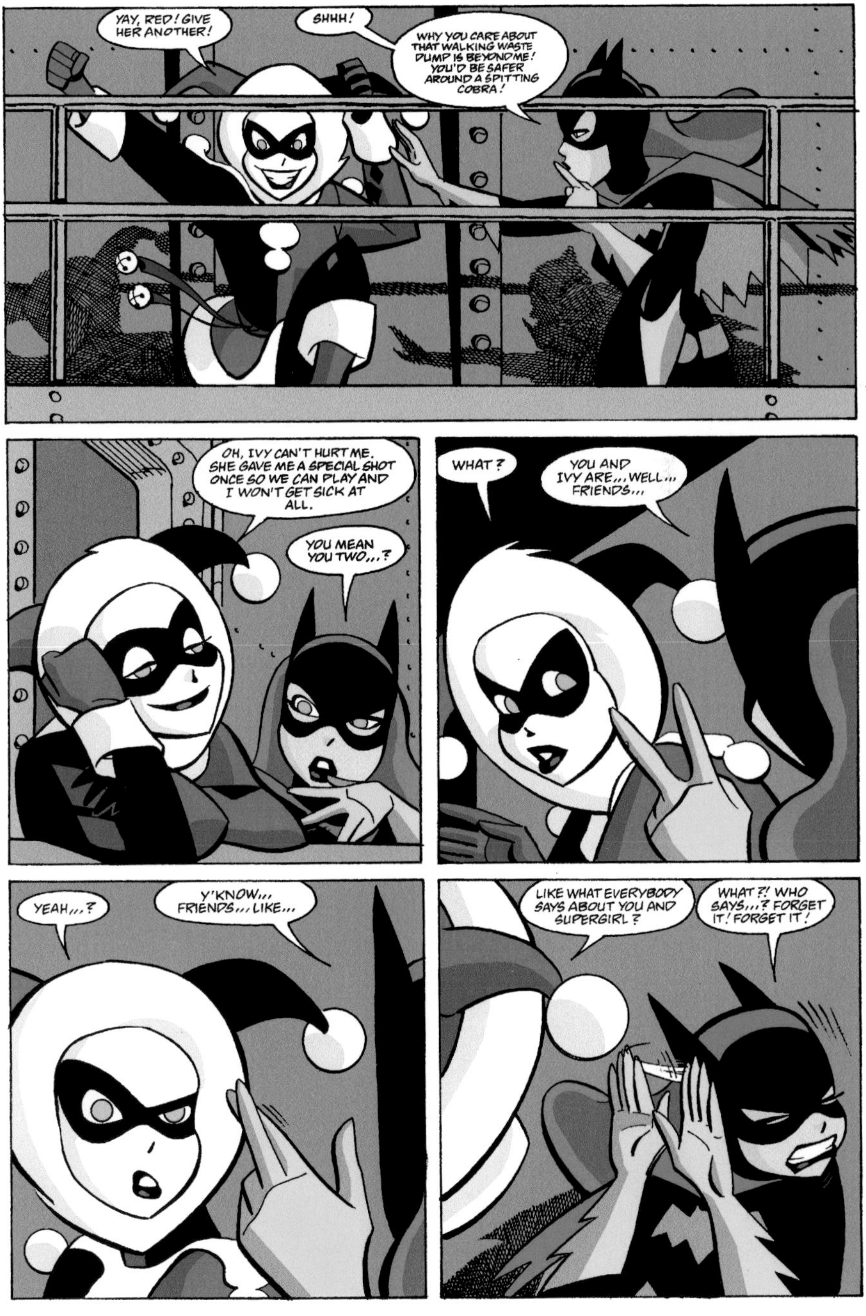
YAY, RED! GIVE HER ANOTHER!
SHHH!
WHY YOU CARE ABOUT THAT WALKING WASTE DUMP IS BEYOND ME! YOU'D BE SAFER AROUND A SPITTING COBRA!
OH, IVY CAN'T HURT ME. SHE GAVE ME A SPECIAL SHOT ONCE SO WE CAN PLAY AND I WON'T GET SICK AT ALL.
YOU MEAN YOU TWO,,,?
WHAT?
YOU AND IVY ARE,,, WELL,,, FRIENDS,,,
YEAH,,,?
Y'KNOW,,, FRIENDS,,, LIKE,,,
LIKE WHAT EVERYBODY SAYS ABOUT YOU AND SUPERGIRL?
WHAT?! WHO SAYS,,,? FORGET IT! FORGET IT!

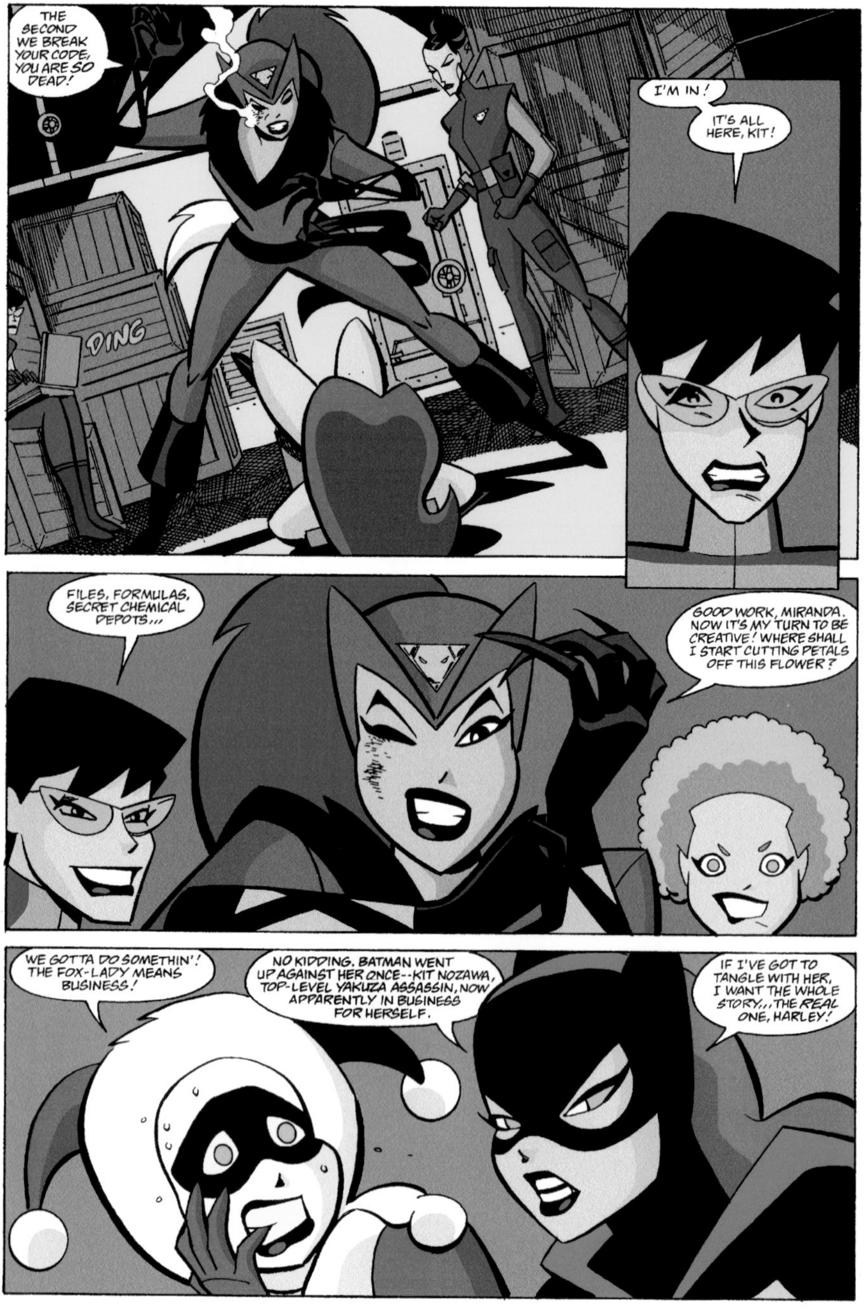
THE SECOND WE BREAK YOUR CODE, YOU ARE SO DEAD!
I'M IN!
IT'S ALL HERE, KIT!
DING
FILES, FORMULAS, SECRET CHEMICAL DEPOTS...
GOOD WORK, MIRANDA. NOW IT'S MY TURN TO BE CREATIVE! WHERE SHALL I START CUTTING PETALS OFF THIS FLOWER?
WE GOTTA DO SOMETHIN'! THE FOX-LADY MEANS BUSINESS!
NO KIDDING. BATMAN WENT UP AGAINST HER ONCE--KIT NOZAWA, TOP-LEVEL YAKUZA ASSASSIN, NOW APPARENTLY IN BUSINESS FOR HERSELF.
IF I'VE GOT TO TANGLE WITH HER, I WANT THE WHOLE STORY... THE REAL ONE, HARLEY!

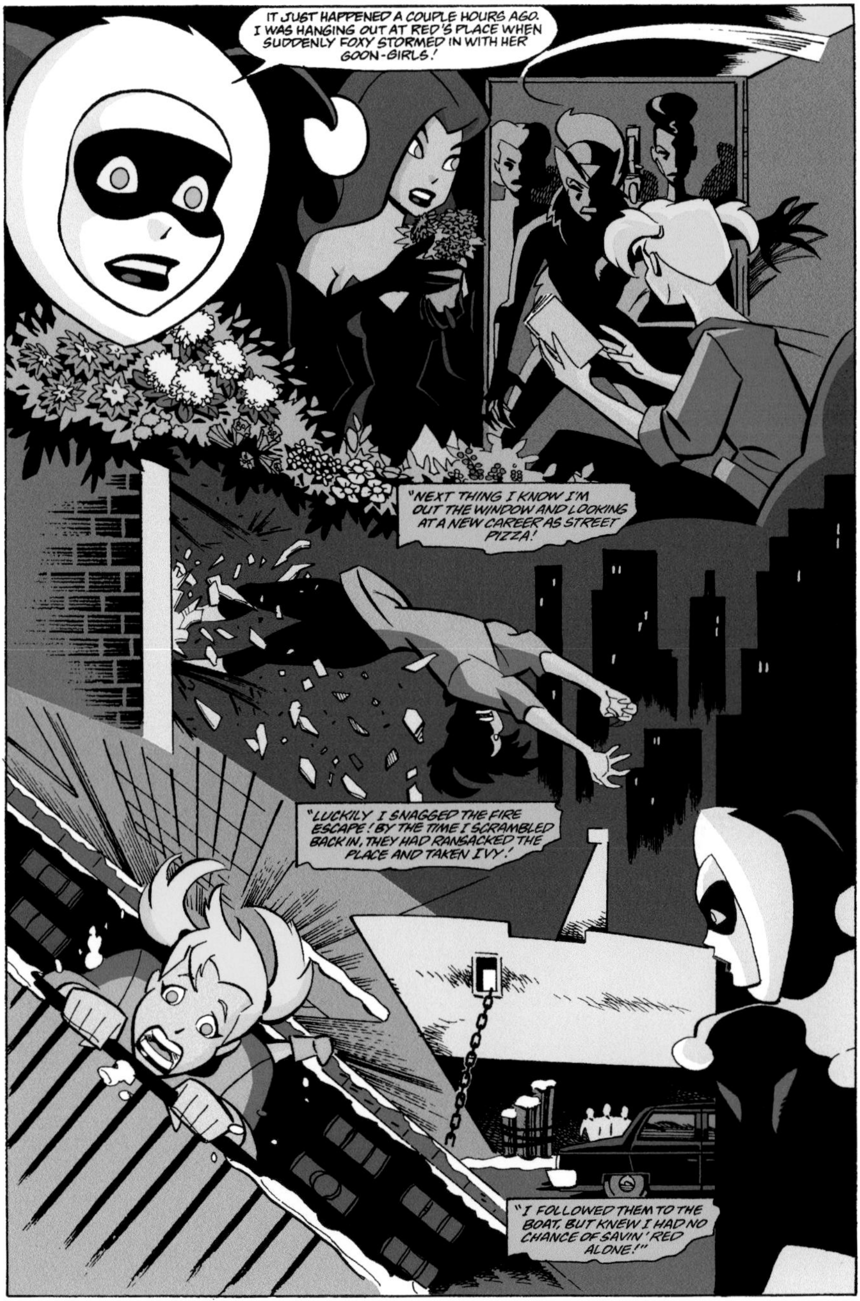
IT JUST HAPPENED A COUPLE HOURS AGO. I WAS HANGING OUT AT RED'S PLACE WHEN SUDDENLY FOXY STORMED IN WITH HER GOON-GIRLS!
"NEXT THING I KNOW I'M OUT THE WINDOW AND LOOKING AT A NEW CAREER AS STREET PIZZA!
"LUCKILY I SNAGGED THE FIRE ESCAPE! BY THE TIME I SCRAMBLED BACK IN, THEY HAD RANSACKED THE PLACE AND TAKEN IVY!
"I FOLLOWED THEM TO THE BOAT, BUT KNEW I HAD NO CHANCE OF SAVIN' RED ALONE!"

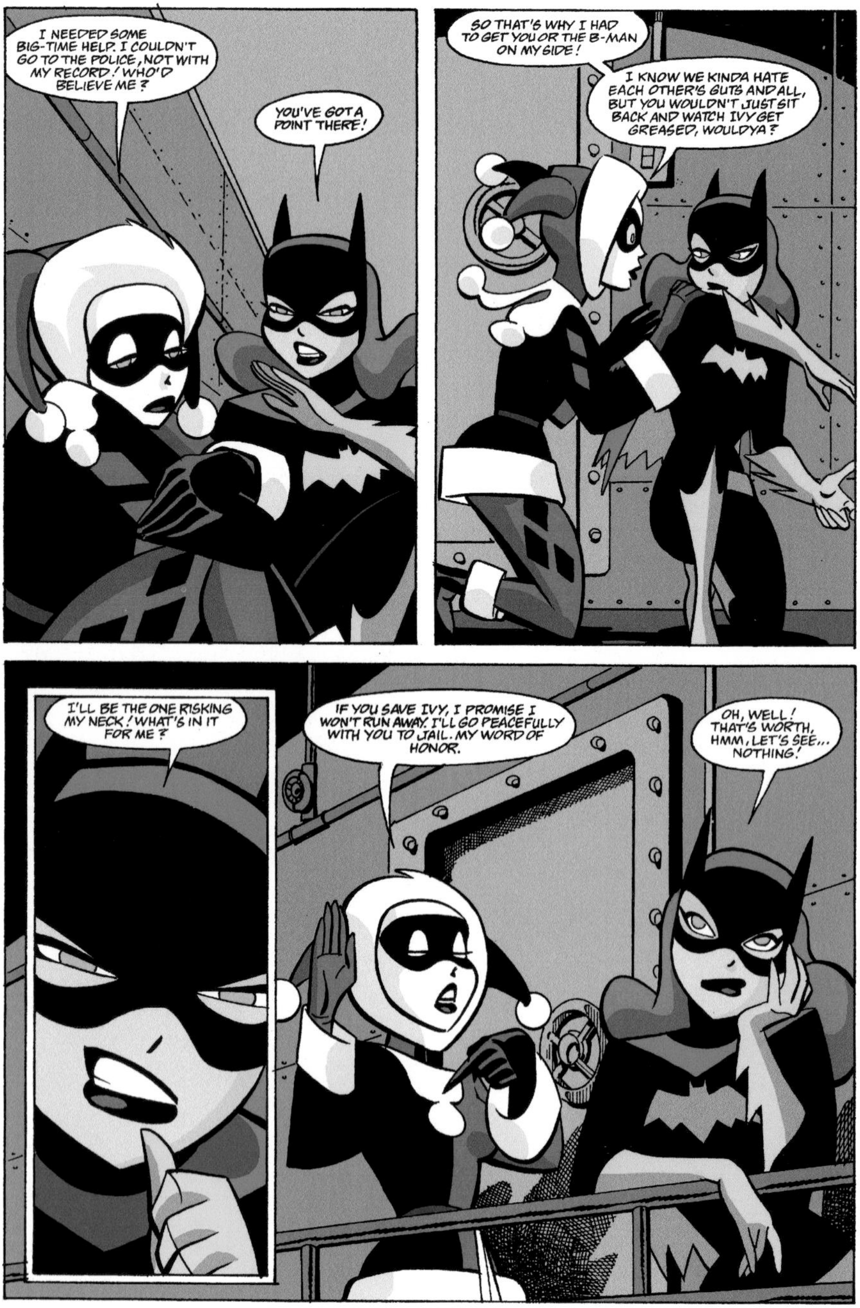
I NEEDED SOME BIG-TIME HELP. I COULDN'T GO TO THE POLICE, NOT WITH MY RECORD! WHO'D BELIEVE ME?
YOU'VE GOT A POINT THERE!
SO THAT'S WHY I HAD TO GET YOU OR THE B-MAN ON MY SIDE!
I KNOW WE KINDA HATE EACH OTHER'S GUTS AND ALL, BUT YOU WOULDN'T JUST SIT BACK AND WATCH IVY GET GREASED, WOULDYA?
I'LL BE THE ONE RISKING MY NECK! WHAT'S IN IT FOR ME?
IF YOU SAVE IVY, I PROMISE I WON'T RUN AWAY. I'LL GO PEACEFULLY WITH YOU TO JAIL. MY WORD OF HONOR.
OH, WELL! THAT'S WORTH, HMM, LET'S SEE... NOTHING!

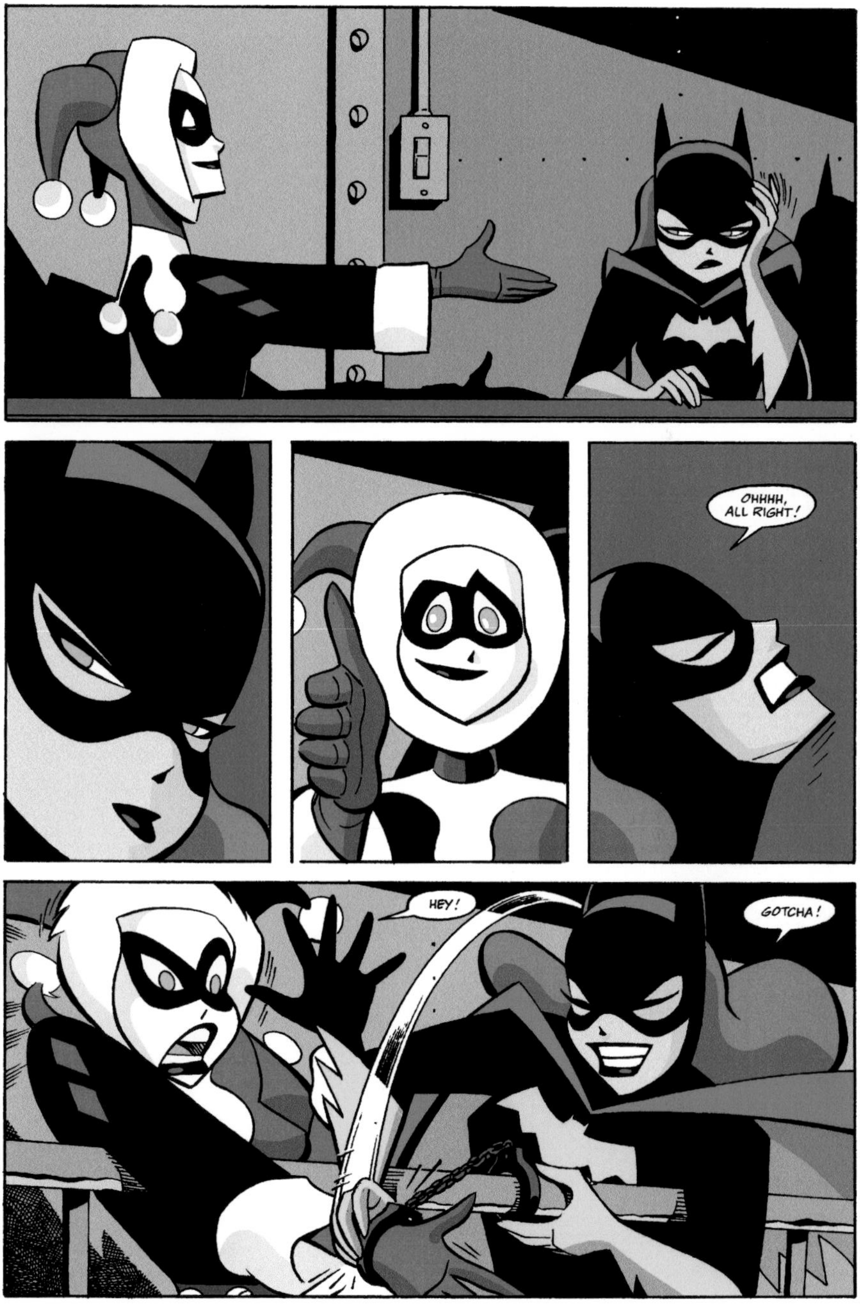
OHHHH, ALL RIGHT!
HEY!
GOTCHA!

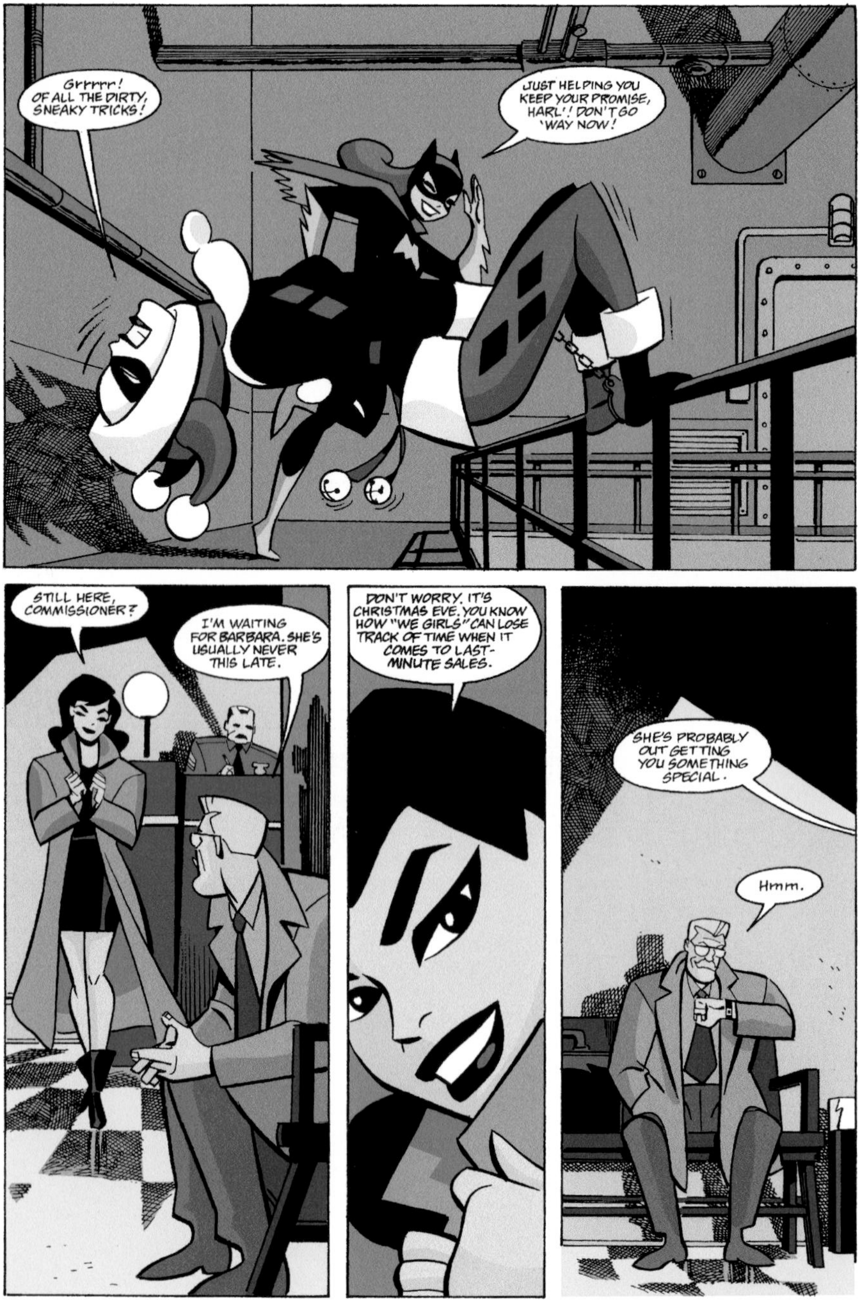

Grrrrr! OF ALL THE DIRTY, SNEAKY TRICKS!
JUST HELPING YOU KEEP YOUR PROMISE, HARL'! DON'T GO 'WAY NOW!
STILL HERE, COMMISSIONER?
I'M WAITING FOR BARBARA. SHE'S USUALLY NEVER THIS LATE.
DON'T WORRY. IT'S CHRISTMAS EVE. YOU KNOW HOW "WE GIRLS" CAN LOSE TRACK OF TIME WHEN IT COMES TO LAST-MINUTE SALES.
SHE'S PROBABLY OUT GETTING YOU SOMETHING SPECIAL.
Hmm.

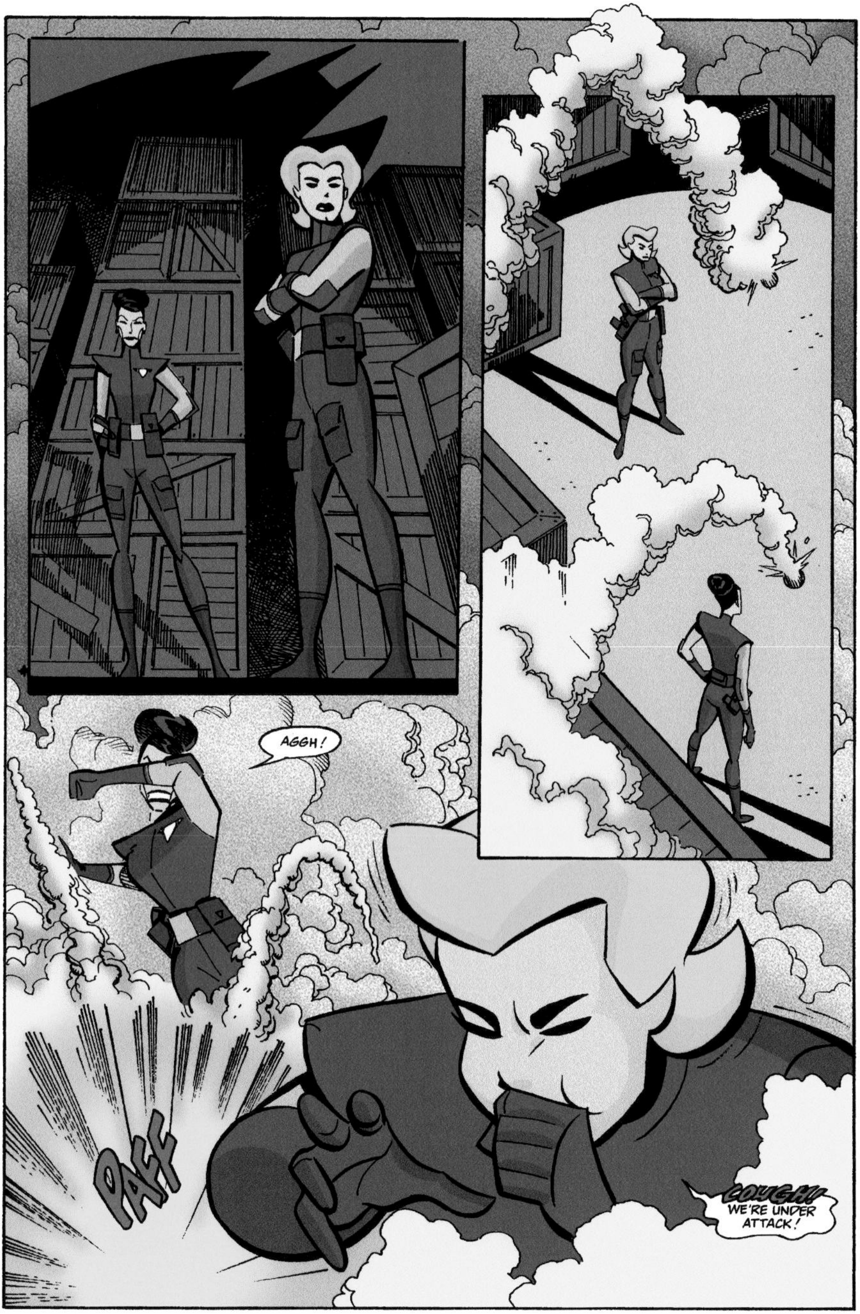
AGGH!
PAFF
COUGH! WE'RE UNDER ATTACK!

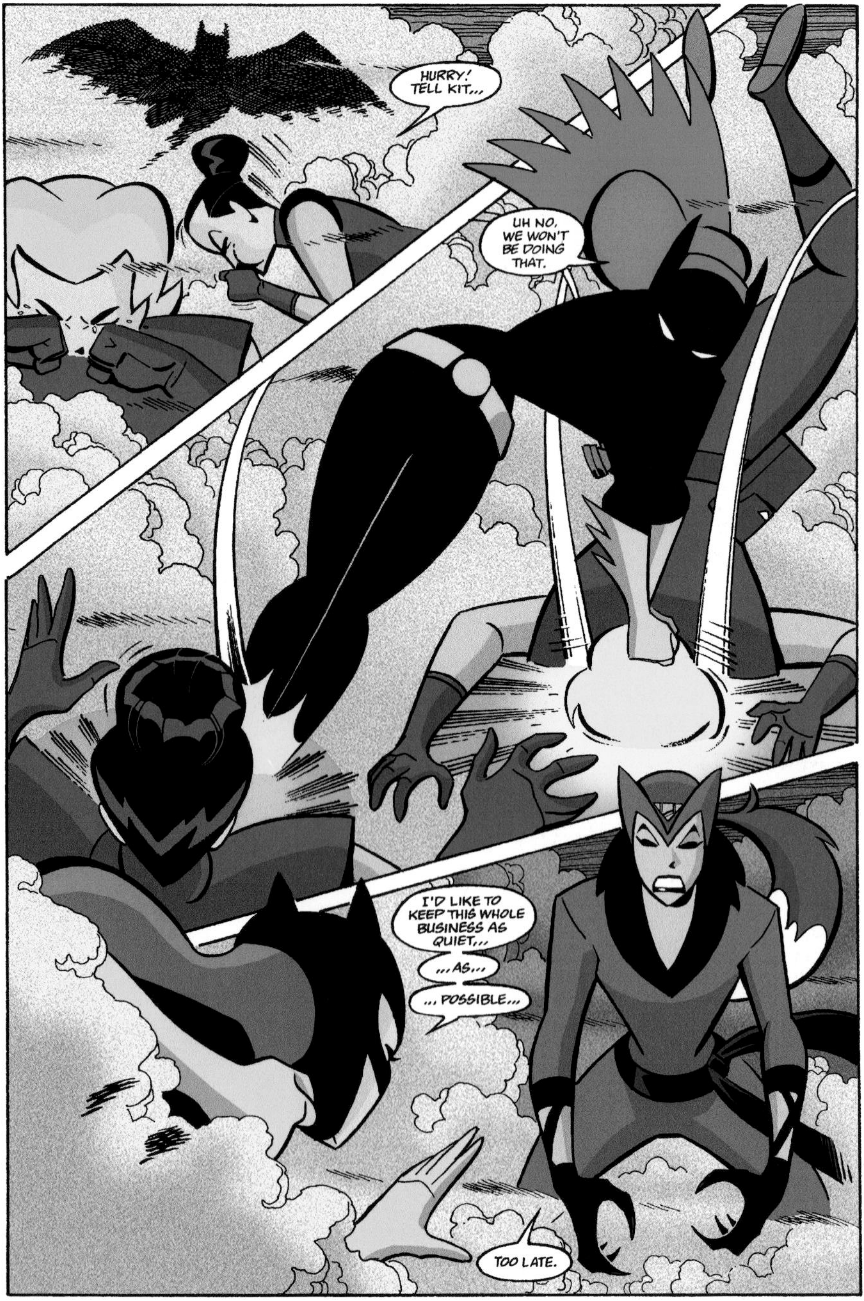
HURRY! TELL KIT...
UH NO, WE WON'T BE DOING THAT.
I'D LIKE TO KEEP THIS WHOLE BUSINESS AS QUIET...
...AS...
...POSSIBLE...
TOO LATE.

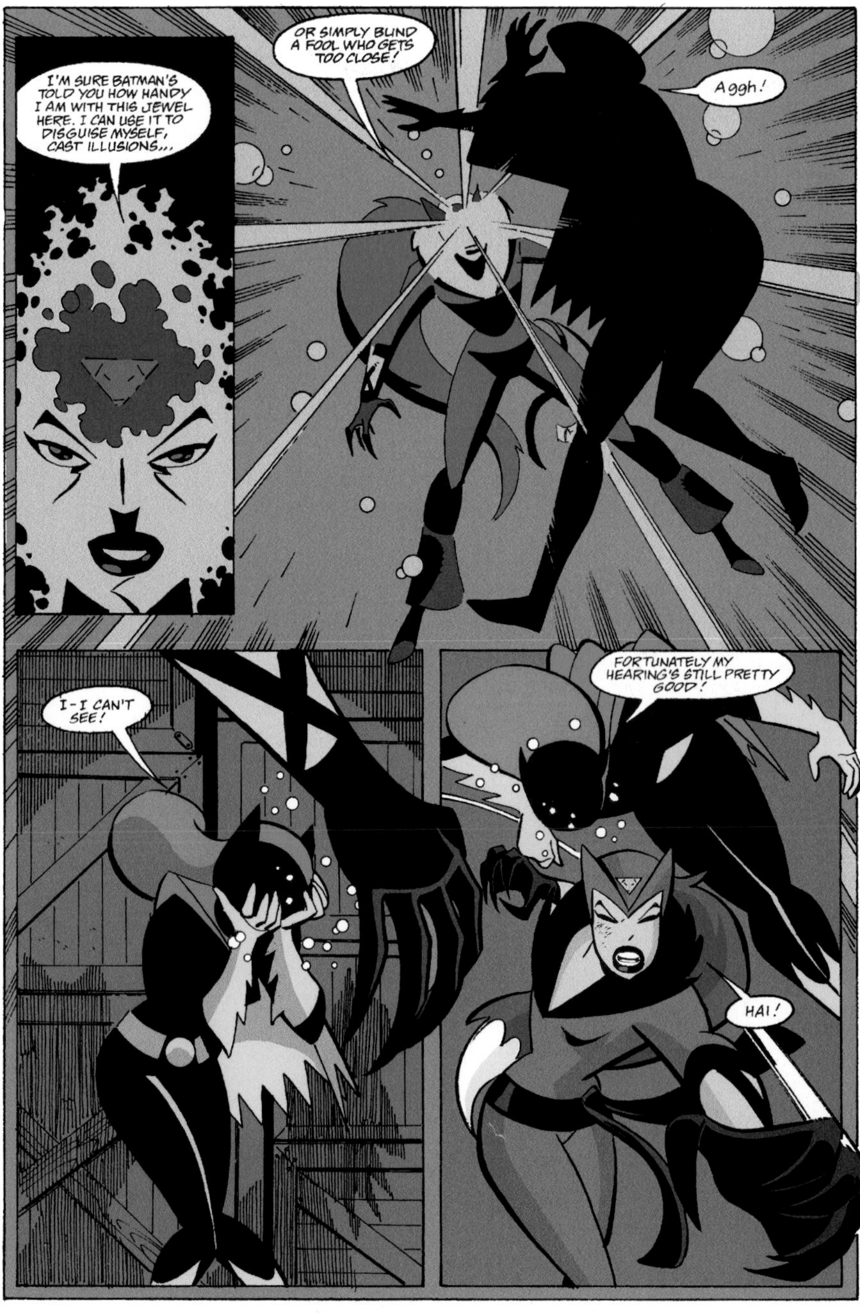

I'M SURE BATMAN'S TOLD YOU HOW HANDY I AM WITH THIS JEWEL HERE. I CAN USE IT TO DISGUISE MYSELF, CAST ILLUSIONS...
OR SIMPLY BLIND A FOOL WHO GETS TOO CLOSE!
Aggh!
I-I CAN'T SEE!
FORTUNATELY MY HEARING'S STILL PRETTY GOOD!
HAI!

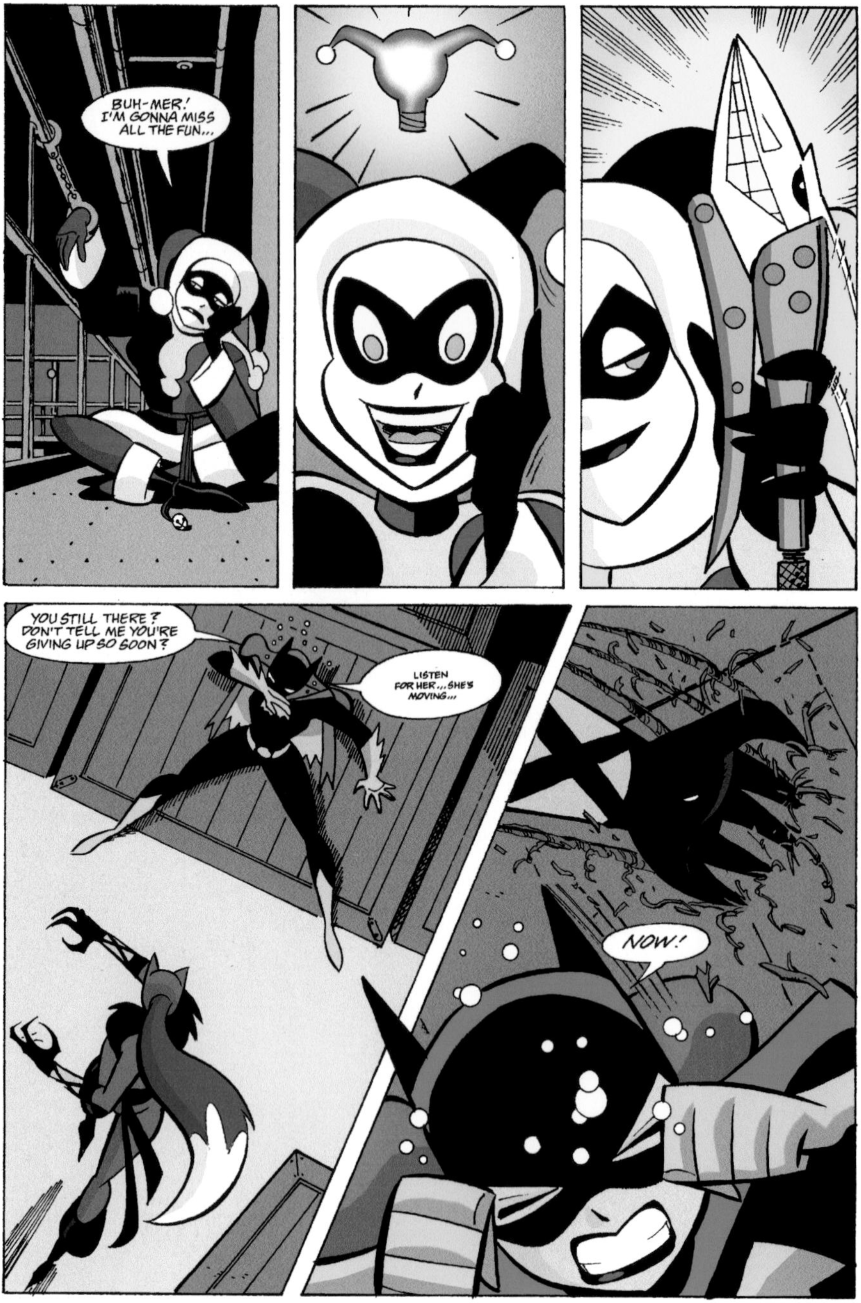
BUH-MER! I'M GONNA MISS ALL THE FUN...
YOU STILL THERE? DON'T TELL ME YOU'RE GIVING UP SO SOON?
LISTEN FOR HER... SHE'S MOVING...
NOW!

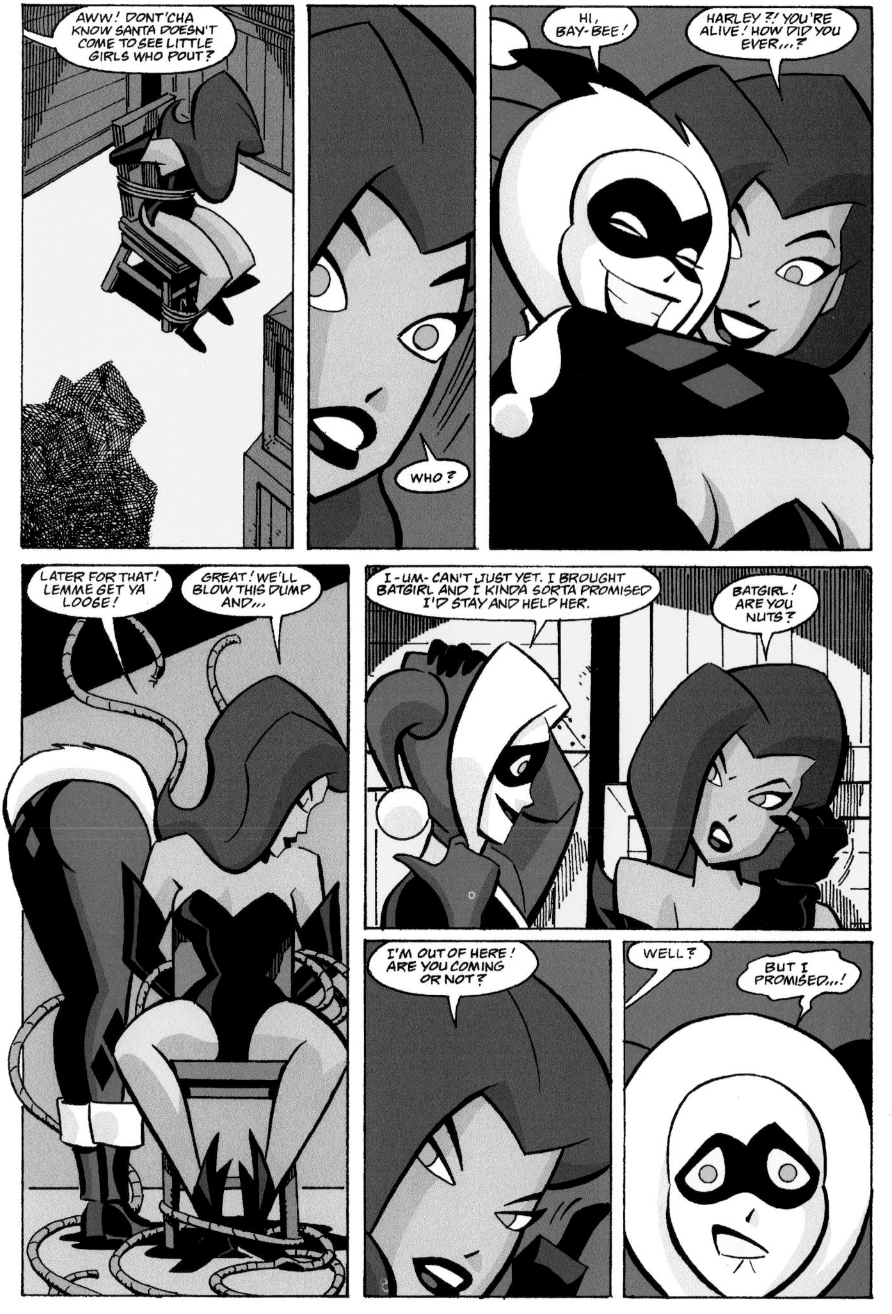
AWW! DONT'CHA KNOW SANTA DOESN'T COME TO SEE LITTLE GIRLS WHO POUT?
WHO?
HI, BAY-BEE!
HARLEY?! YOU'RE ALIVE! HOW DID YOU EVER,,,?
LATER FOR THAT! LEMME GET YA LOOSE!
GREAT! WE'LL BLOW THIS DUMP AND,,,
I-UM- CAN'T JUST YET. I BROUGHT BATGIRL AND I KINDA SORTA PROMISED I'D STAY AND HELP HER.
BATGIRL! ARE YOU NUTS?
I'M OUT OF HERE! ARE YOU COMING OR NOT?
WELL?
BUT I PROMISED,,,!

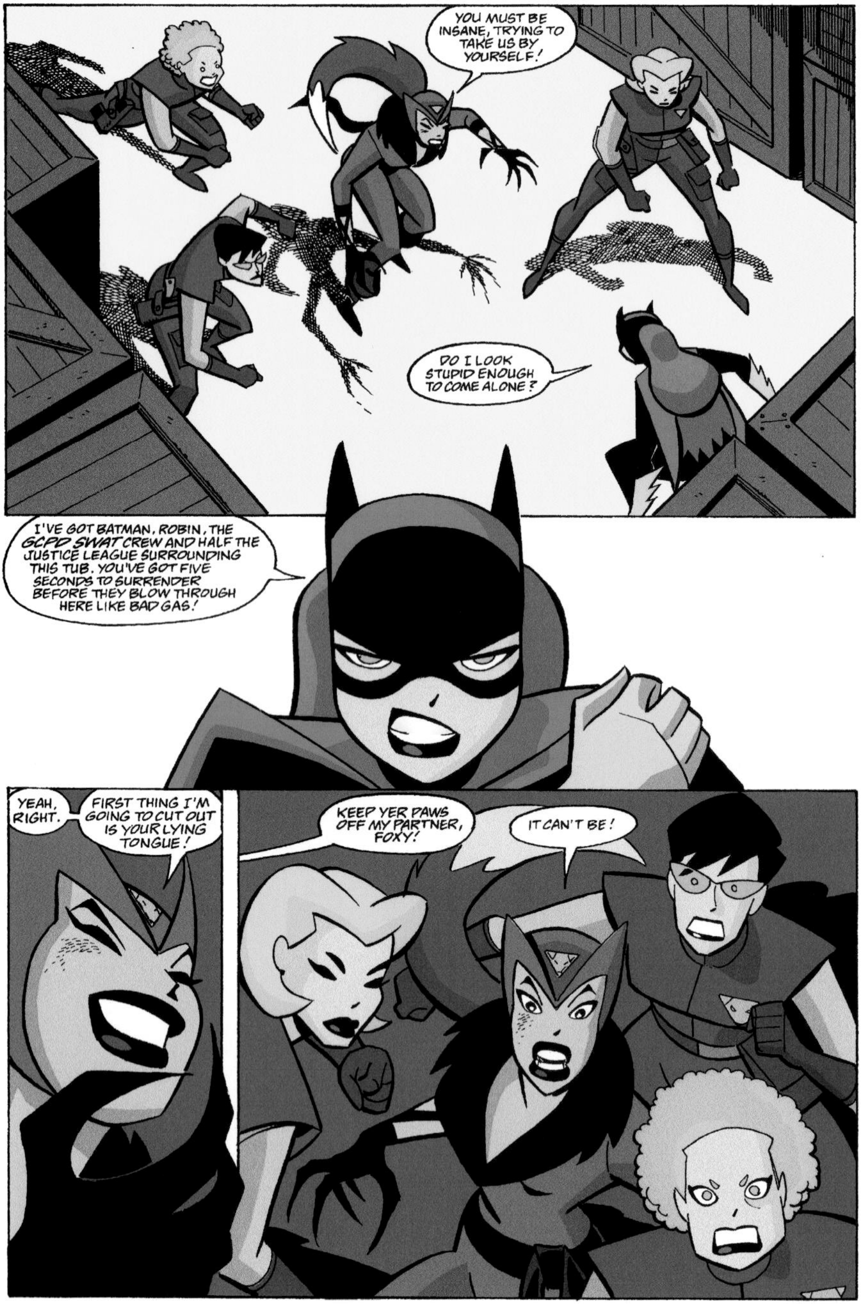
YOU MUST BE INSANE, TRYING TO TAKE US BY YOURSELF!
DO I LOOK STUPID ENOUGH TO COME ALONE?
I'VE GOT BATMAN, ROBIN, THE GCPD SWAT CREW AND HALF THE JUSTICE LEAGUE SURROUNDING THIS TUB. YOU'VE GOT FIVE SECONDS TO SURRENDER BEFORE THEY BLOW THROUGH HERE LIKE BAD GAS!
YEAH, RIGHT.
FIRST THING I'M GOING TO CUT OUT IS YOUR LYING TONGUE!
KEEP YER PAWS OFF MY PARTNER, FOXY!
IT CAN'T BE!

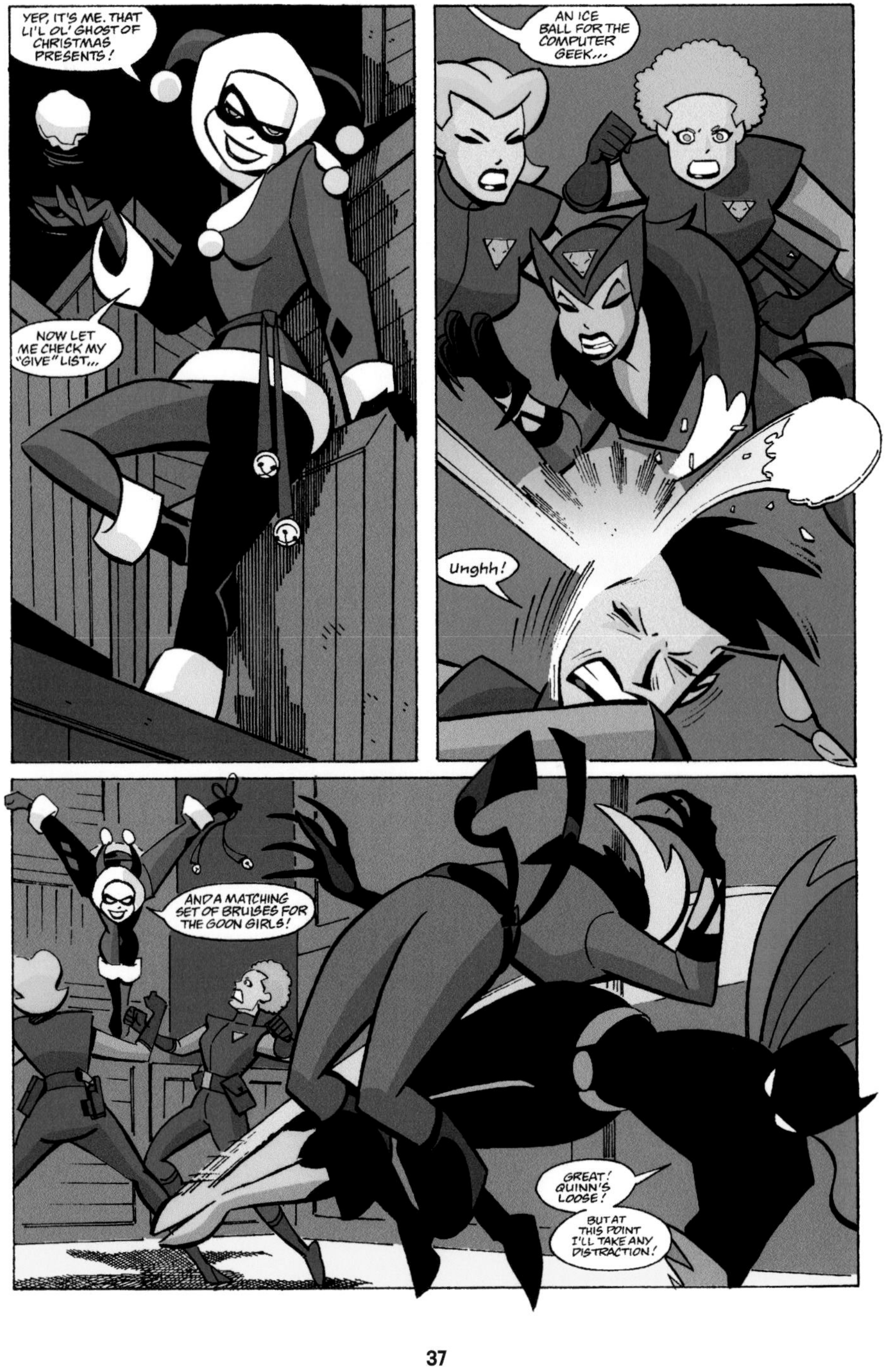
YEP, IT'S ME. THAT LI'L OL' GHOST OF CHRISTMAS PRESENTS!
NOW LET ME CHECK MY "GIVE" LIST...
AN ICE BALL FOR THE COMPUTER GEEK...
Unghh!
AND A MATCHING SET OF BRUISES FOR THE GOON GIRLS!
GREAT! QUINN'S LOOSE!
BUT AT THIS POINT I'LL TAKE ANY DISTRACTION!

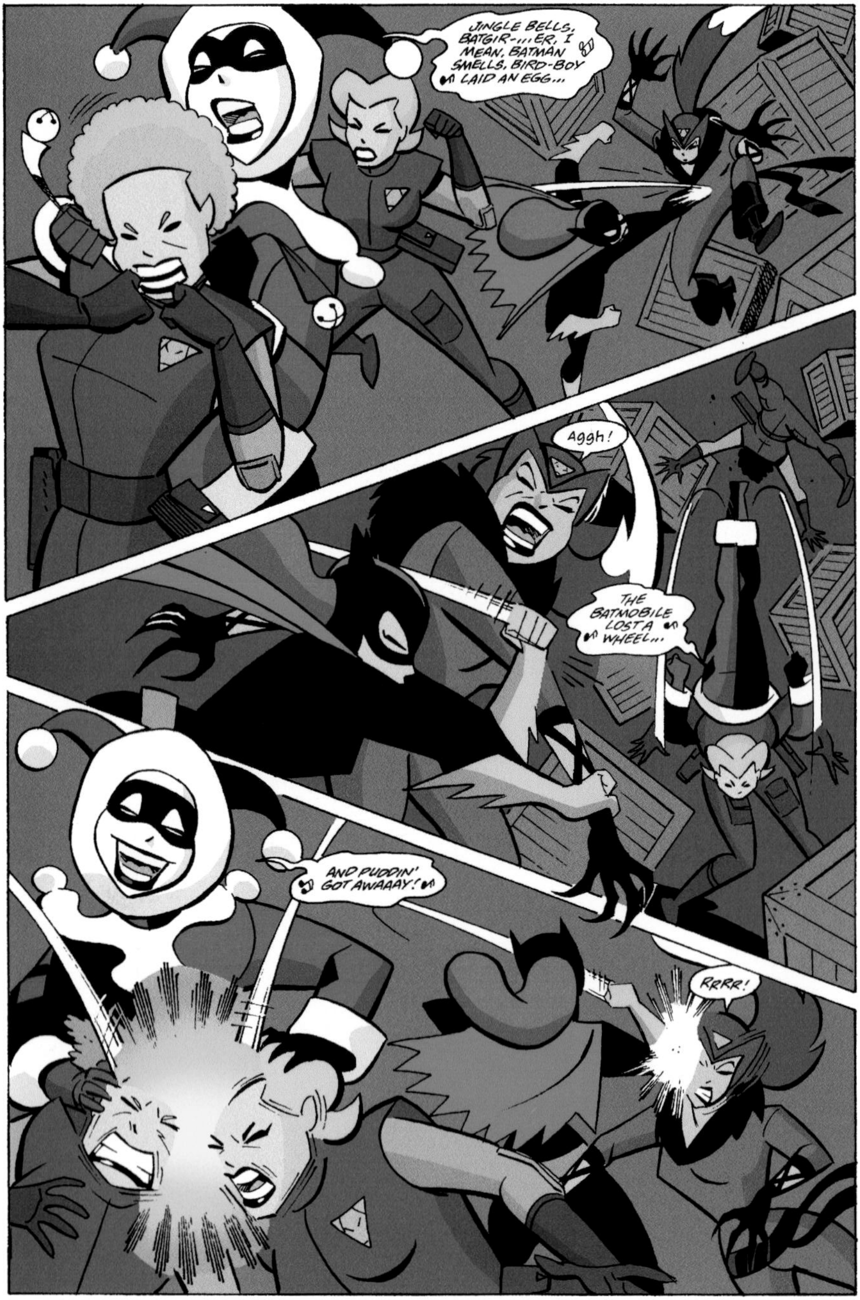
JINGLE BELLS, BATGIR-... ER, I MEAN, BATMAN SMELLS, BIRD-BOY LAID AN EGG...
Aggh!
THE BATMOBILE LOST A WHEEL...
AND PUDDIN' GOT AWAAAY!
RRRR!

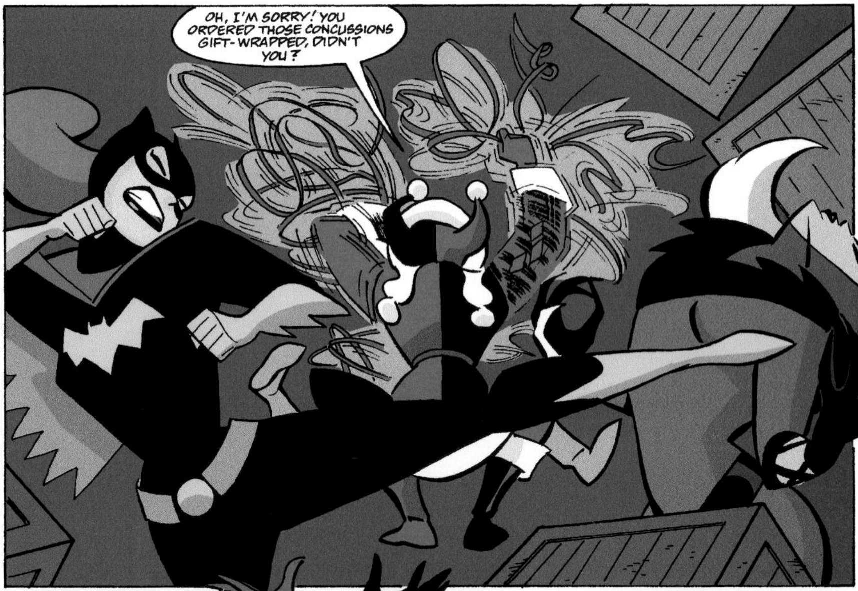
OH, I'M SORRY! YOU ORDERED THOSE CONCUSSIONS GIFT-WRAPPED, DIDN'T YOU?

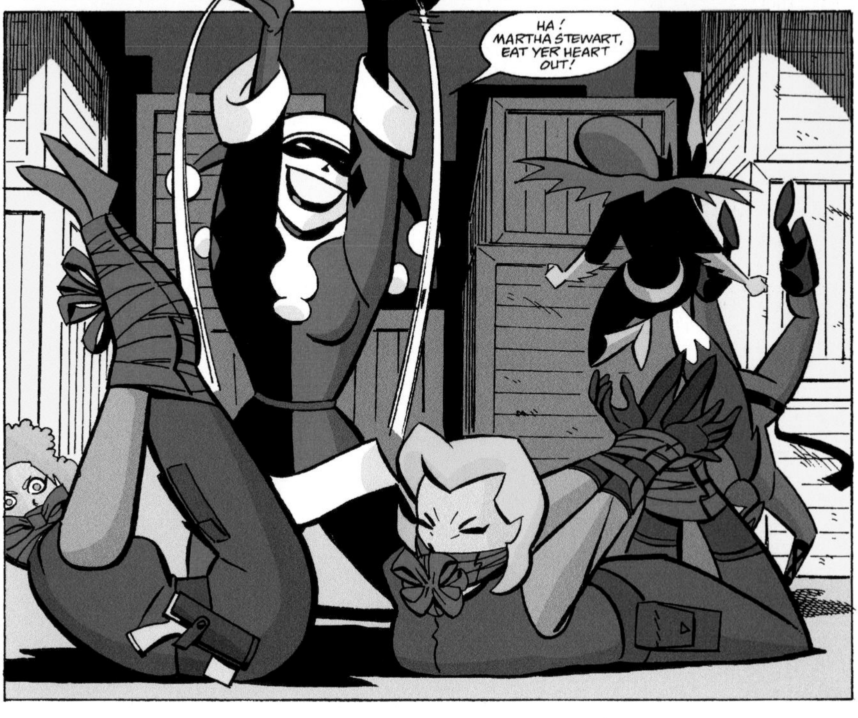
HA! MARTHA STEWART, EAT YER HEART OUT!

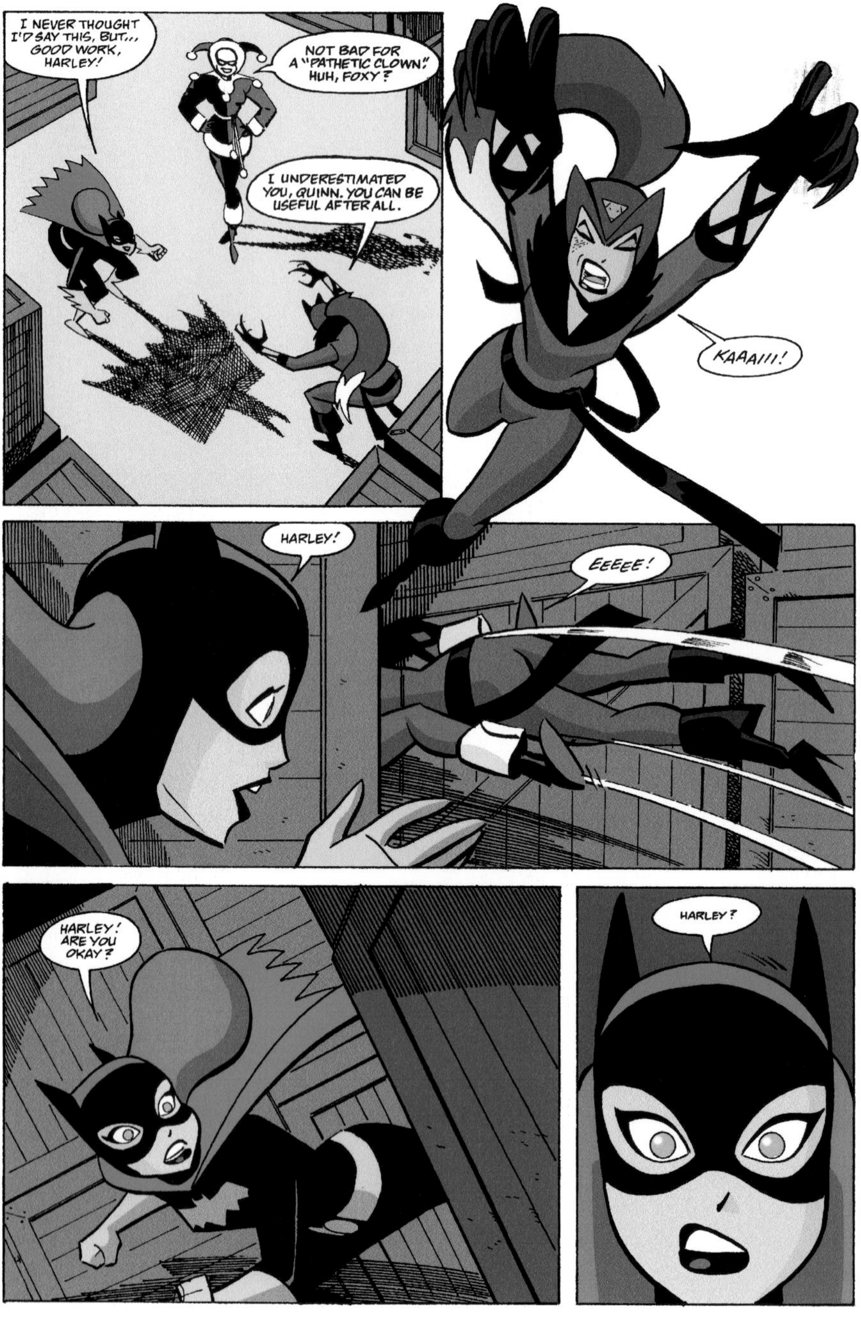
I NEVER THOUGHT I'D SAY THIS, BUT... GOOD WORK, HARLEY!
NOT BAD FOR A "PATHETIC CLOWN," HUH, FOXY?
I UNDERESTIMATED YOU, QUINN. YOU CAN BE USEFUL AFTER ALL.
KAAAIII!
HARLEY!
EEEEE!
HARLEY! ARE YOU OKAY?
HARLEY?

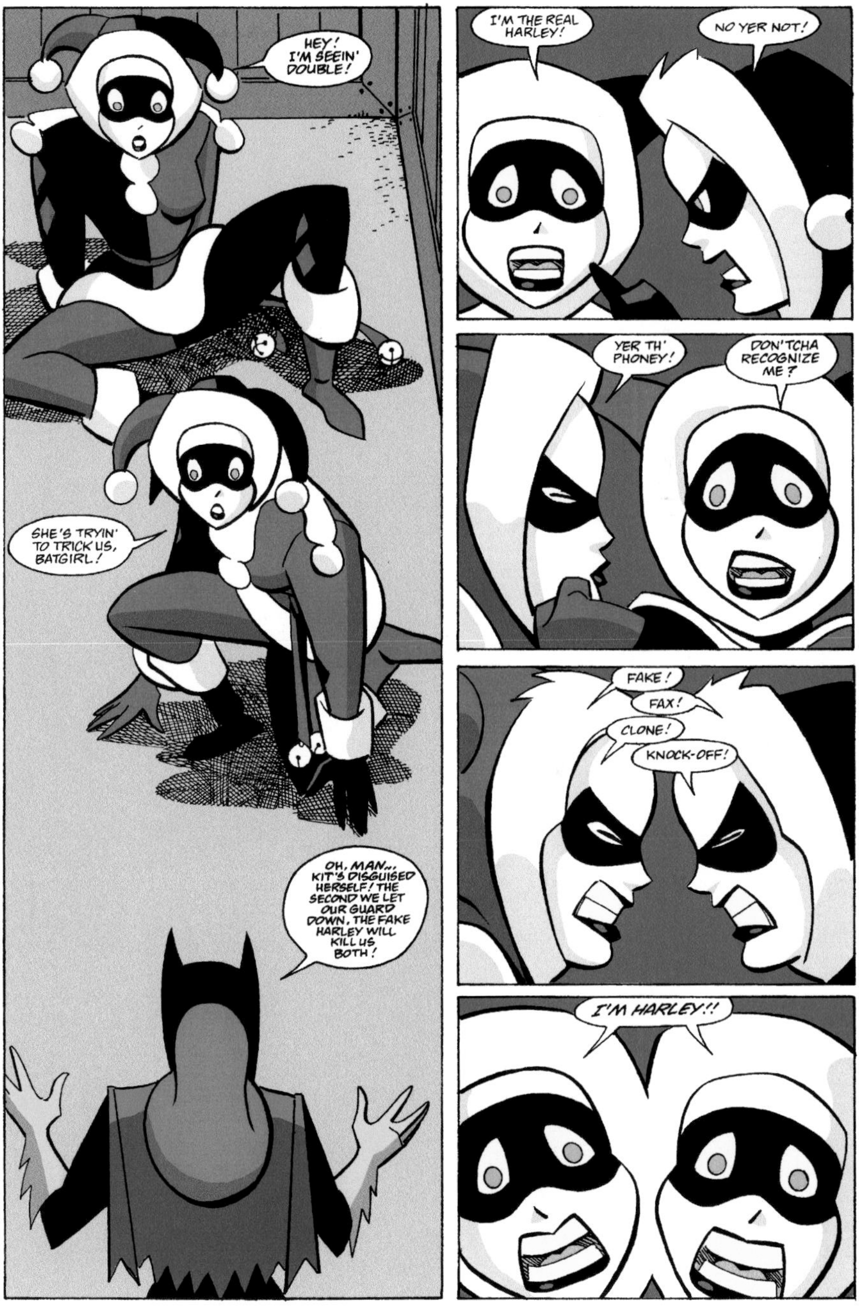
HEY! I'M SEEIN' DOUBLE!
SHE'S TRYIN' TO TRICK US, BATGIRL!
OH, MAN... KIT'S DISGUISED HERSELF! THE SECOND WE LET OUR GUARD DOWN, THE FAKE HARLEY WILL KILL US BOTH!
I'M THE REAL HARLEY!
NO YER NOT!
YER TH' PHONEY!
DON'TCHA RECOGNIZE ME?
FAKE!
FAX!
CLONE!
KNOCK-OFF!
I'M HARLEY!!

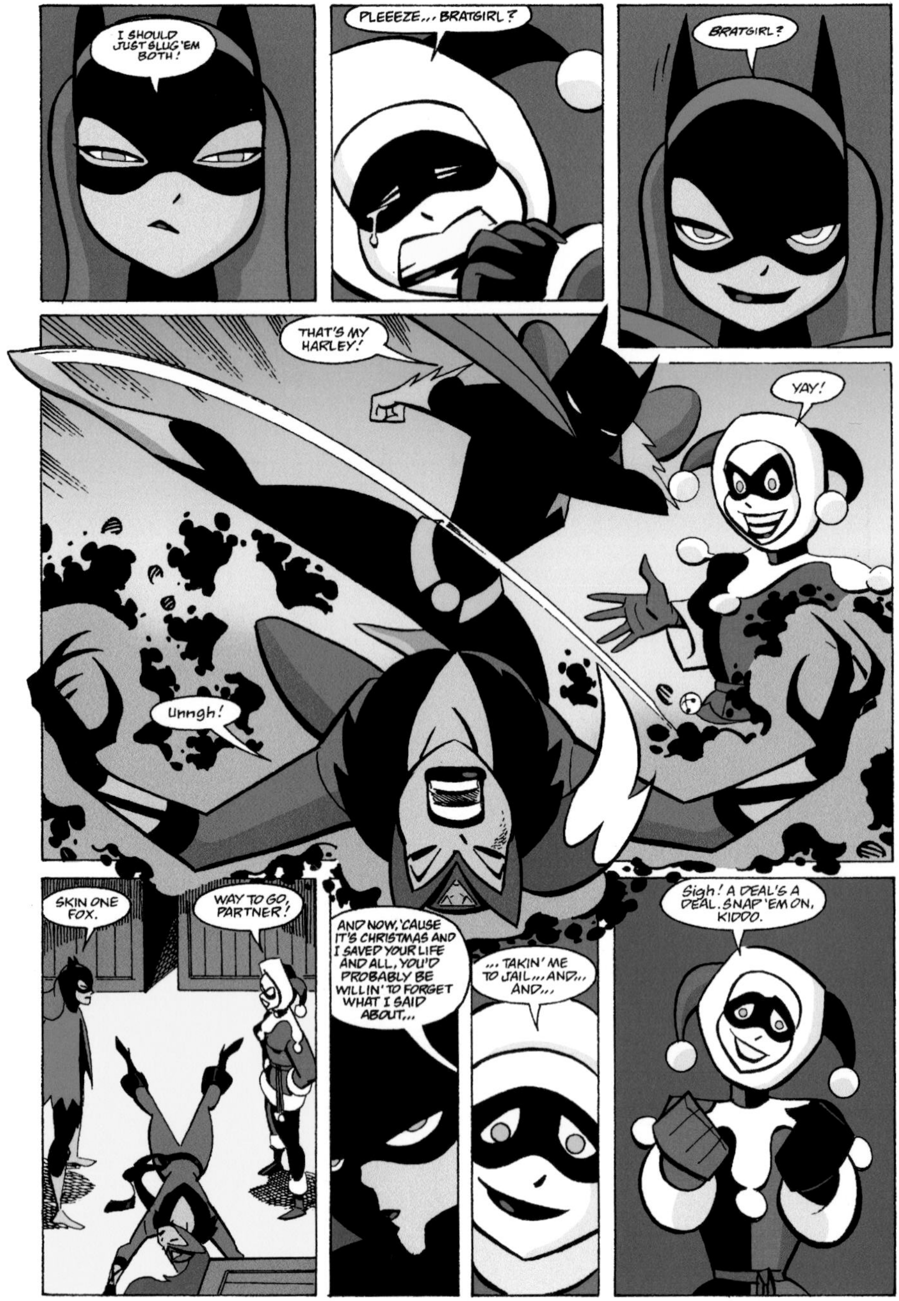
I SHOULD JUST SLUG 'EM BOTH!
PLEEEZE... BRATGIRL?
BRATGIRL?
THAT'S MY HARLEY!
YAY!
Unngh!
SKIN ONE FOX.
WAY TO GO, PARTNER!
AND NOW, 'CAUSE IT'S CHRISTMAS AND I SAVED YOUR LIFE AND ALL, YOU'D PROBABLY BE WILLIN' TO FORGET WHAT I SAID ABOUT...
...TAKIN' ME TO JAIL... AND... AND...
Sigh! A DEAL'S A DEAL. SNAP 'EM ON, KIDDO.

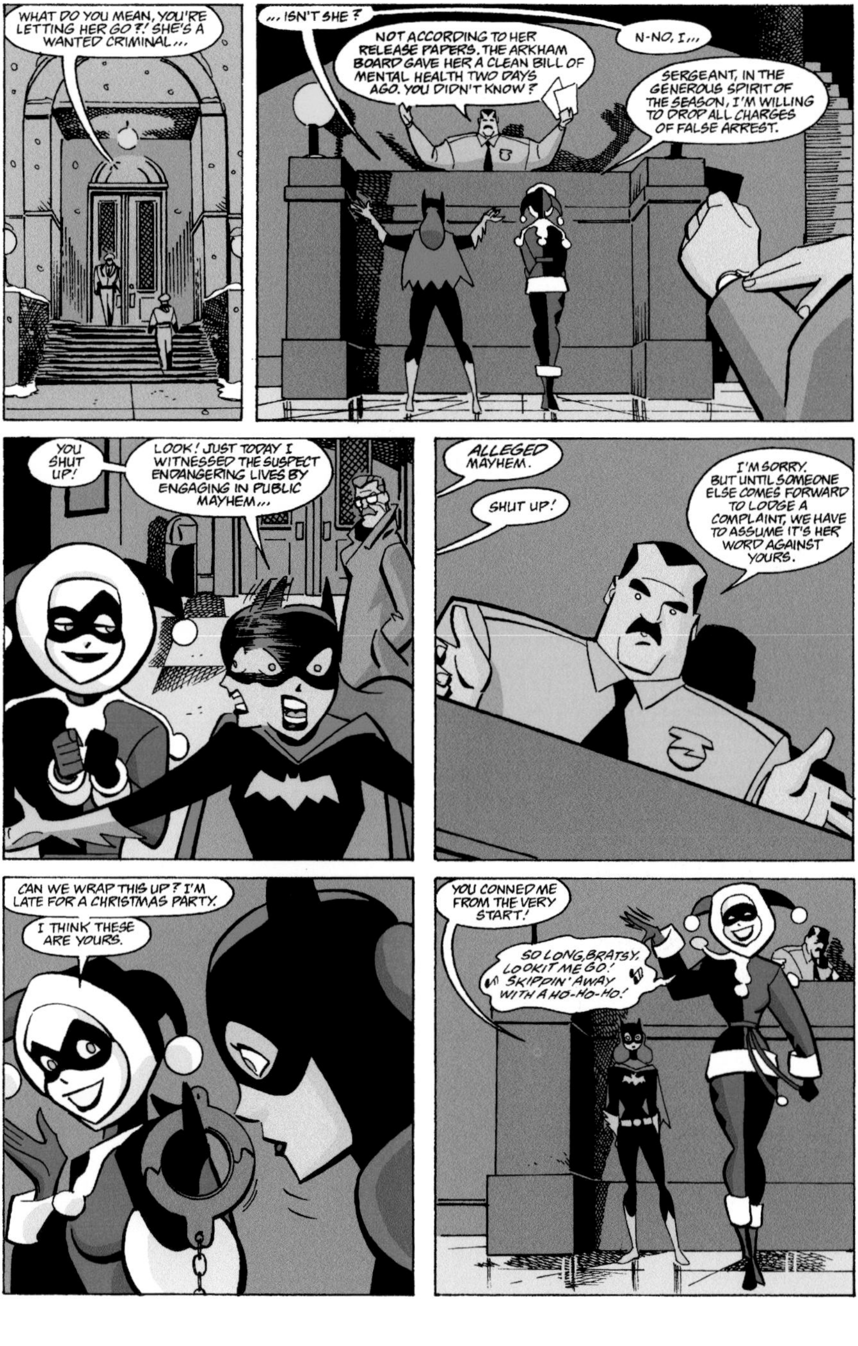
WHAT DO YOU MEAN, YOU'RE LETTING HER GO?! SHE'S A WANTED CRIMINAL...
...ISN'T SHE?
NOT ACCORDING TO HER RELEASE PAPERS. THE ARKHAM BOARD GAVE HER A CLEAN BILL OF MENTAL HEALTH TWO DAYS AGO. YOU DIDN'T KNOW?
N-NO, I...
SERGEANT, IN THE GENEROUS SPIRIT OF THE SEASON, I'M WILLING TO DROP ALL CHARGES OF FALSE ARREST.
YOU SHUT UP!
LOOK! JUST TODAY I WITNESSED THE SUSPECT ENDANGERING LIVES BY ENGAGING IN PUBLIC MAYHEM...
ALLEGED MAYHEM.
SHUT UP!
I'M SORRY. BUT UNTIL SOMEONE ELSE COMES FORWARD TO LODGE A COMPLAINT, WE HAVE TO ASSUME IT'S HER WORD AGAINST YOURS.
CAN WE WRAP THIS UP? I'M LATE FOR A CHRISTMAS PARTY.
I THINK THESE ARE YOURS.
YOU CONNED ME FROM THE VERY START!
SO LONG, BRATSY. LOOKIT ME GO! SKIPPIN' AWAY WITH A HO-HO-HO!

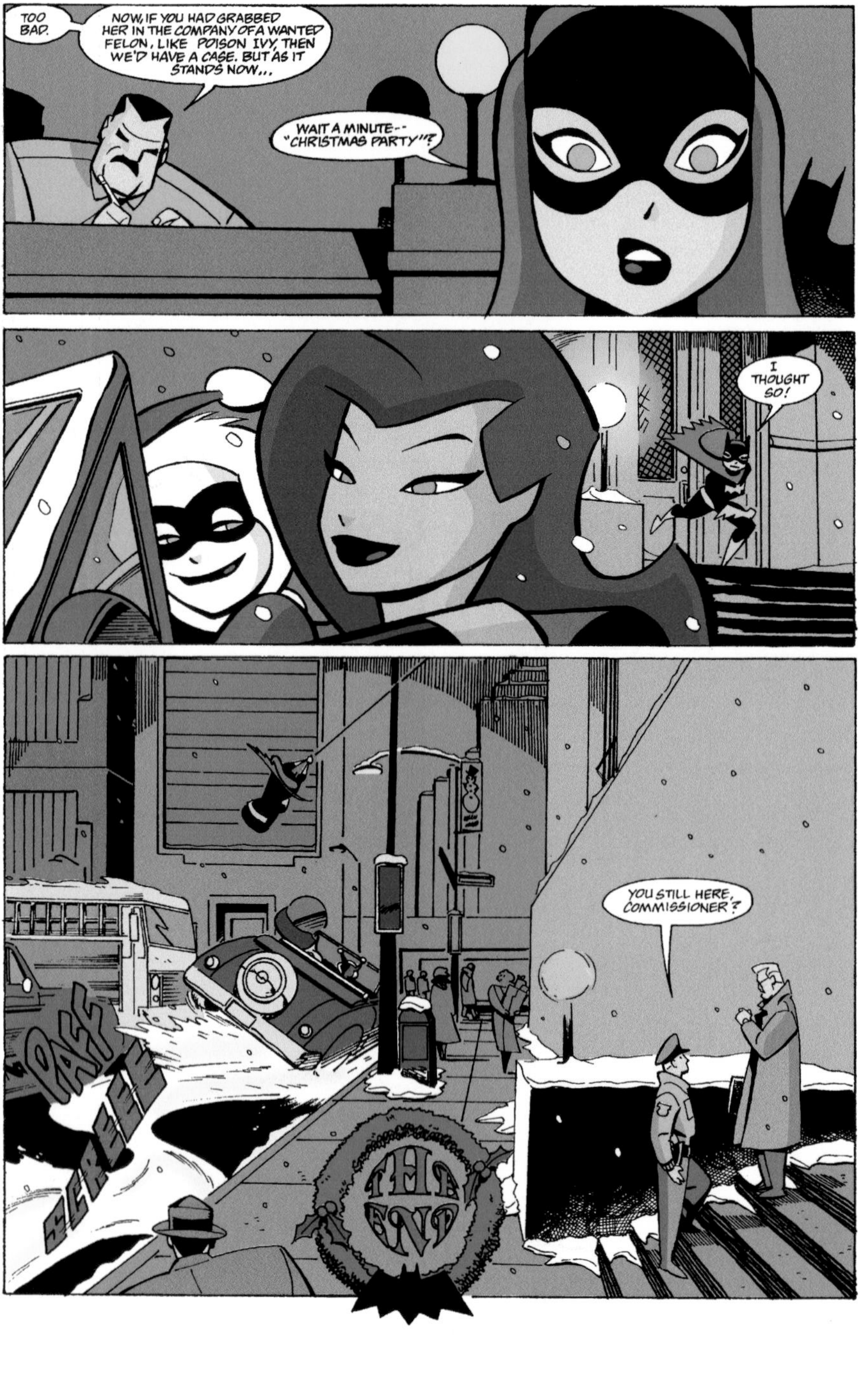
TOO BAD.
NOW, IF YOU HAD GRABBED HER IN THE COMPANY OF A WANTED FELON, LIKE POISON IVY, THEN WE'D HAVE A CASE. BUT AS IT STANDS NOW...
WAIT A MINUTE-- "CHRISTMAS PARTY"?
I THOUGHT SO!
PAFF
SCREEEE
YOU STILL HERE, COMMISSIONER?
THE END

CHAPTER 2: THE HUNCHBACK OF NOTRE DAME

BATGIRL

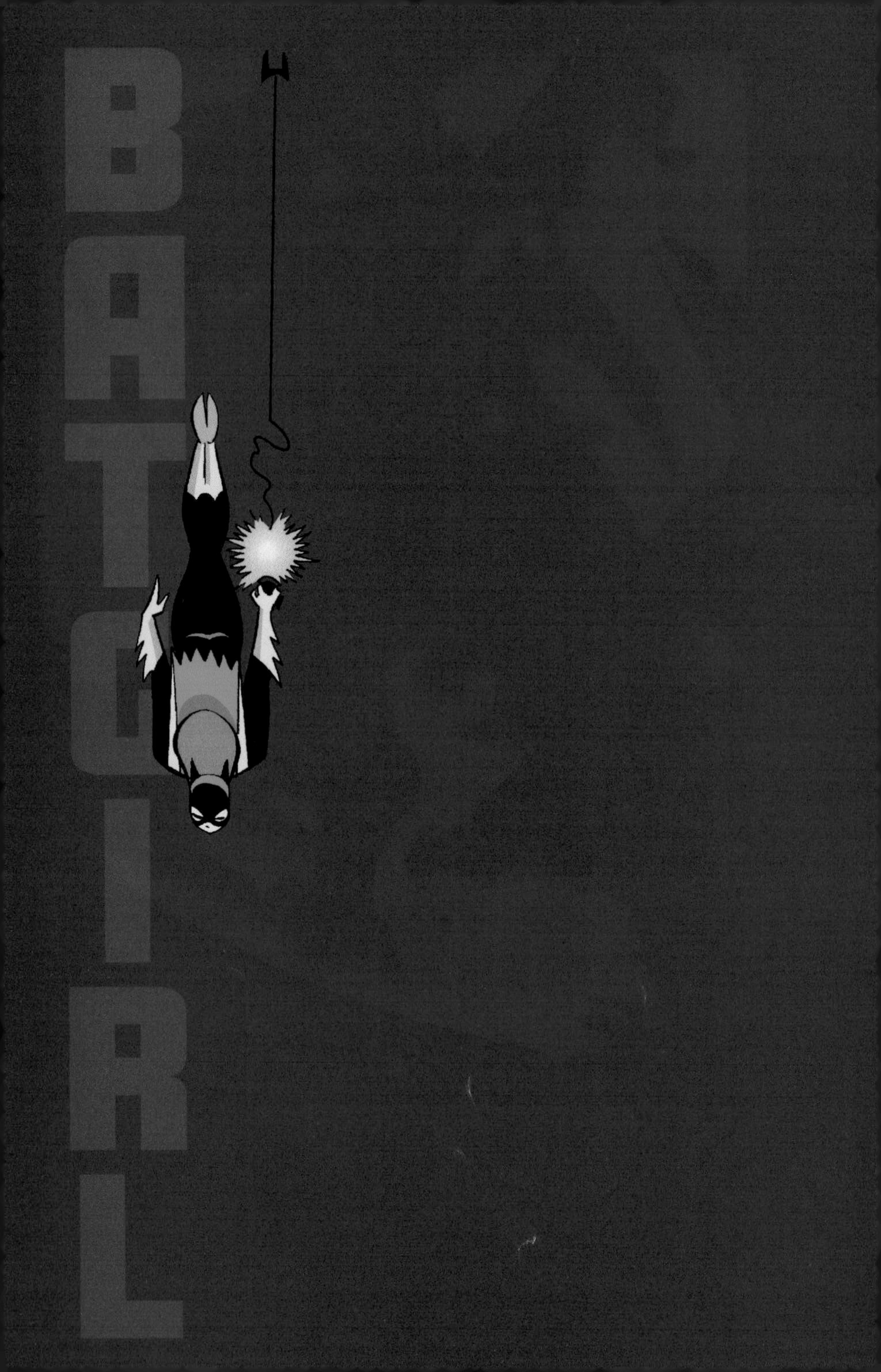
BATGIRL

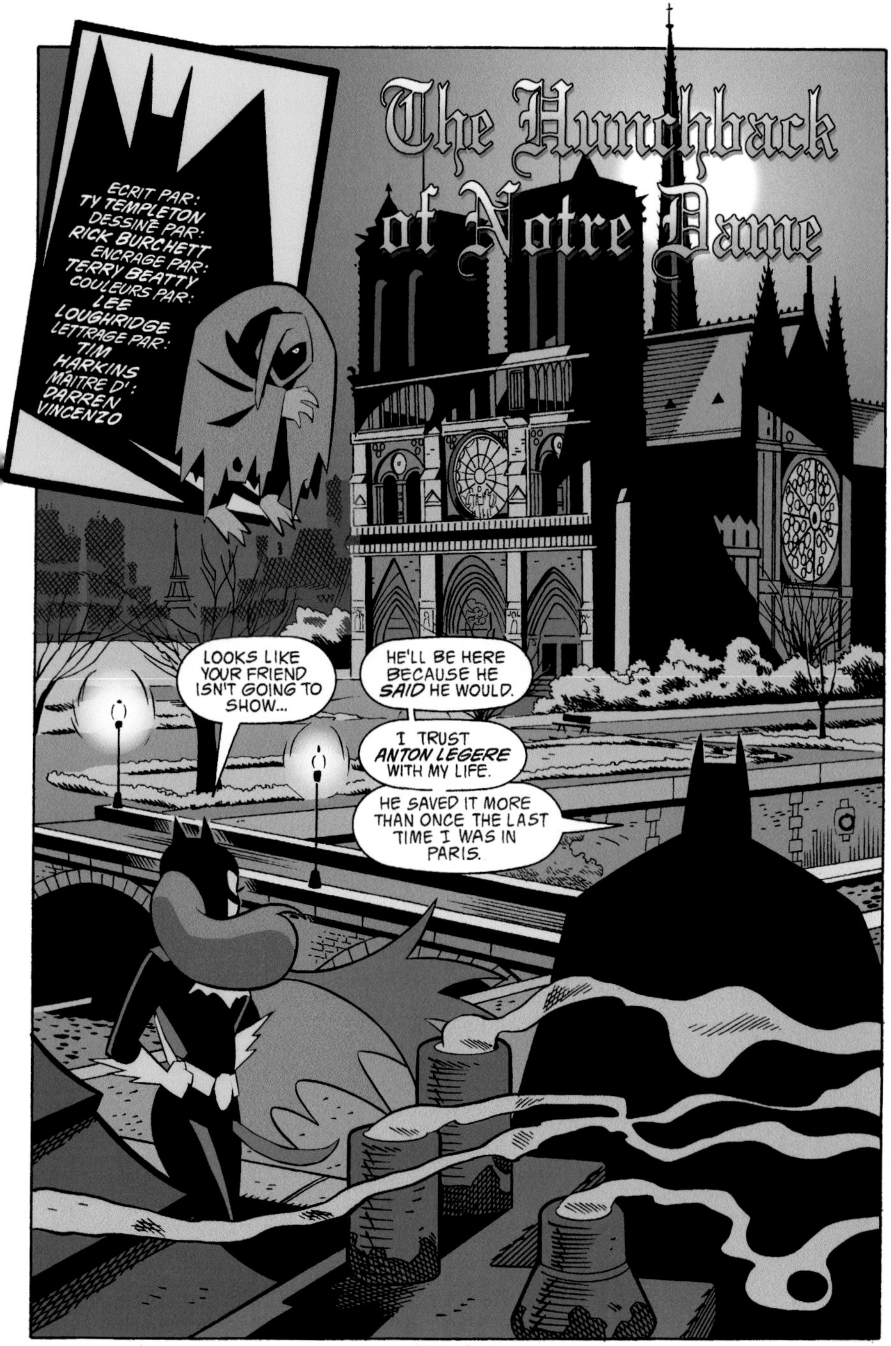

The Hunchback of Notre Dame
ECRIT PAR: TY TEMPLETON
DESSINÉ PAR: RICK BURCHETT
ENCRAGE PAR: TERRY BEATTY
COULEURS PAR: LEE LOUGHRIDGE
LETTRAGE PAR: TIM HARKINS
MAITRE D': DARREN VINCENZO
LOOKS LIKE YOUR FRIEND ISN'T GOING TO SHOW...
HE'LL BE HERE BECAUSE HE *SAID* HE WOULD.
I TRUST *ANTON LEGERE* WITH MY LIFE.
HE SAVED IT MORE THAN ONCE THE LAST TIME I WAS IN PARIS.

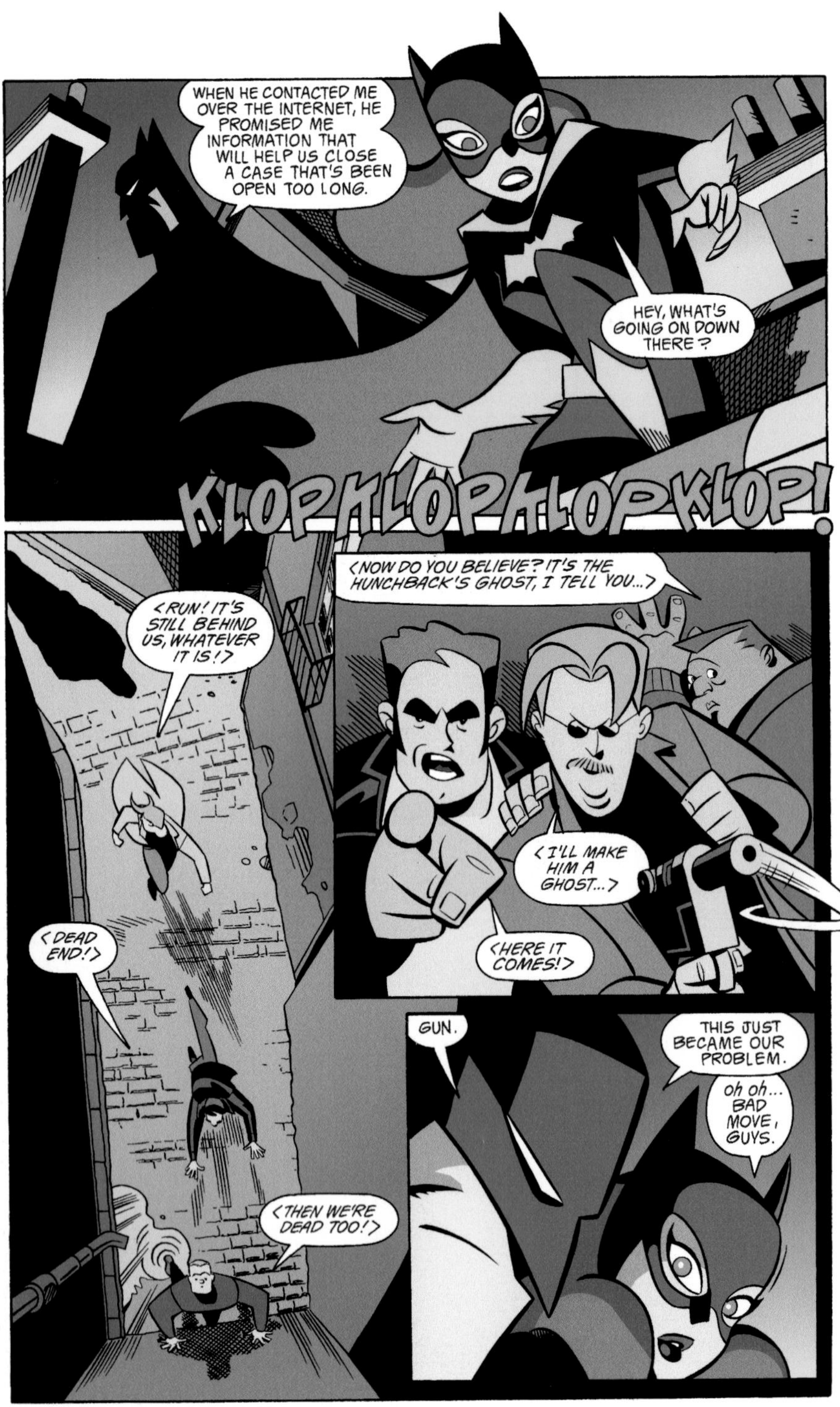
WHEN HE CONTACTED ME OVER THE INTERNET, HE PROMISED ME INFORMATION THAT WILL HELP US CLOSE A CASE THAT'S BEEN OPEN TOO LONG.
HEY, WHAT'S GOING ON DOWN THERE?
KLOPKLOPKLOPKLOP!
<RUN! IT'S STILL BEHIND US, WHATEVER IT IS!>
<DEAD END!>
<THEN WE'RE DEAD TOO!>
<NOW DO YOU BELIEVE? IT'S THE HUNCHBACK'S GHOST, I TELL YOU...>
<I'LL MAKE HIM A GHOST...>
<HERE IT COMES!>
GUN.
THIS JUST BECAME OUR PROBLEM.
oh oh... BAD MOVE, GUYS.

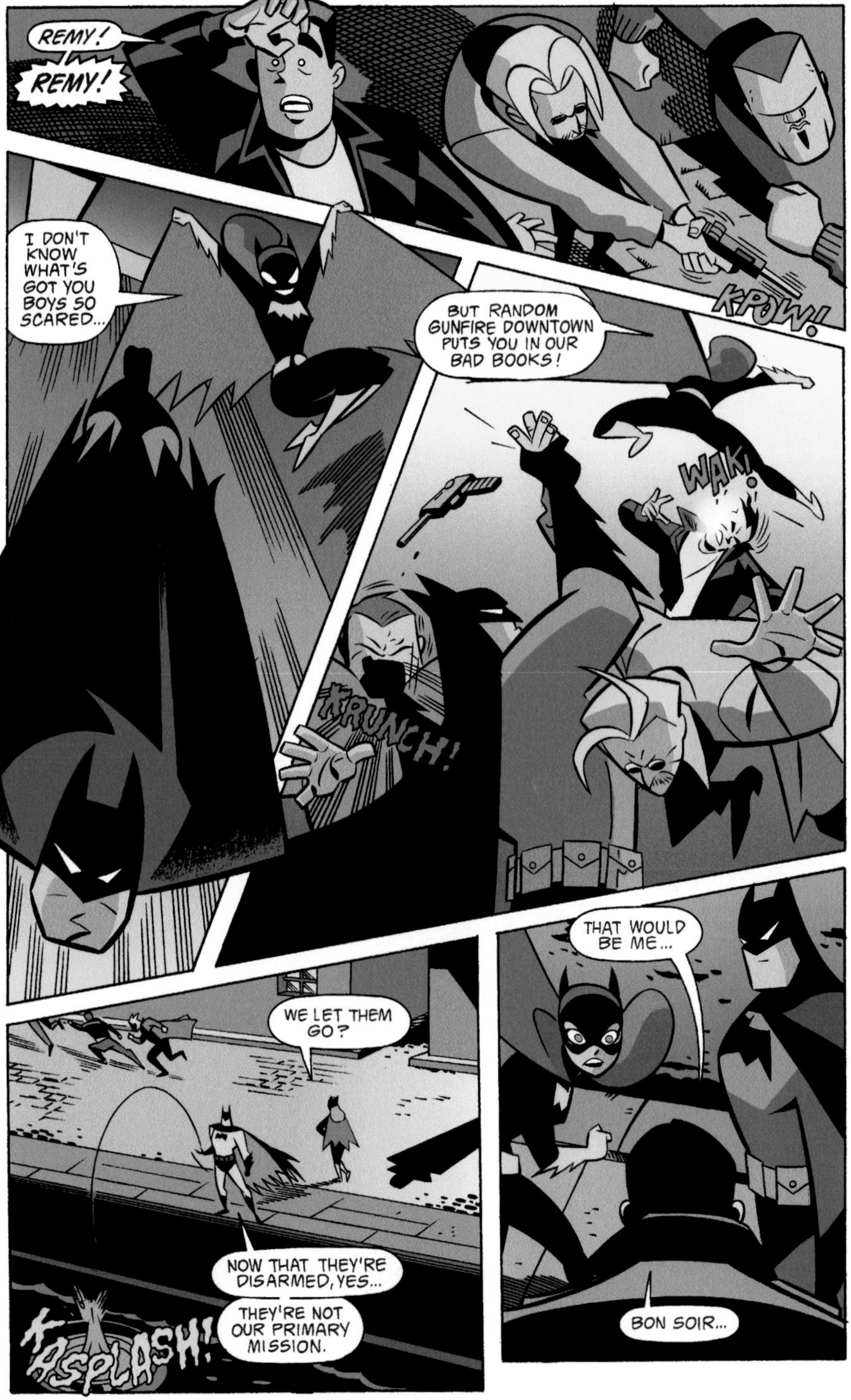
REMY!
REMY!
KPOW!
I DON'T KNOW WHAT'S GOT YOU BOYS SO SCARED...
BUT RANDOM GUNFIRE DOWNTOWN PUTS YOU IN OUR BAD BOOKS!
WAK!
KRUNCH!
WE LET THEM GO?
NOW THAT THEY'RE DISARMED, YES...
THEY'RE NOT OUR PRIMARY MISSION.
KASPLASH!
THAT WOULD BE ME...
BON SOIR...

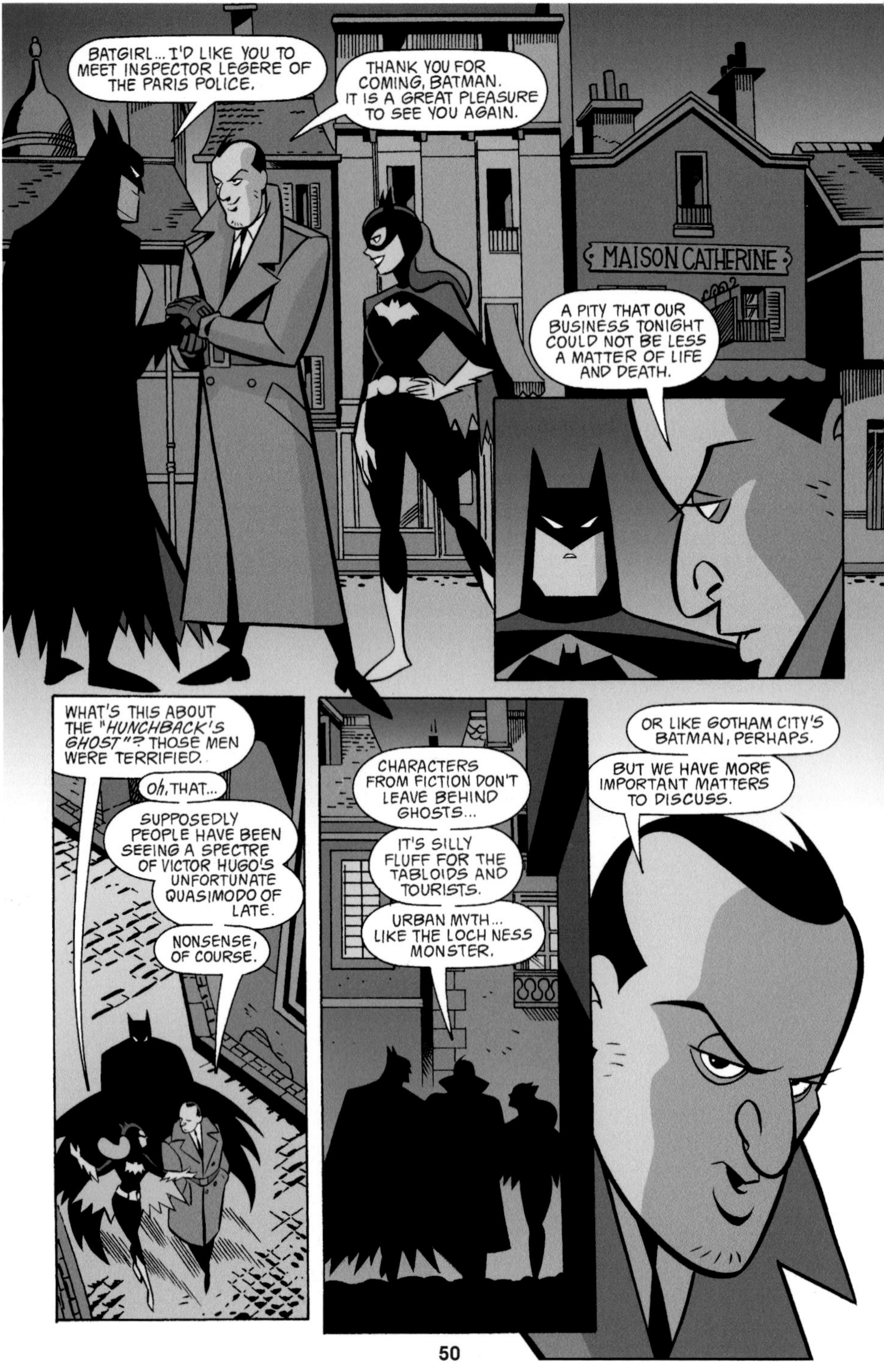
BATGIRL... I'D LIKE YOU TO MEET INSPECTOR LEGERE OF THE PARIS POLICE.
THANK YOU FOR COMING, BATMAN. IT IS A GREAT PLEASURE TO SEE YOU AGAIN.
MAISON CATHERINE
A PITY THAT OUR BUSINESS TONIGHT COULD NOT BE LESS A MATTER OF LIFE AND DEATH.
WHAT'S THIS ABOUT THE "HUNCHBACK'S GHOST"? THOSE MEN WERE TERRIFIED.
Oh, THAT...
SUPPOSEDLY PEOPLE HAVE BEEN SEEING A SPECTRE OF VICTOR HUGO'S UNFORTUNATE QUASIMODO OF LATE.
NONSENSE, OF COURSE.
CHARACTERS FROM FICTION DON'T LEAVE BEHIND GHOSTS...
IT'S SILLY FLUFF FOR THE TABLOIDS AND TOURISTS.
URBAN MYTH... LIKE THE LOCH NESS MONSTER.
OR LIKE GOTHAM CITY'S BATMAN, PERHAPS.
BUT WE HAVE MORE IMPORTANT MATTERS TO DISCUSS.

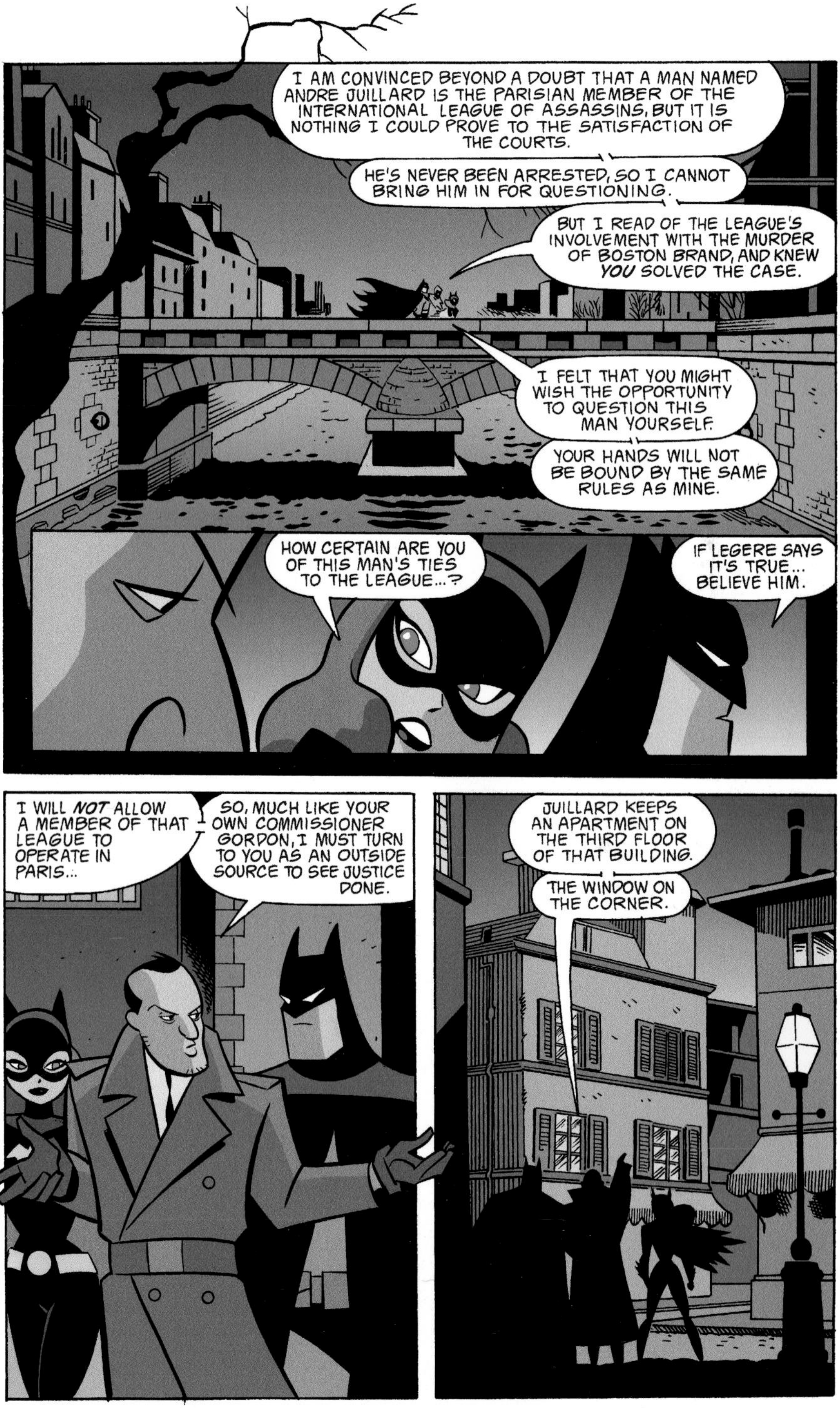
I AM CONVINCED BEYOND A DOUBT THAT A MAN NAMED ANDRE JUILLARD IS THE PARISIAN MEMBER OF THE INTERNATIONAL LEAGUE OF ASSASSINS, BUT IT IS NOTHING I COULD PROVE TO THE SATISFACTION OF THE COURTS.
HE'S NEVER BEEN ARRESTED, SO I CANNOT BRING HIM IN FOR QUESTIONING.
BUT I READ OF THE LEAGUE'S INVOLVEMENT WITH THE MURDER OF BOSTON BRAND, AND KNEW *YOU* SOLVED THE CASE.
I FELT THAT YOU MIGHT WISH THE OPPORTUNITY TO QUESTION THIS MAN YOURSELF.
YOUR HANDS WILL NOT BE BOUND BY THE SAME RULES AS MINE.
HOW CERTAIN ARE YOU OF THIS MAN'S TIES TO THE LEAGUE...?
IF LEGERE SAYS IT'S TRUE... BELIEVE HIM.
I WILL *NOT* ALLOW A MEMBER OF THAT LEAGUE TO OPERATE IN PARIS...
SO, MUCH LIKE YOUR OWN COMMISSIONER GORDON, I MUST TURN TO YOU AS AN OUTSIDE SOURCE TO SEE JUSTICE DONE.
JUILLARD KEEPS AN APARTMENT ON THE THIRD FLOOR OF THAT BUILDING.
THE WINDOW ON THE CORNER.

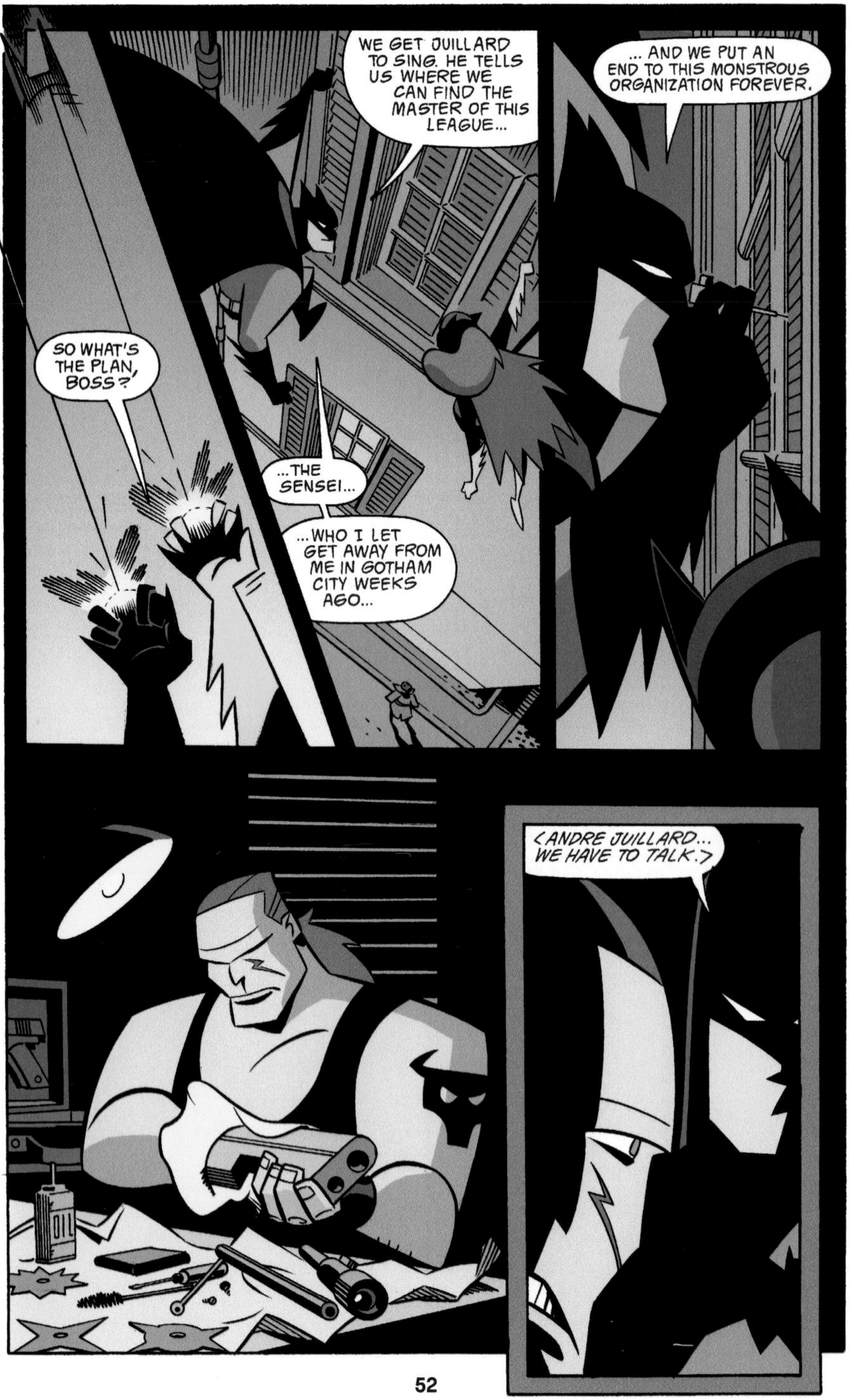
SO WHAT'S THE PLAN, BOSS?
WE GET JUILLARD TO SING. HE TELLS US WHERE WE CAN FIND THE MASTER OF THIS LEAGUE...
...THE SENSEI...
...WHO I LET GET AWAY FROM ME IN GOTHAM CITY WEEKS AGO...
... AND WE PUT AN END TO THIS MONSTROUS ORGANIZATION FOREVER.
OIL
<ANDRE JUILLARD... WE HAVE TO TALK.>

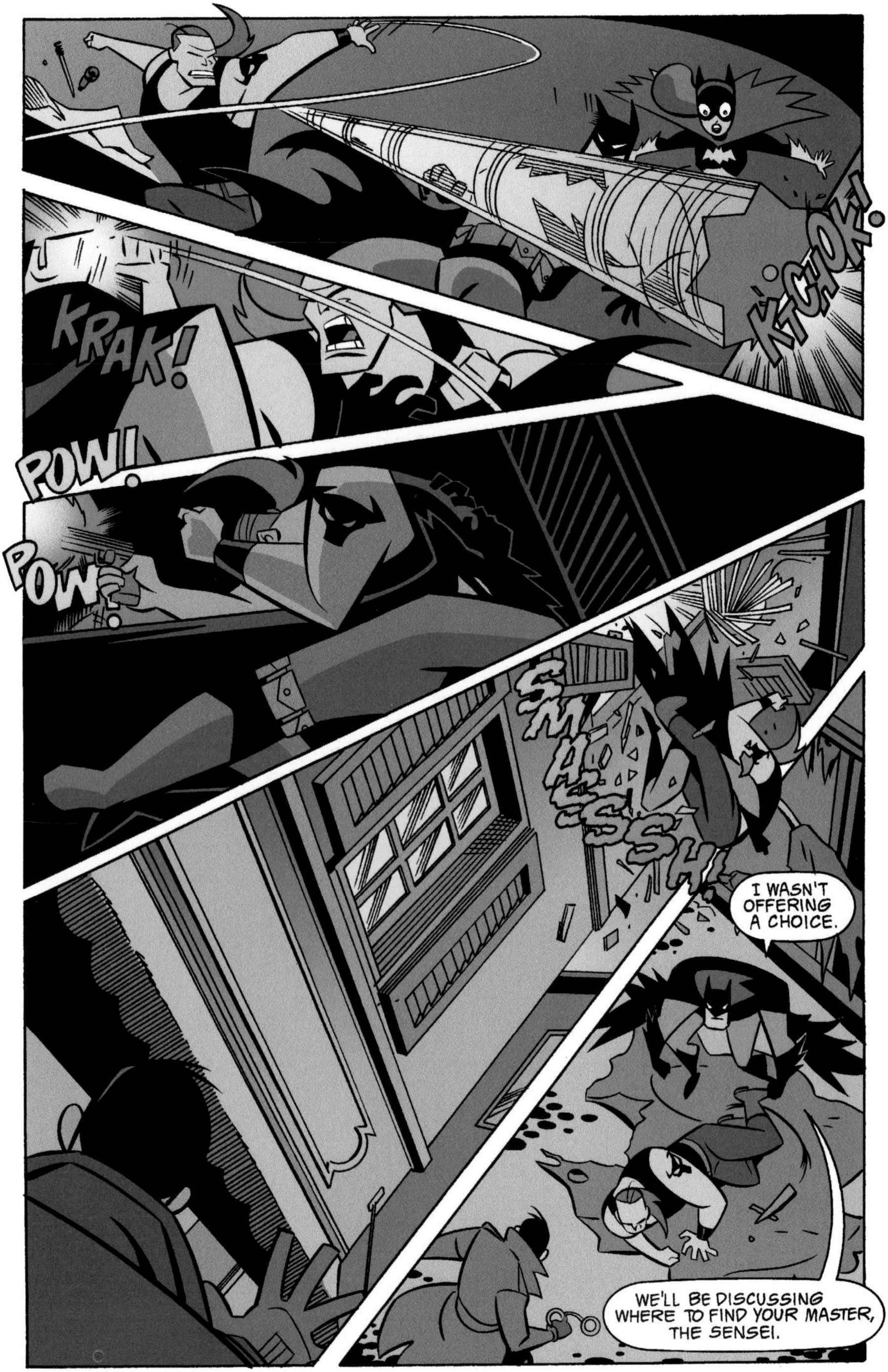
K'CHOK!
KRAK!
POW!
POW!
SMASSSH!
I WASN'T OFFERING A CHOICE.
WE'LL BE DISCUSSING WHERE TO FIND YOUR MASTER, THE SENSEI.

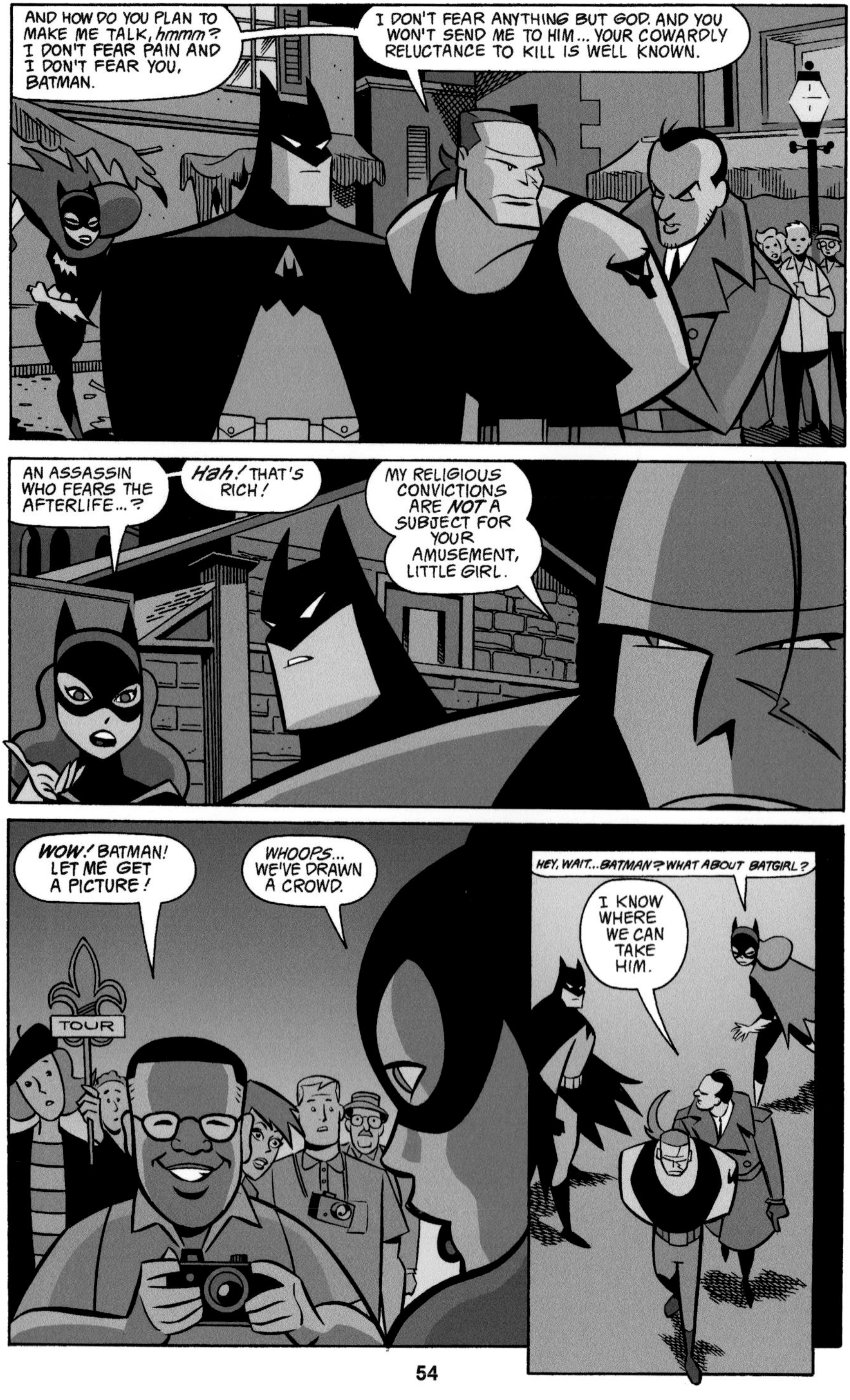
AND HOW DO YOU PLAN TO MAKE ME TALK, *hmmm*? I DON'T FEAR PAIN AND I DON'T FEAR YOU, BATMAN.
I DON'T FEAR ANYTHING BUT GOD. AND YOU WON'T SEND ME TO HIM... YOUR COWARDLY RELUCTANCE TO KILL IS WELL KNOWN.
AN ASSASSIN WHO FEARS THE AFTERLIFE...?
Hah! THAT'S RICH!
MY RELIGIOUS CONVICTIONS ARE *NOT* A SUBJECT FOR YOUR AMUSEMENT, LITTLE GIRL.
WOW! BATMAN! LET ME GET A PICTURE!
WHOOPS... WE'VE DRAWN A CROWD.
TOUR
HEY, WAIT... BATMAN? WHAT ABOUT BATGIRL?
I KNOW WHERE WE CAN TAKE HIM.

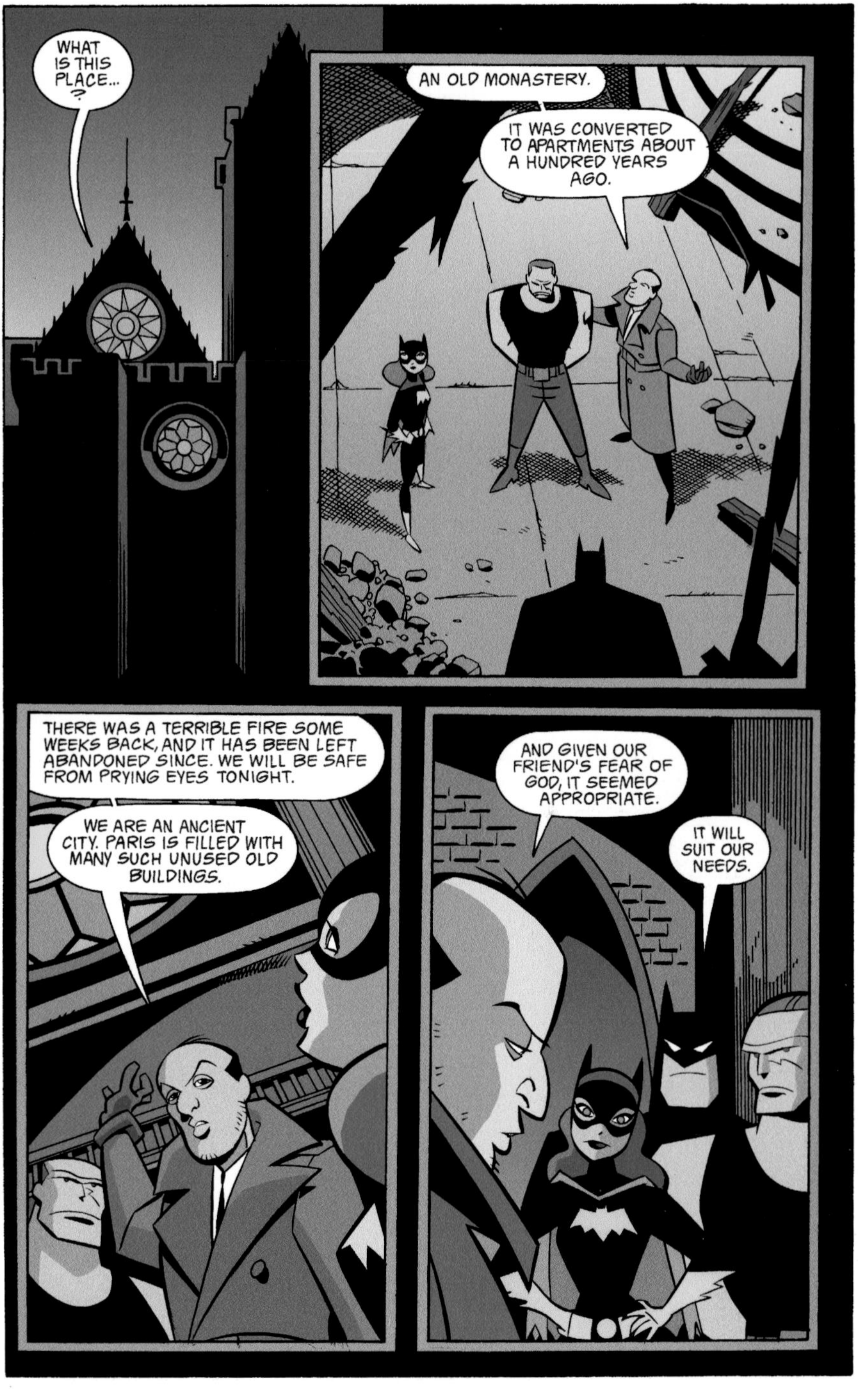
WHAT IS THIS PLACE...?
AN OLD MONASTERY.
IT WAS CONVERTED TO APARTMENTS ABOUT A HUNDRED YEARS AGO.
THERE WAS A TERRIBLE FIRE SOME WEEKS BACK, AND IT HAS BEEN LEFT ABANDONED SINCE. WE WILL BE SAFE FROM PRYING EYES TONIGHT.
WE ARE AN ANCIENT CITY. PARIS IS FILLED WITH MANY SUCH UNUSED OLD BUILDINGS.
AND GIVEN OUR FRIEND'S FEAR OF GOD, IT SEEMED APPROPRIATE.
IT WILL SUIT OUR NEEDS.

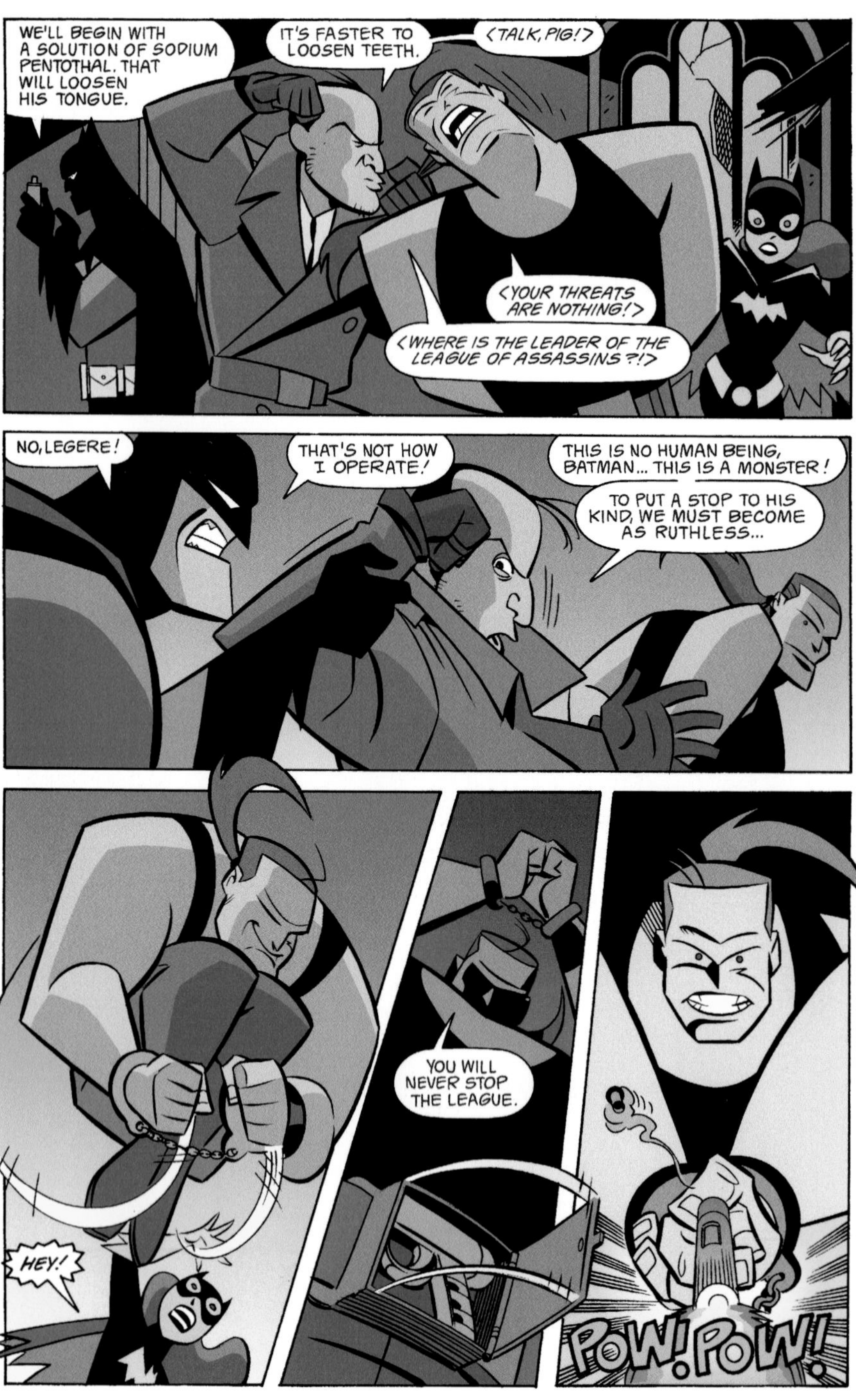
WE'LL BEGIN WITH A SOLUTION OF SODIUM PENTOTHAL. THAT WILL LOOSEN HIS TONGUE.
IT'S FASTER TO LOOSEN TEETH.
<TALK, PIG!>
<YOUR THREATS ARE NOTHING!>
<WHERE IS THE LEADER OF THE LEAGUE OF ASSASSINS?!>
NO, LEGERE!
THAT'S NOT HOW I OPERATE!
THIS IS NO HUMAN BEING, BATMAN... THIS IS A MONSTER!
TO PUT A STOP TO HIS KIND, WE MUST BECOME AS RUTHLESS...
HEY!
YOU WILL NEVER STOP THE LEAGUE.
POW! POW!

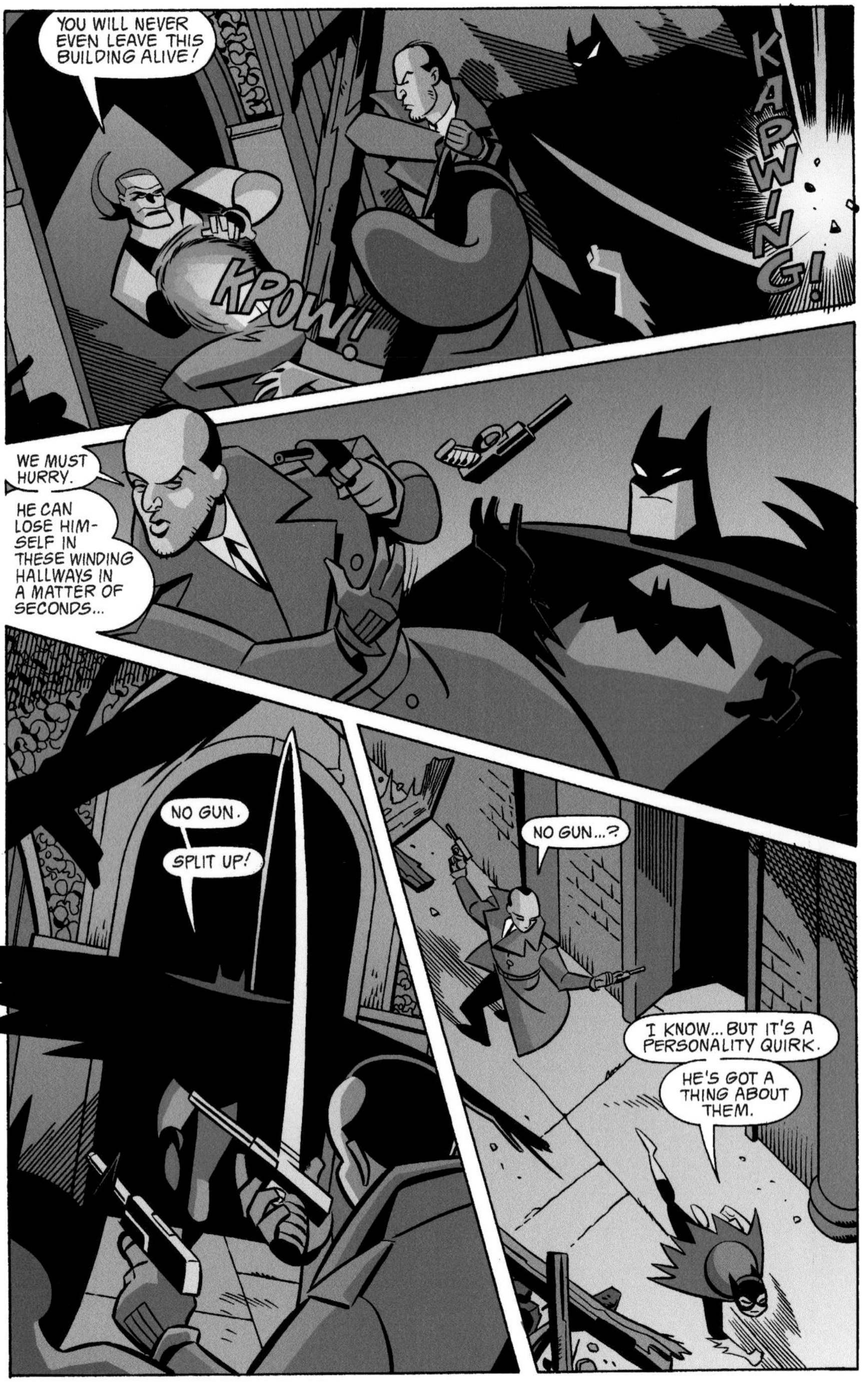
YOU WILL NEVER EVEN LEAVE THIS BUILDING ALIVE!
KAPWING!
KPOW!
WE MUST HURRY.
HE CAN LOSE HIM-SELF IN THESE WINDING HALLWAYS IN A MATTER OF SECONDS...
NO GUN.
SPLIT UP!
NO GUN...?
I KNOW... BUT IT'S A PERSONALITY QUIRK.
HE'S GOT A THING ABOUT THEM.

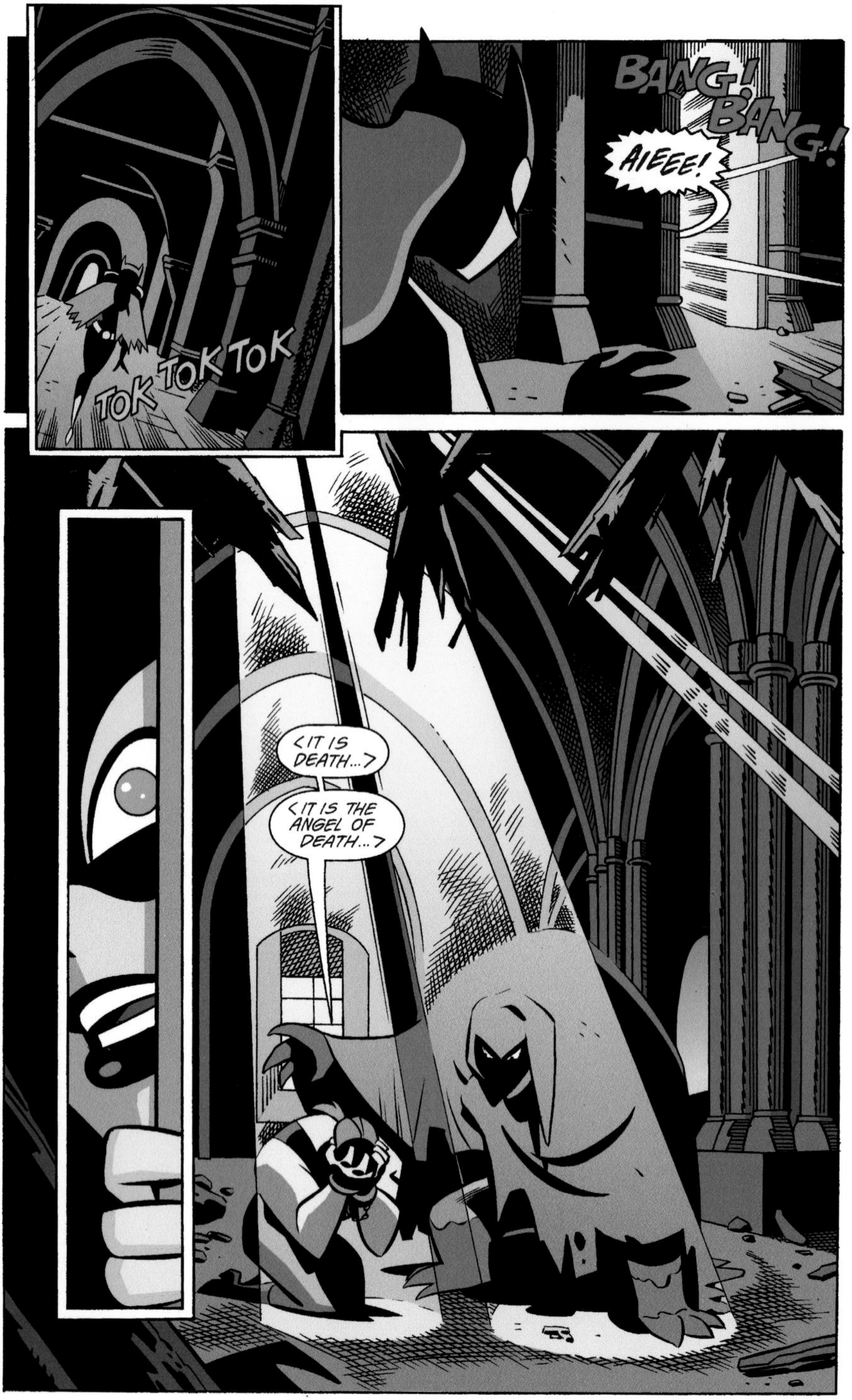
TOK TOK TOK
BANG! BANG!
AIEEE!
<IT IS DEATH...>
<IT IS THE ANGEL OF DEATH...>

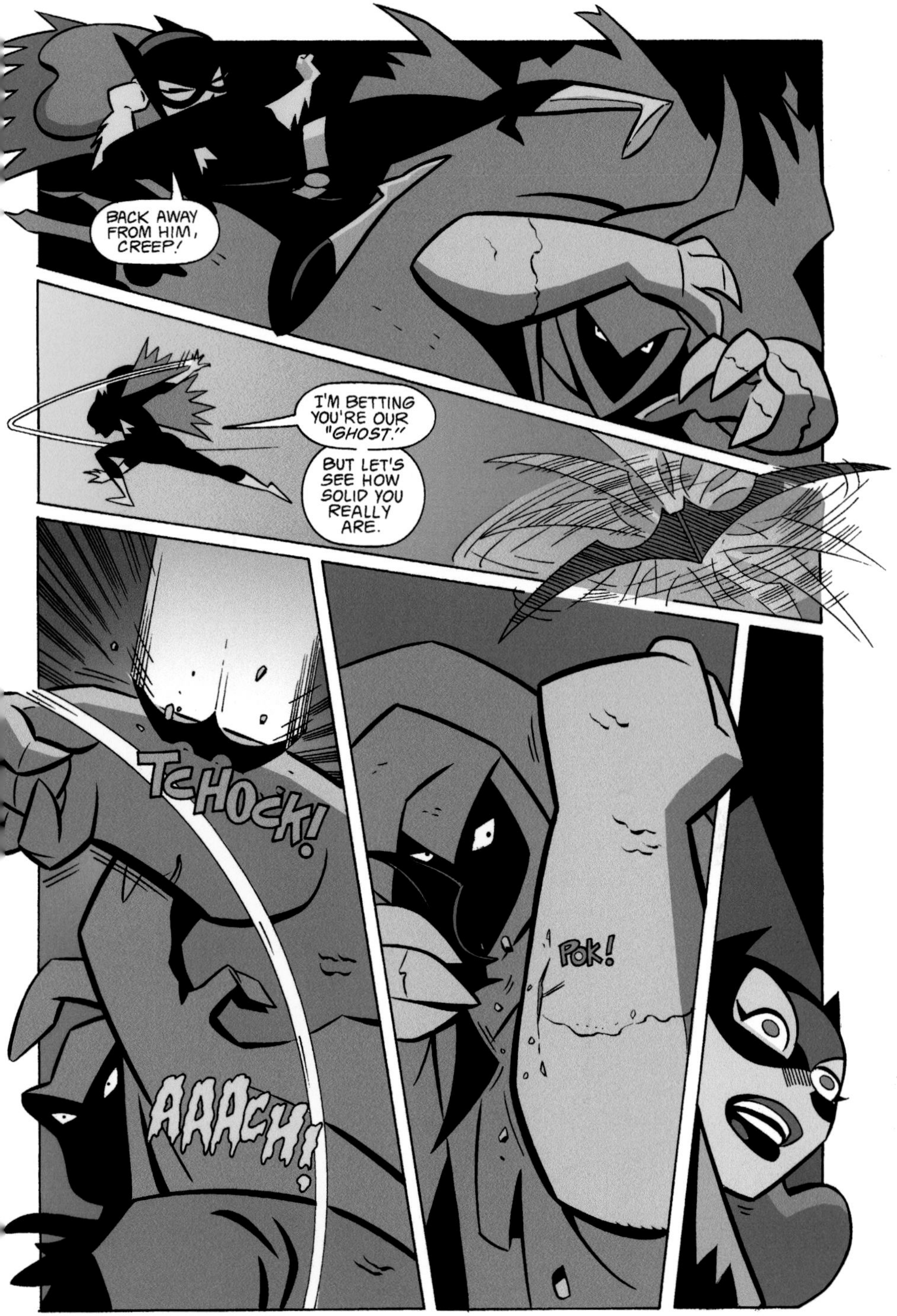
BACK AWAY FROM HIM, CREEP!
I'M BETTING YOU'RE OUR "GHOST."
BUT LET'S SEE HOW SOLID YOU REALLY ARE.
TCHOCK!
POK!
AAACH!

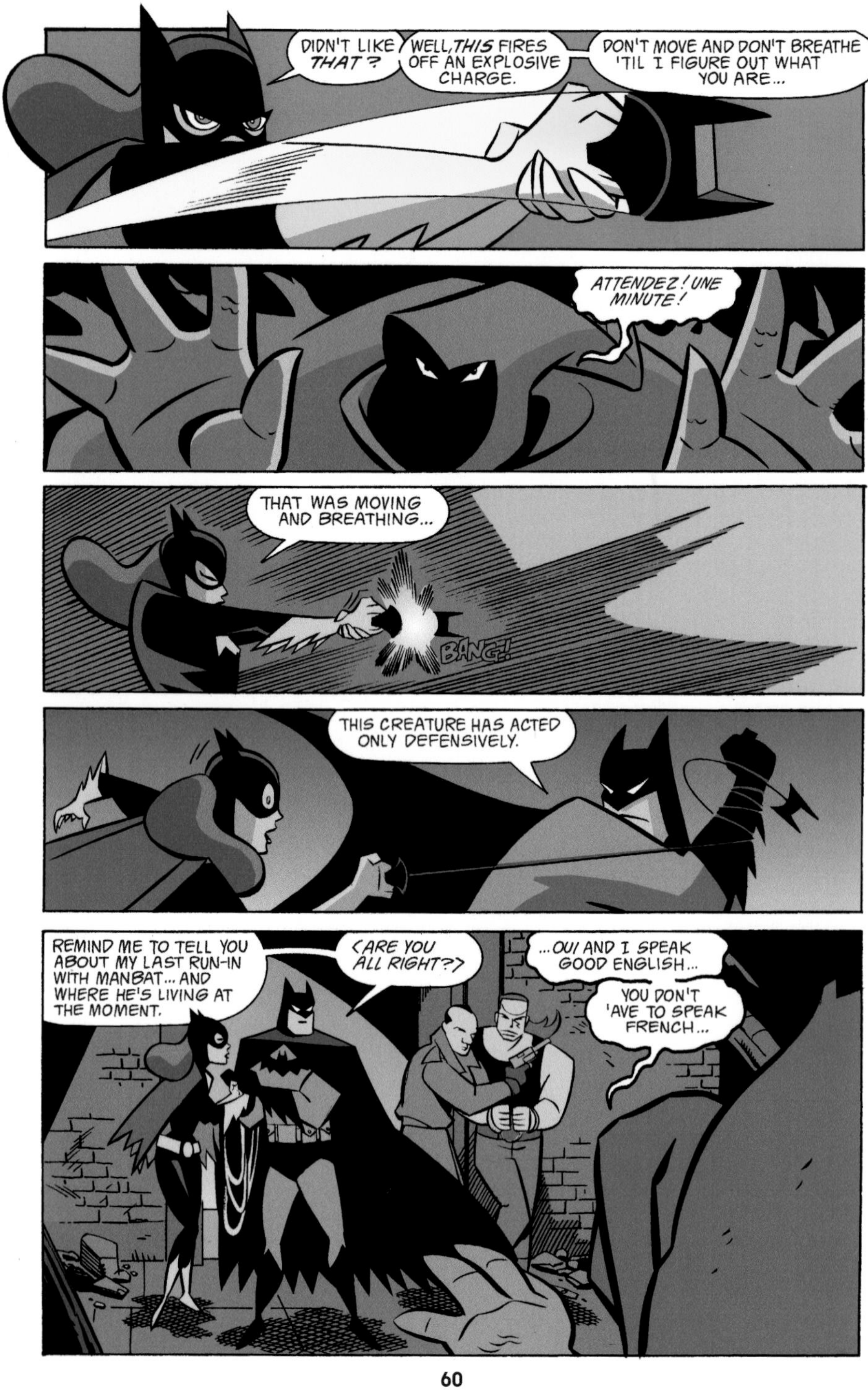
DIDN'T LIKE THAT?
WELL, THIS FIRES OFF AN EXPLOSIVE CHARGE.
DON'T MOVE AND DON'T BREATHE 'TIL I FIGURE OUT WHAT YOU ARE...
ATTENDEZ! UNE MINUTE!
THAT WAS MOVING AND BREATHING...
BANG!
THIS CREATURE HAS ACTED ONLY DEFENSIVELY.
REMIND ME TO TELL YOU ABOUT MY LAST RUN-IN WITH MANBAT... AND WHERE HE'S LIVING AT THE MOMENT.
<ARE YOU ALL RIGHT?>
...OUI AND I SPEAK GOOD ENGLISH...
YOU DON'T 'AVE TO SPEAK FRENCH...

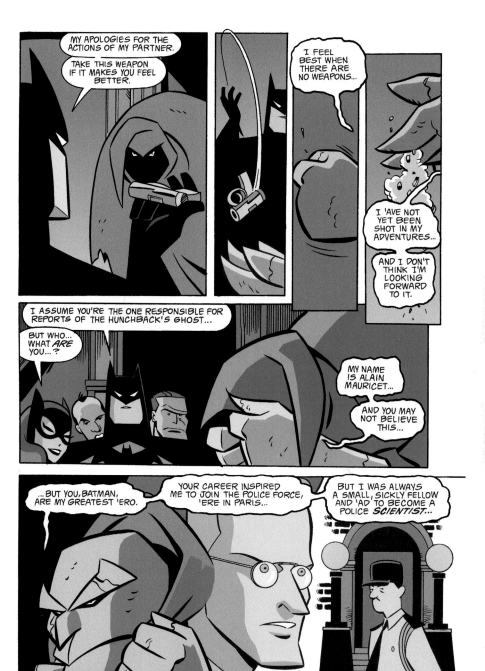

MY APOLOGIES FOR THE ACTIONS OF MY PARTNER.

TAKE THIS WEAPON IF IT MAKES YOU FEEL BETTER.

I FEEL BEST WHEN THERE ARE NO WEAPONS...

I 'AVE NOT YET BEEN SHOT IN MY ADVENTURES...

AND I DON'T THINK I'M LOOKING FORWARD TO IT.

I ASSUME YOU'RE THE ONE RESPONSIBLE FOR REPORTS OF THE HUNCHBACK'S GHOST...

BUT WHO... WHAT *ARE* YOU...?

MY NAME IS ALAIN MAURICET...

AND YOU MAY NOT BELIEVE THIS...

...BUT YOU, BATMAN, ARE MY GREATEST 'ERO.

YOUR CAREER INSPIRED ME TO JOIN THE POLICE FORCE, 'ERE IN PARIS...

BUT I WAS ALWAYS A SMALL, SICKLY FELLOW AND 'AD TO BECOME A POLICE *SCIENTIST*...

61

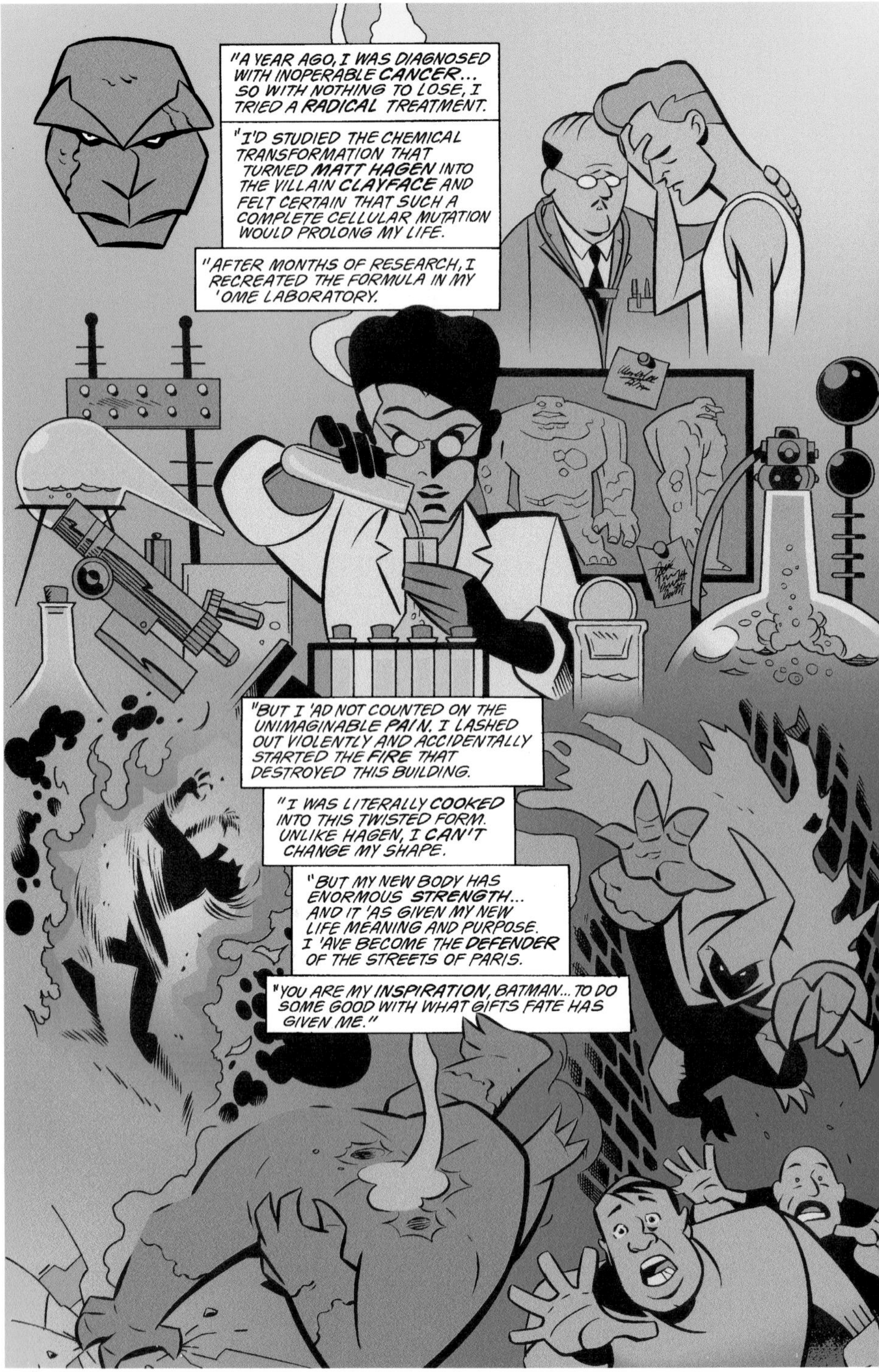
"A YEAR AGO, I WAS DIAGNOSED WITH INOPERABLE CANCER... SO WITH NOTHING TO LOSE, I TRIED A RADICAL TREATMENT.
"I'D STUDIED THE CHEMICAL TRANSFORMATION THAT TURNED MATT HAGEN INTO THE VILLAIN CLAYFACE AND FELT CERTAIN THAT SUCH A COMPLETE CELLULAR MUTATION WOULD PROLONG MY LIFE.
"AFTER MONTHS OF RESEARCH, I RECREATED THE FORMULA IN MY 'OME LABORATORY.
"BUT I 'AD NOT COUNTED ON THE UNIMAGINABLE PAIN. I LASHED OUT VIOLENTLY AND ACCIDENTALLY STARTED THE FIRE THAT DESTROYED THIS BUILDING.
"I WAS LITERALLY COOKED INTO THIS TWISTED FORM. UNLIKE HAGEN, I CAN'T CHANGE MY SHAPE.
"BUT MY NEW BODY HAS ENORMOUS STRENGTH... AND IT 'AS GIVEN MY NEW LIFE MEANING AND PURPOSE. I 'AVE BECOME THE DEFENDER OF THE STREETS OF PARIS.
"YOU ARE MY INSPIRATION, BATMAN... TO DO SOME GOOD WITH WHAT GIFTS FATE HAS GIVEN ME."

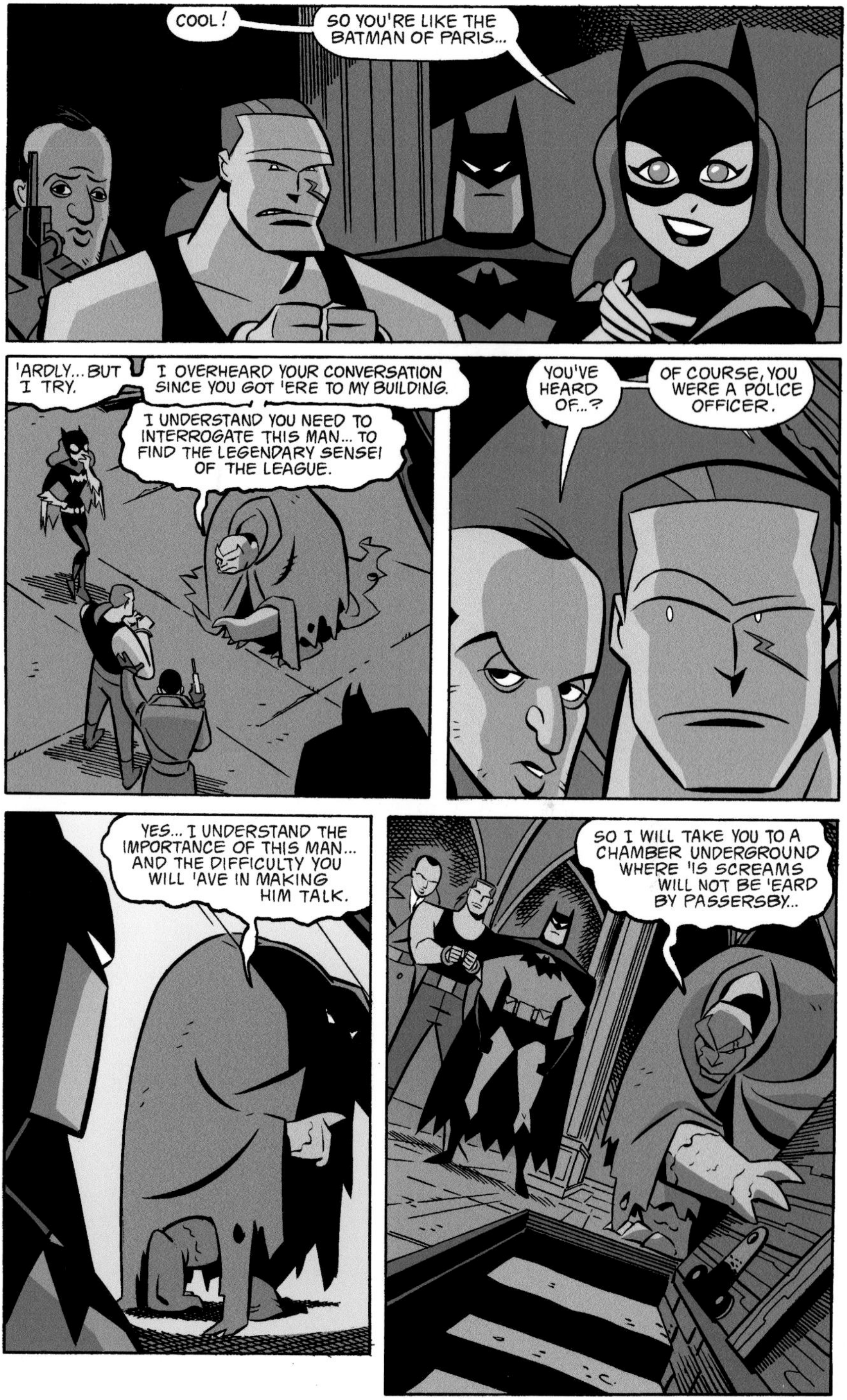
COOL!
SO YOU'RE LIKE THE BATMAN OF PARIS...
'ARDLY... BUT I TRY.
I OVERHEARD YOUR CONVERSATION SINCE YOU GOT 'ERE TO MY BUILDING.
I UNDERSTAND YOU NEED TO INTERROGATE THIS MAN... TO FIND THE LEGENDARY SENSEI OF THE LEAGUE.
YOU'VE HEARD OF...?
OF COURSE, YOU WERE A POLICE OFFICER.
YES... I UNDERSTAND THE IMPORTANCE OF THIS MAN... AND THE DIFFICULTY YOU WILL 'AVE IN MAKING HIM TALK.
SO I WILL TAKE YOU TO A CHAMBER UNDERGROUND WHERE 'IS SCREAMS WILL NOT BE 'EARD BY PASSERSBY...

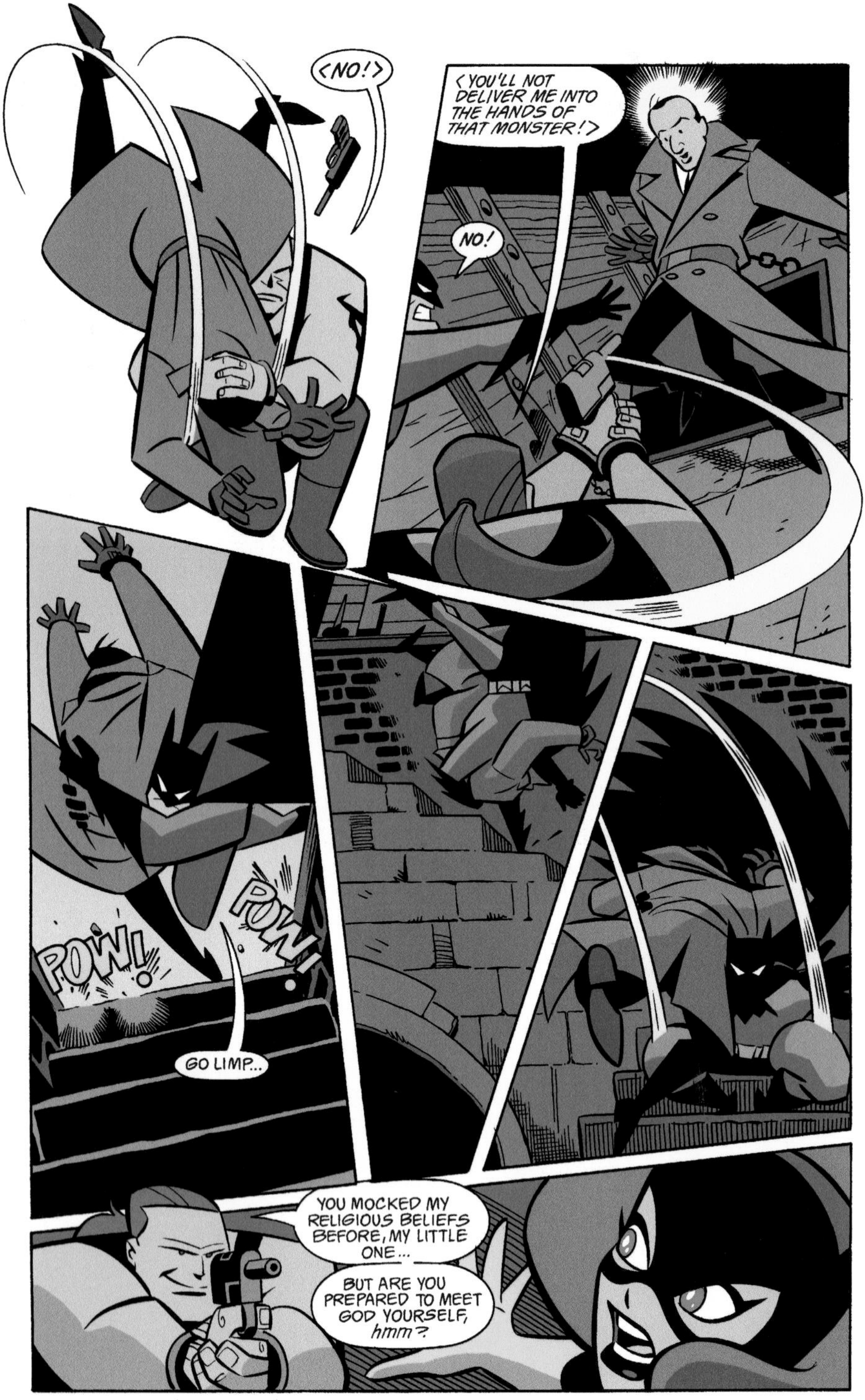
<NO!>
<YOU'LL NOT DELIVER ME INTO THE HANDS OF THAT MONSTER!>
NO!
POW!
POW!
GO LIMP...
YOU MOCKED MY RELIGIOUS BELIEFS BEFORE, MY LITTLE ONE...
BUT ARE YOU PREPARED TO MEET GOD YOURSELF, *hmm*?

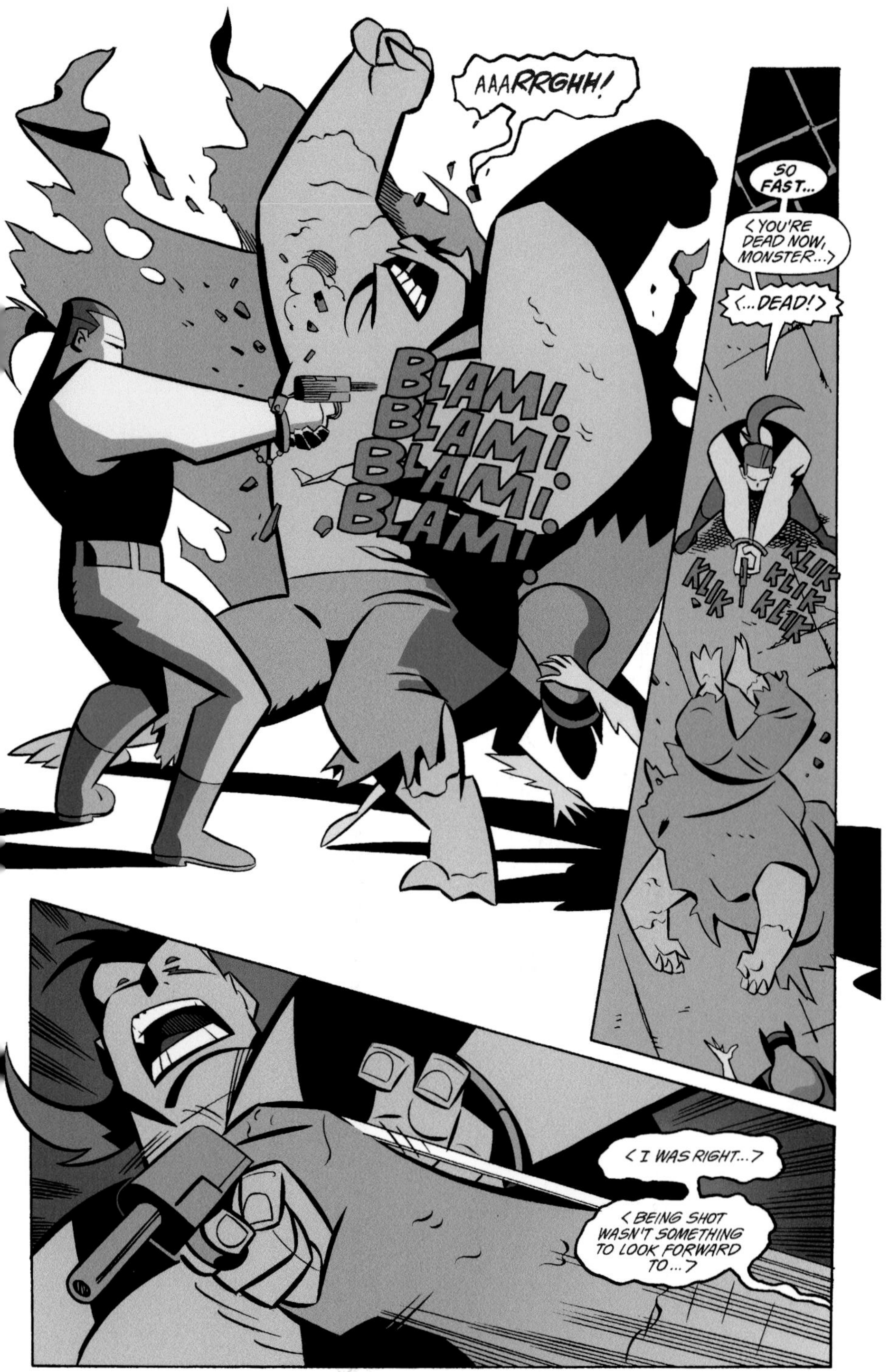

AAARRGHH!
BLAM! BLAM! BLAM! BLAM!
SO FAST...
< YOU'RE DEAD NOW, MONSTER... >
< ...DEAD! >
KLIK KLIK KLIK KLIK
< I WAS RIGHT... >
< BEING SHOT WASN'T SOMETHING TO LOOK FORWARD TO... >

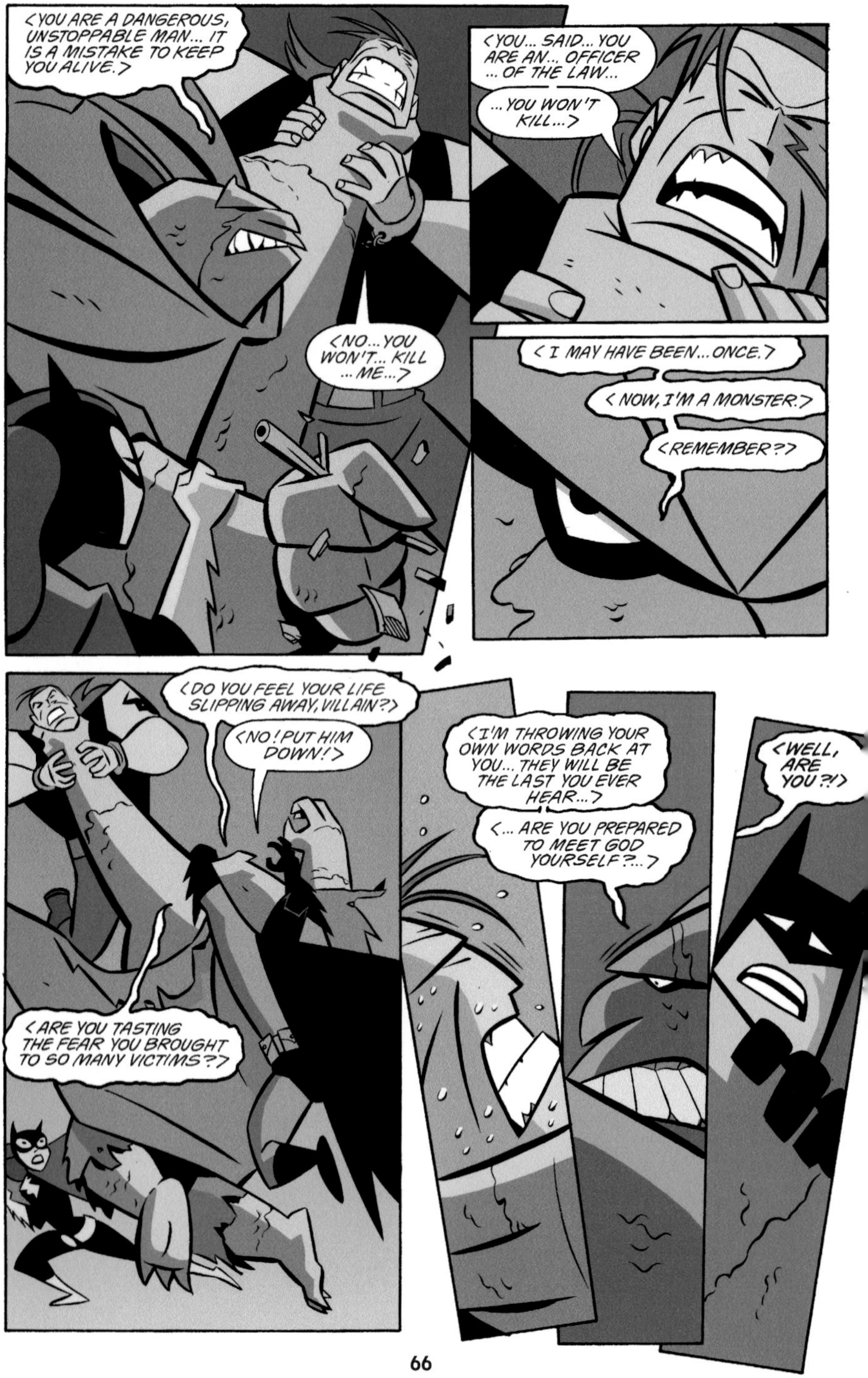
<YOU ARE A DANGEROUS, UNSTOPPABLE MAN... IT IS A MISTAKE TO KEEP YOU ALIVE.>
<NO... YOU WON'T... KILL ...ME...>
<YOU... SAID... YOU ARE AN... OFFICER ... OF THE LAW...
...YOU WON'T KILL...>
<I MAY HAVE BEEN... ONCE.>
<NOW, I'M A MONSTER.>
<REMEMBER?>
<DO YOU FEEL YOUR LIFE SLIPPING AWAY, VILLAIN?>
<NO! PUT HIM DOWN!>
<ARE YOU TASTING THE FEAR YOU BROUGHT TO SO MANY VICTIMS?>
<I'M THROWING YOUR OWN WORDS BACK AT YOU... THEY WILL BE THE LAST YOU EVER HEAR...>
<... ARE YOU PREPARED TO MEET GOD YOURSELF?...>
<WELL, ARE YOU?!>

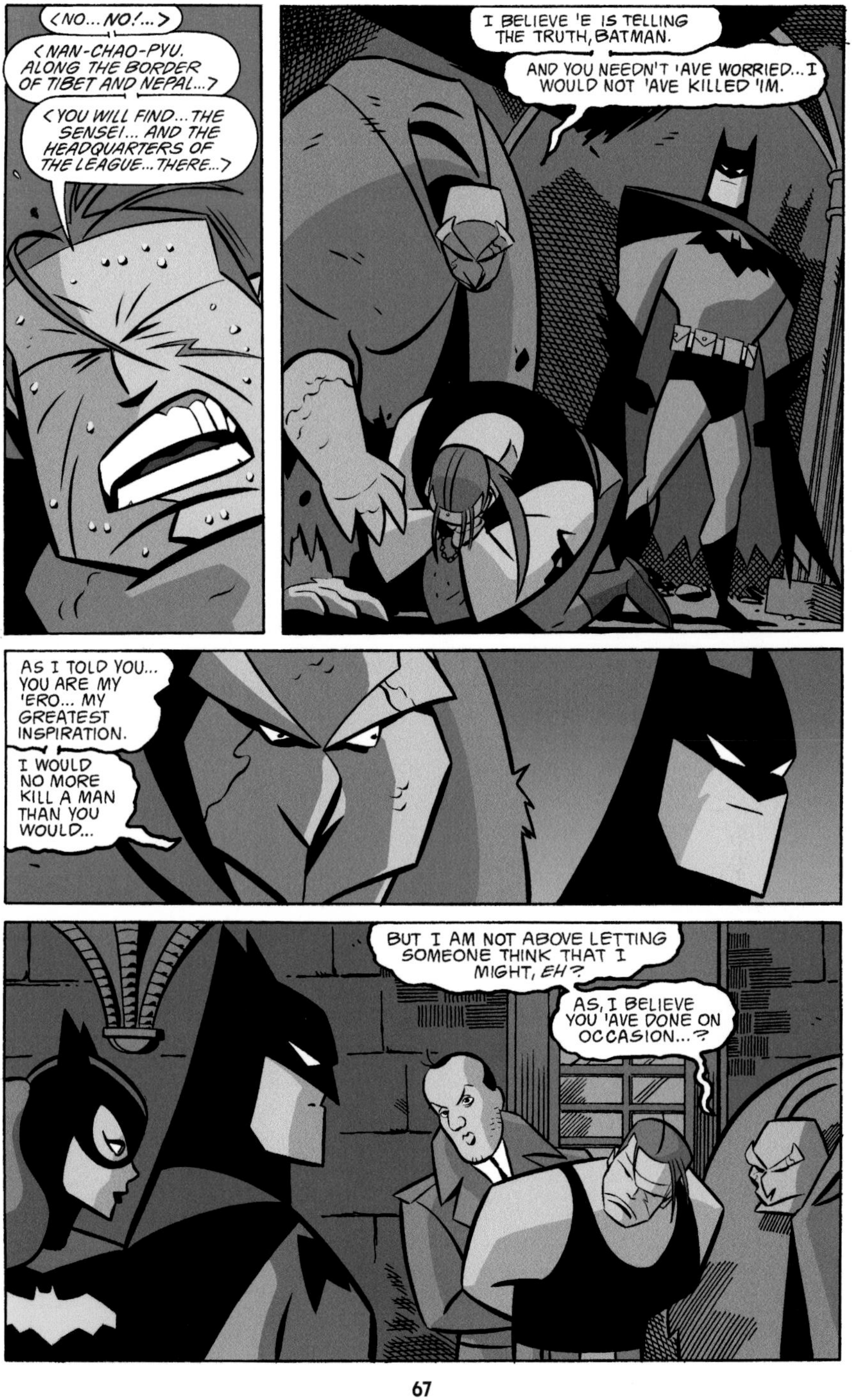

<NO... NO!...>
<NAN-CHAO-PYU. ALONG THE BORDER OF TIBET AND NEPAL...>
<YOU WILL FIND... THE SENSEI... AND THE HEADQUARTERS OF THE LEAGUE... THERE...>
I BELIEVE 'E IS TELLING THE TRUTH, BATMAN.
AND YOU NEEDN'T 'AVE WORRIED... I WOULD NOT 'AVE KILLED 'IM.
AS I TOLD YOU... YOU ARE MY 'ERO... MY GREATEST INSPIRATION.
I WOULD NO MORE KILL A MAN THAN YOU WOULD...
BUT I AM NOT ABOVE LETTING SOMEONE THINK THAT I MIGHT, EH?
AS, I BELIEVE YOU 'AVE DONE ON OCCASION...?

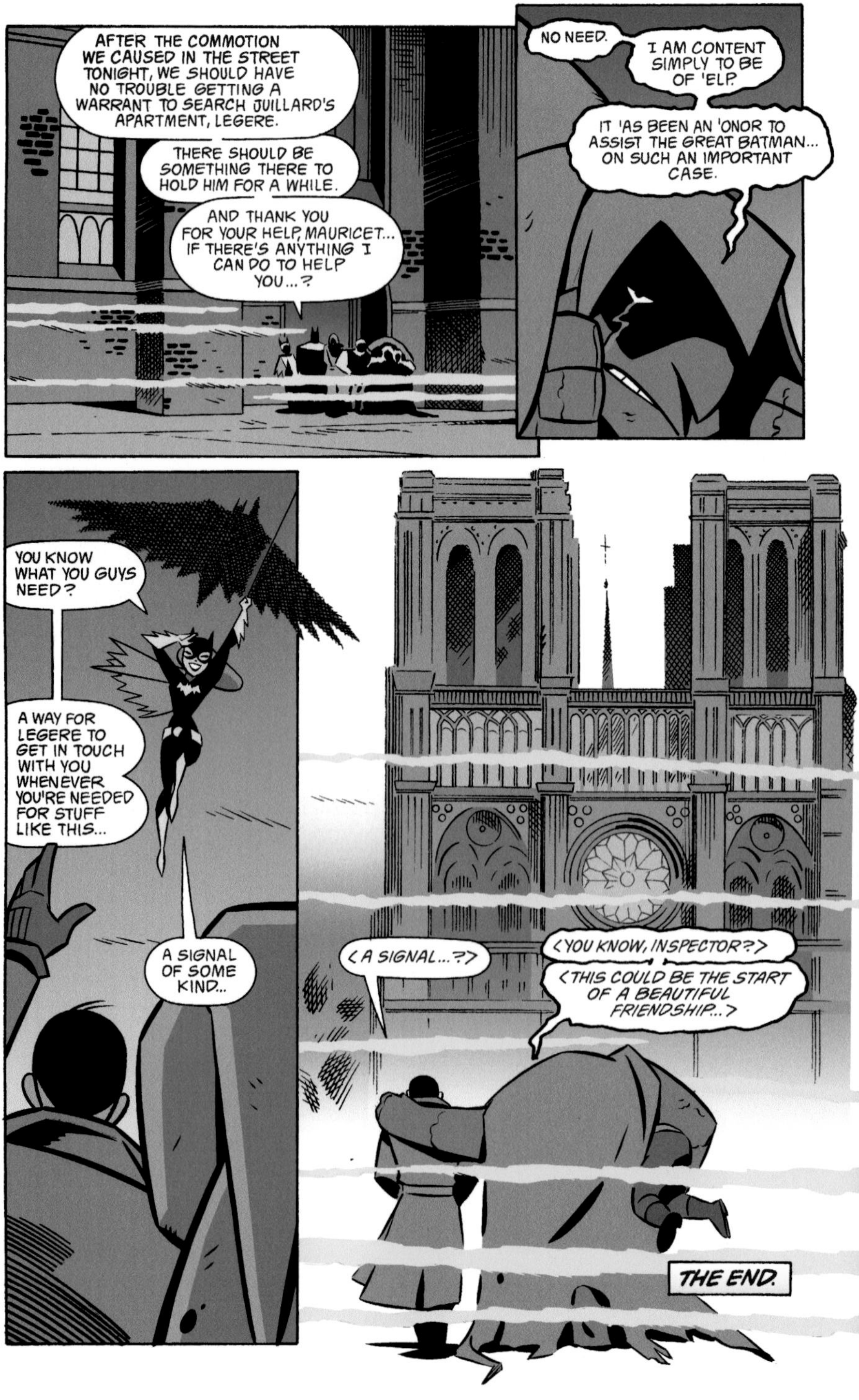
AFTER THE COMMOTION WE CAUSED IN THE STREET TONIGHT, WE SHOULD HAVE NO TROUBLE GETTING A WARRANT TO SEARCH JUILLARD'S APARTMENT, LEGERE.
THERE SHOULD BE SOMETHING THERE TO HOLD HIM FOR A WHILE.
AND THANK YOU FOR YOUR HELP, MAURICET... IF THERE'S ANYTHING I CAN DO TO HELP YOU...?
NO NEED.
I AM CONTENT SIMPLY TO BE OF 'ELP.
IT 'AS BEEN AN 'ONOR TO ASSIST THE GREAT BATMAN... ON SUCH AN IMPORTANT CASE.
YOU KNOW WHAT YOU GUYS NEED?
A WAY FOR LEGERE TO GET IN TOUCH WITH YOU WHENEVER YOU'RE NEEDED FOR STUFF LIKE THIS...
A SIGNAL OF SOME KIND...
<A SIGNAL...?>
<YOU KNOW, INSPECTOR?>
<THIS COULD BE THE START OF A BEAUTIFUL FRIENDSHIP...>
THE END.

CHAPTER 3: A LEAGUE OF HIS OWN!

BATGIRL

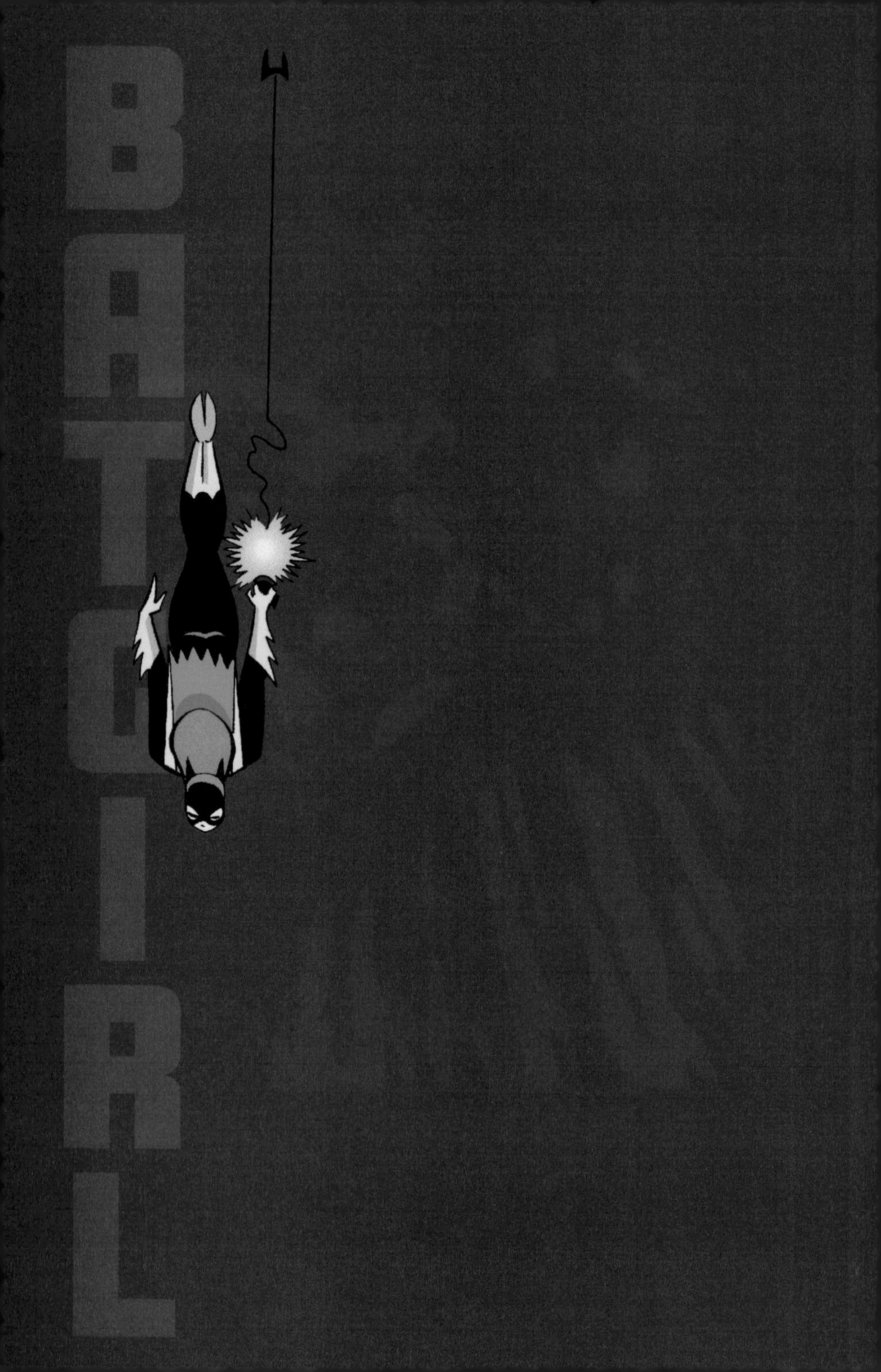
BATGIRL

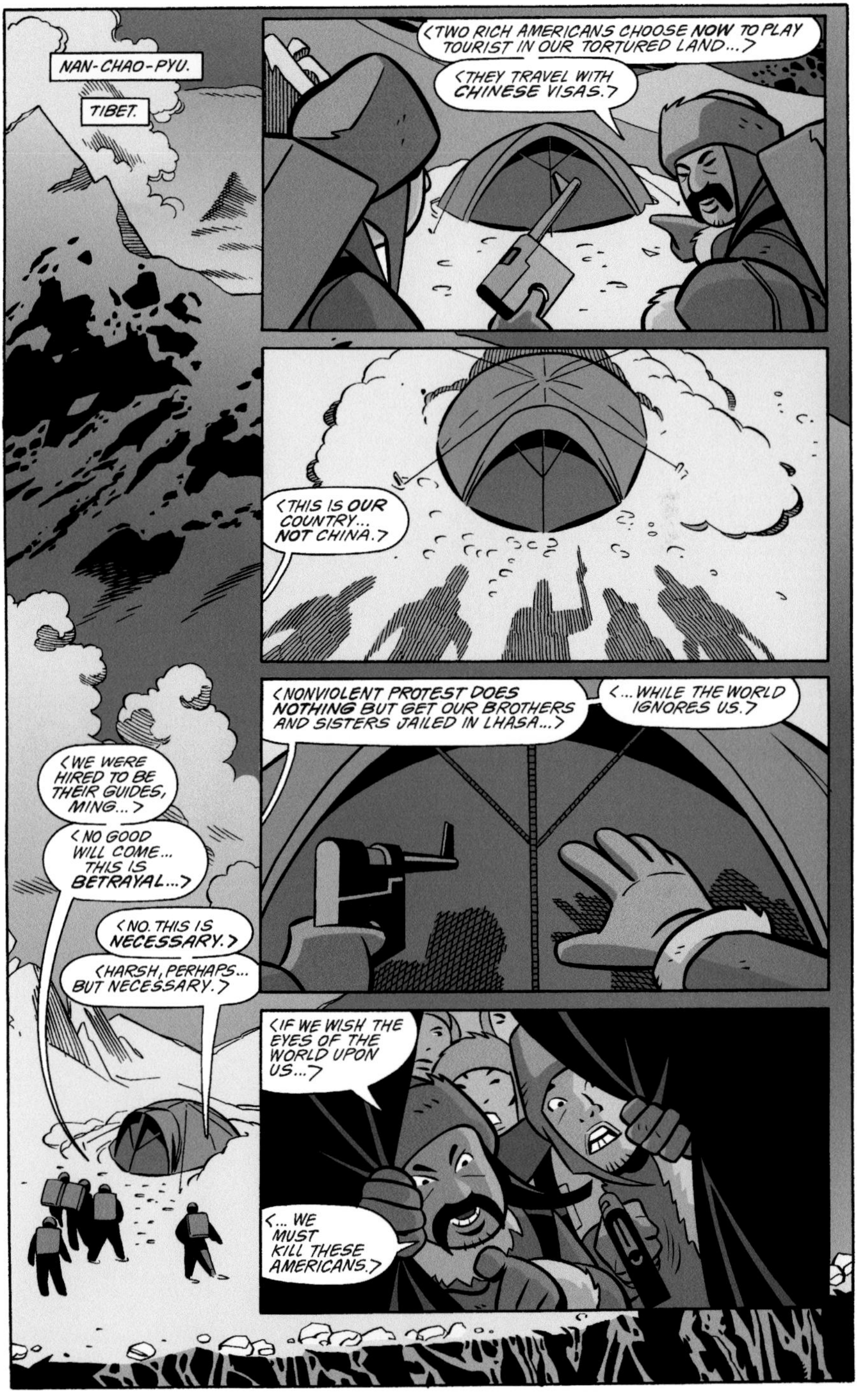
NAN-CHAO-PYU.
TIBET.
<TWO RICH AMERICANS CHOOSE NOW TO PLAY TOURIST IN OUR TORTURED LAND...>
<THEY TRAVEL WITH CHINESE VISAS.>
<THIS IS OUR COUNTRY... NOT CHINA.>
<NONVIOLENT PROTEST DOES NOTHING BUT GET OUR BROTHERS AND SISTERS JAILED IN LHASA...>
<...WHILE THE WORLD IGNORES US.>
<WE WERE HIRED TO BE THEIR GUIDES, MING...>
<NO GOOD WILL COME... THIS IS BETRAYAL...>
<NO. THIS IS NECESSARY.>
<HARSH, PERHAPS... BUT NECESSARY.>
<IF WE WISH THE EYES OF THE WORLD UPON US...>
<... WE MUST KILL THESE AMERICANS.>

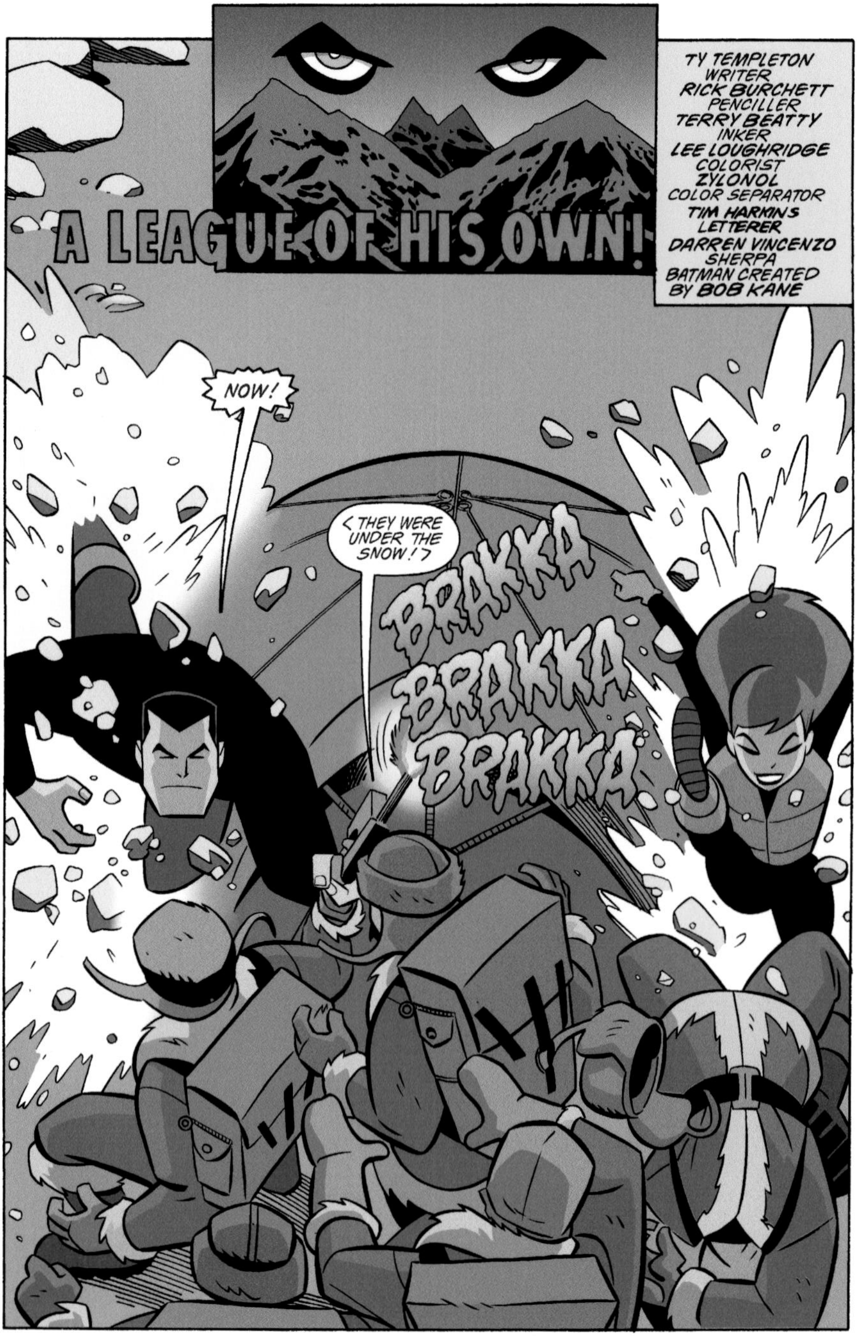
A LEAGUE OF HIS OWN!
TY TEMPLETON WRITER
RICK BURCHETT PENCILLER
TERRY BEATTY INKER
LEE LOUGHRIDGE COLORIST
ZYLONOL COLOR SEPARATOR
TIM HARKINS LETTERER
DARREN VINCENZO SHERPA
BATMAN CREATED BY BOB KANE
NOW!
<THEY WERE UNDER THE SNOW!>
BRAKKA
BRAKKA
BRAKKA

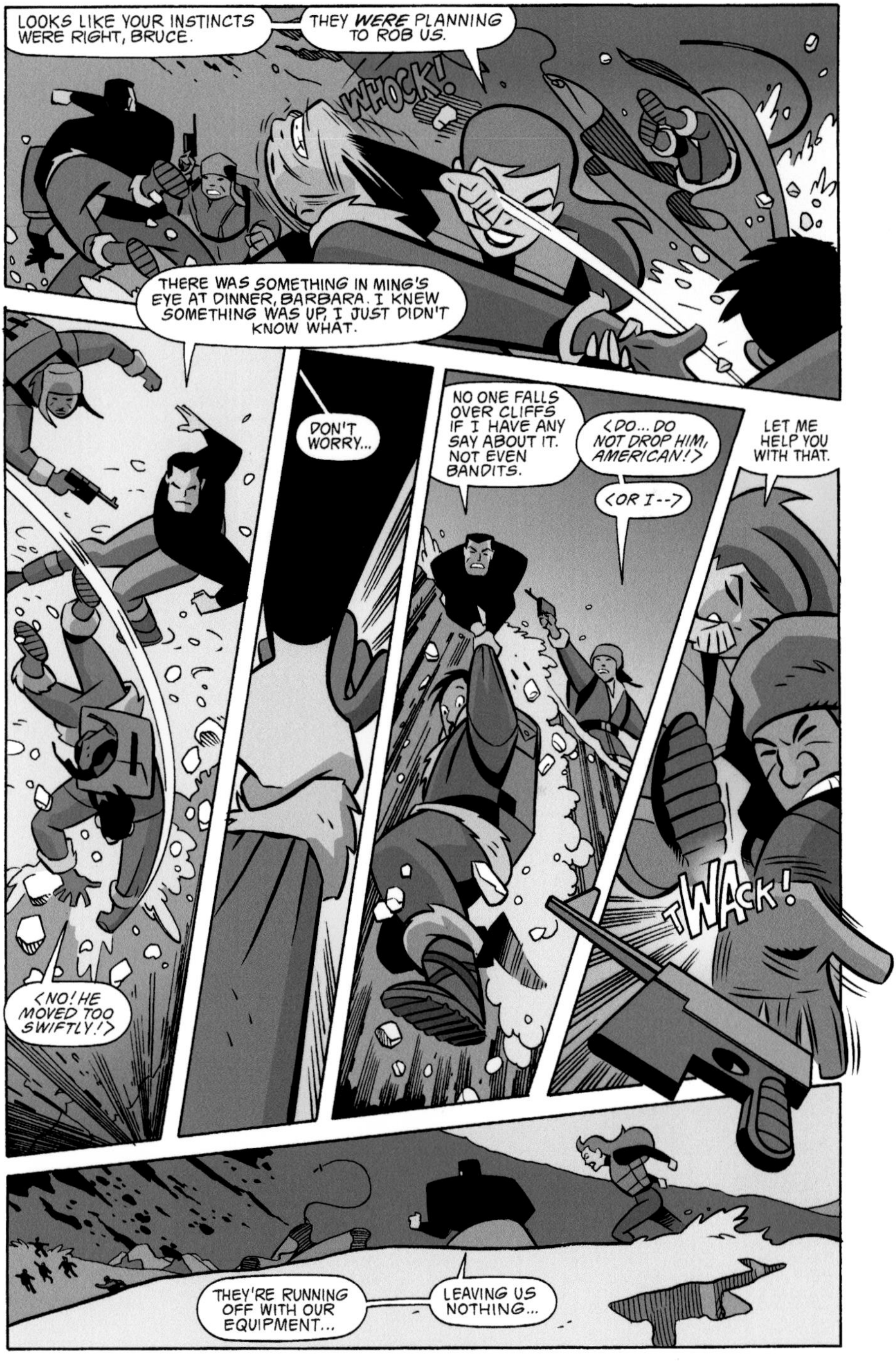

LOOKS LIKE YOUR INSTINCTS WERE RIGHT, BRUCE.
THEY *WERE* PLANNING TO ROB US.
WHOCK!
THERE WAS SOMETHING IN MING'S EYE AT DINNER, BARBARA. I KNEW SOMETHING WAS UP, I JUST DIDN'T KNOW WHAT.
<NO! HE MOVED TOO SWIFTLY!>
DON'T WORRY...
NO ONE FALLS OVER CLIFFS IF I HAVE ANY SAY ABOUT IT. NOT EVEN BANDITS.
<DO... DO NOT DROP HIM, AMERICAN!>
<OR I-->
LET ME HELP YOU WITH THAT.
TWACK!
THEY'RE RUNNING OFF WITH OUR EQUIPMENT...
LEAVING US NOTHING...

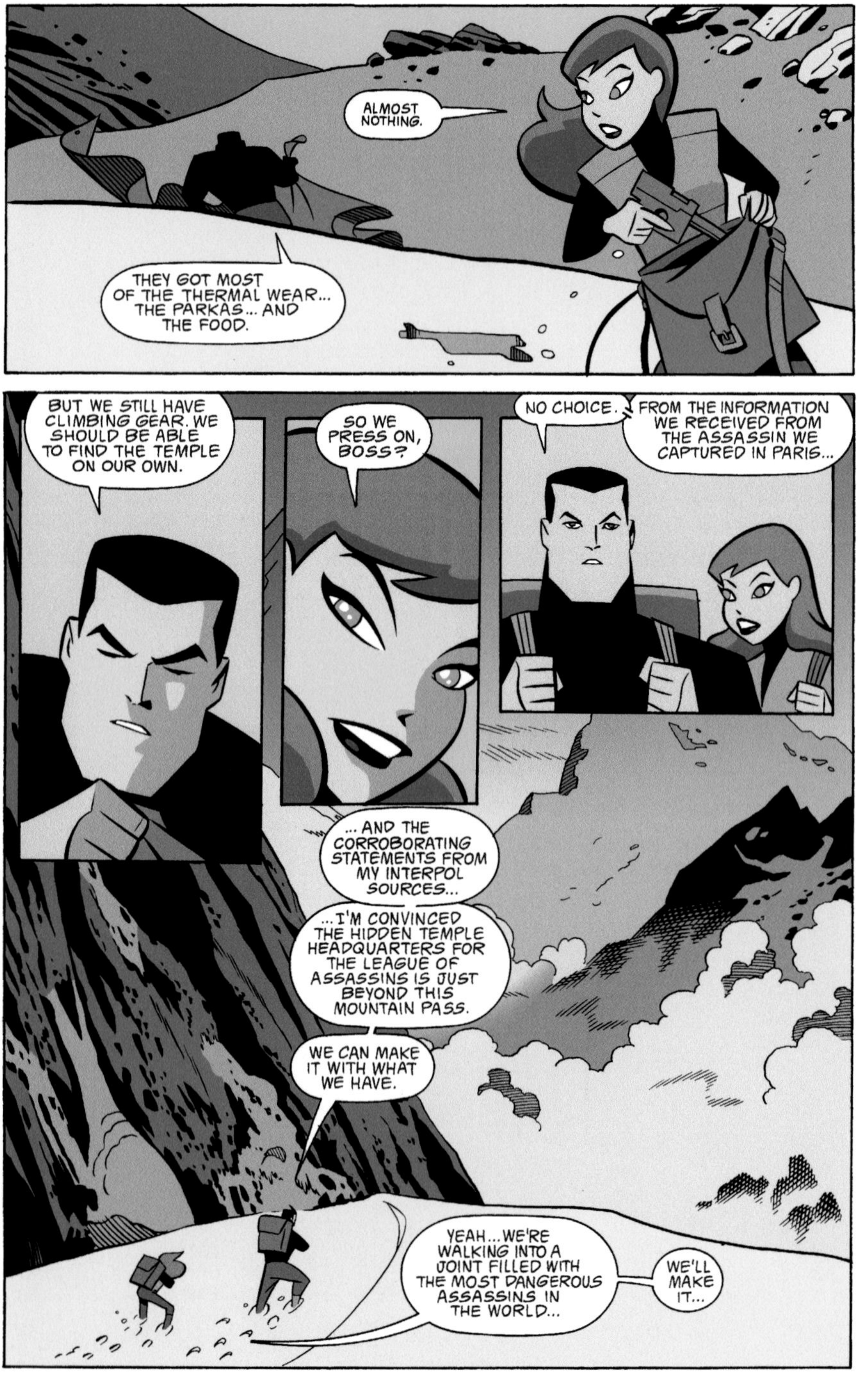
ALMOST NOTHING.
THEY GOT MOST OF THE THERMAL WEAR... THE PARKAS... AND THE FOOD.
BUT WE STILL HAVE CLIMBING GEAR. WE SHOULD BE ABLE TO FIND THE TEMPLE ON OUR OWN.
SO WE PRESS ON, BOSS?
NO CHOICE.
FROM THE INFORMATION WE RECEIVED FROM THE ASSASSIN WE CAPTURED IN PARIS...
...AND THE CORROBORATING STATEMENTS FROM MY INTERPOL SOURCES...
...I'M CONVINCED THE HIDDEN TEMPLE HEADQUARTERS FOR THE LEAGUE OF ASSASSINS IS JUST BEYOND THIS MOUNTAIN PASS.
WE CAN MAKE IT WITH WHAT WE HAVE.
YEAH...WE'RE WALKING INTO A JOINT FILLED WITH THE MOST DANGEROUS ASSASSINS IN THE WORLD...
WE'LL MAKE IT...

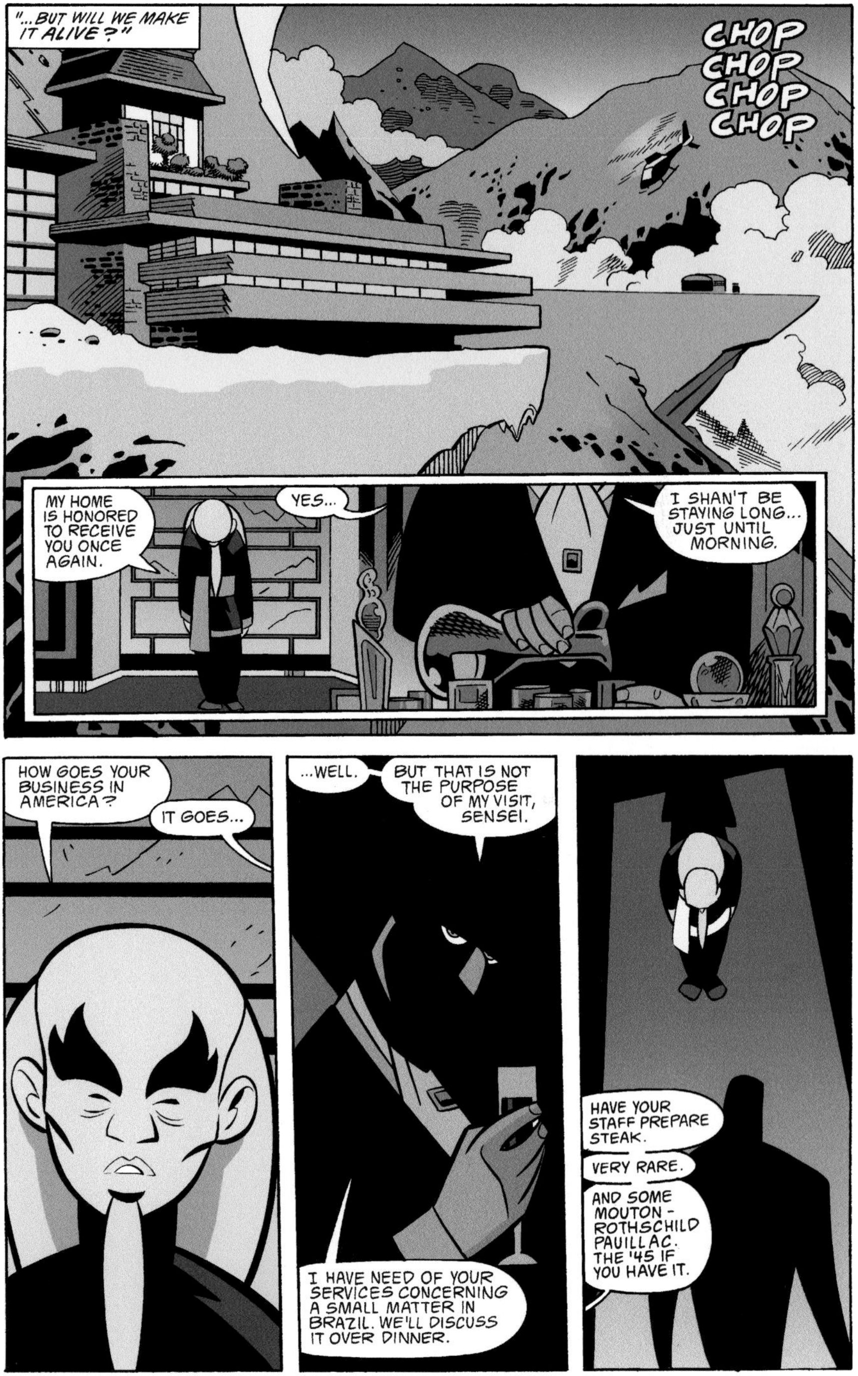
"...BUT WILL WE MAKE IT ALIVE?"
CHOP CHOP CHOP CHOP
MY HOME IS HONORED TO RECEIVE YOU ONCE AGAIN.
YES...
I SHAN'T BE STAYING LONG... JUST UNTIL MORNING.
HOW GOES YOUR BUSINESS IN AMERICA?
IT GOES...
...WELL.
BUT THAT IS NOT THE PURPOSE OF MY VISIT, SENSEI.
I HAVE NEED OF YOUR SERVICES CONCERNING A SMALL MATTER IN BRAZIL. WE'LL DISCUSS IT OVER DINNER.
HAVE YOUR STAFF PREPARE STEAK.
VERY RARE.
AND SOME MOUTON-ROTHSCHILD PAUILLAC. THE '45 IF YOU HAVE IT.

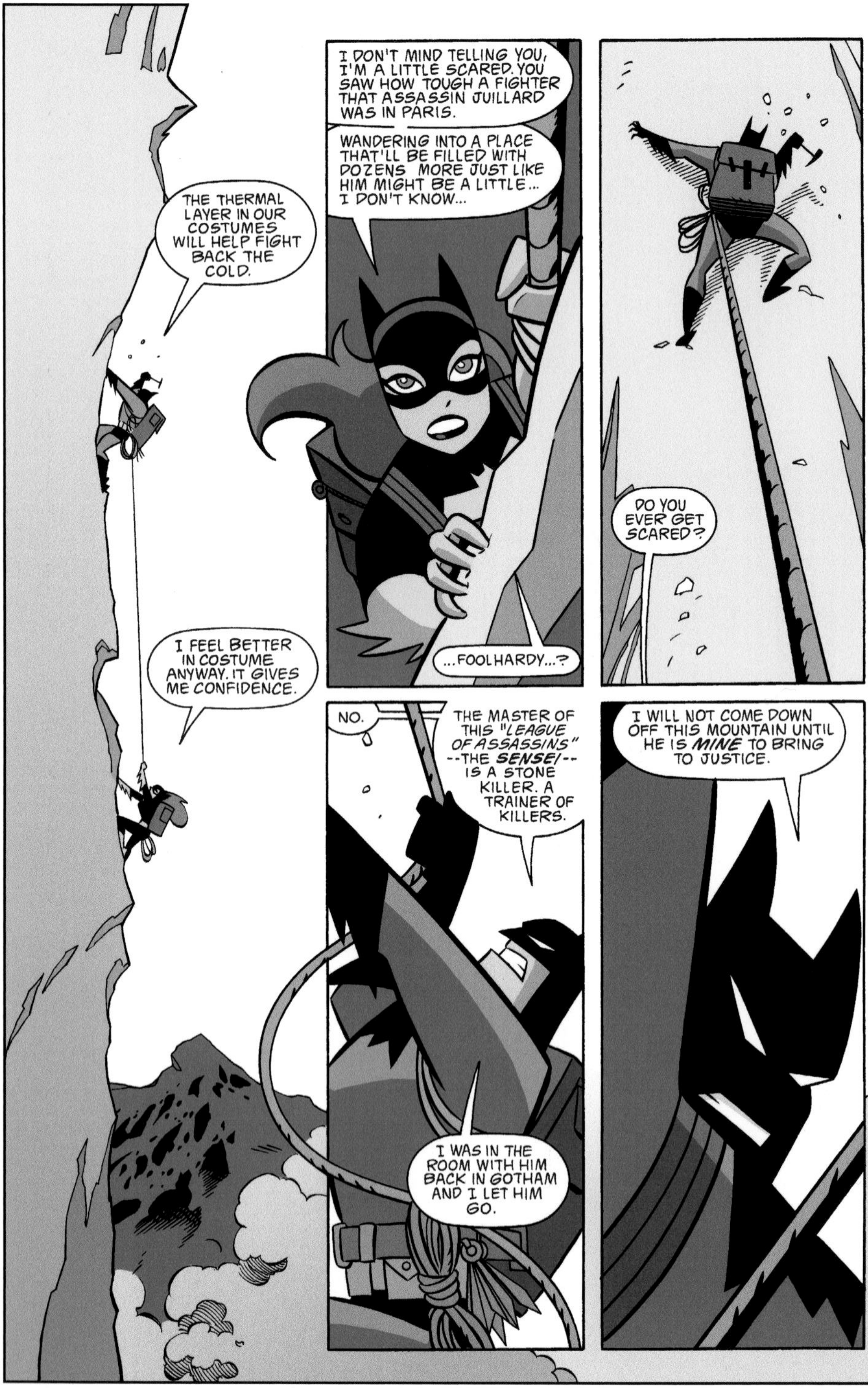

THE THERMAL LAYER IN OUR COSTUMES WILL HELP FIGHT BACK THE COLD.
I FEEL BETTER IN COSTUME ANYWAY. IT GIVES ME CONFIDENCE.
I DON'T MIND TELLING YOU, I'M A LITTLE SCARED. YOU SAW HOW TOUGH A FIGHTER THAT ASSASSIN JUILLARD WAS IN PARIS.
WANDERING INTO A PLACE THAT'LL BE FILLED WITH DOZENS MORE JUST LIKE HIM MIGHT BE A LITTLE... I DON'T KNOW...
...FOOLHARDY...?
DO YOU EVER GET SCARED?
NO.
THE MASTER OF THIS "LEAGUE OF ASSASSINS" --THE SENSEI-- IS A STONE KILLER. A TRAINER OF KILLERS.
I WAS IN THE ROOM WITH HIM BACK IN GOTHAM AND I LET HIM GO.
I WILL NOT COME DOWN OFF THIS MOUNTAIN UNTIL HE IS MINE TO BRING TO JUSTICE.

I KNOW... HE'S A BAD GUY, AND WE HAVE TO CATCH HIM...

...BUT THIS MAY BE THE MOST DANGEROUS THING WE'VE EVER DONE.

I HAVE A PISTOL WITH ME, BATMAN.

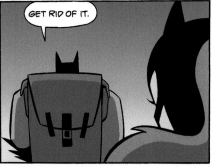

GET RID OF IT.

HEY... YOU FORGET I'M A TRAINED POLICE OFFICER IN MY OTHER IDENTITY. AND MY FATHER IS COMMISSIONER OF POLICE.

I'VE BEEN AROUND GUNS MY WHOLE LIFE. I KNOW WHAT I'M DOING.

IT'S A MISTAKE TO RELY ON ANY ONE WEAPON IN A FIGHT, BATGIRL. YOU MIGHT *LOSE* IT, AND THAT GIVES YOUR OPPONENT THE ADVANTAGE.

YOUR BEST WEAPON IS TO RELY ON YOURSELF.

GET RID OF IT.

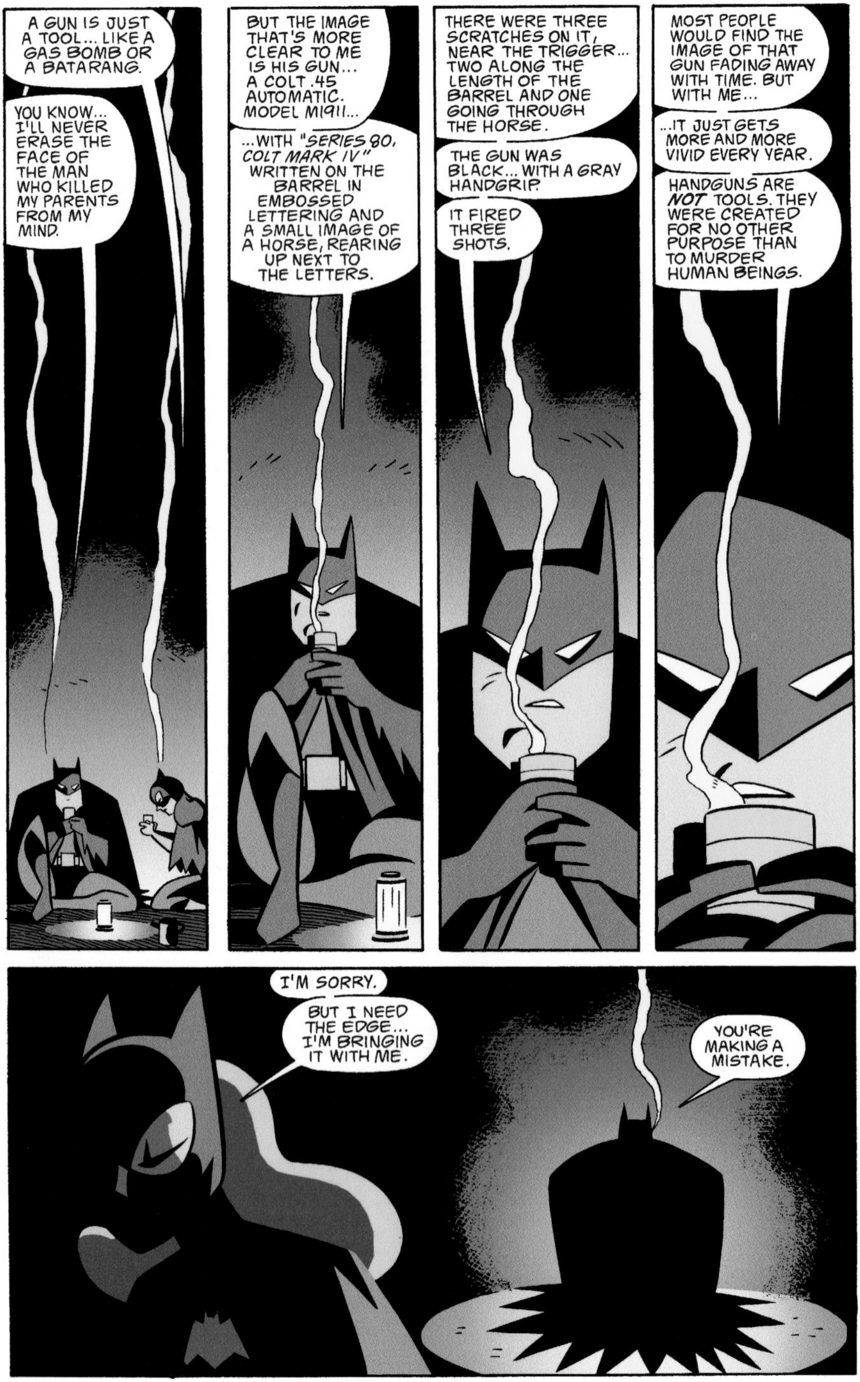

A GUN IS JUST A TOOL... LIKE A GAS BOMB OR A BATARANG.
YOU KNOW... I'LL NEVER ERASE THE FACE OF THE MAN WHO KILLED MY PARENTS FROM MY MIND.
BUT THE IMAGE THAT'S MORE CLEAR TO ME IS HIS GUN... A COLT .45 AUTOMATIC. MODEL M1911...
...WITH "SERIES 80, COLT MARK IV" WRITTEN ON THE BARREL IN EMBOSSED LETTERING AND A SMALL IMAGE OF A HORSE, REARING UP NEXT TO THE LETTERS.
THERE WERE THREE SCRATCHES ON IT, NEAR THE TRIGGER... TWO ALONG THE LENGTH OF THE BARREL AND ONE GOING THROUGH THE HORSE.
THE GUN WAS BLACK... WITH A GRAY HANDGRIP.
IT FIRED THREE SHOTS.
MOST PEOPLE WOULD FIND THE IMAGE OF THAT GUN FADING AWAY WITH TIME. BUT WITH ME...
...IT JUST GETS MORE AND MORE VIVID EVERY YEAR.
HANDGUNS ARE NOT TOOLS. THEY WERE CREATED FOR NO OTHER PURPOSE THAN TO MURDER HUMAN BEINGS.
I'M SORRY.
BUT I NEED THE EDGE... I'M BRINGING IT WITH ME.
YOU'RE MAKING A MISTAKE.

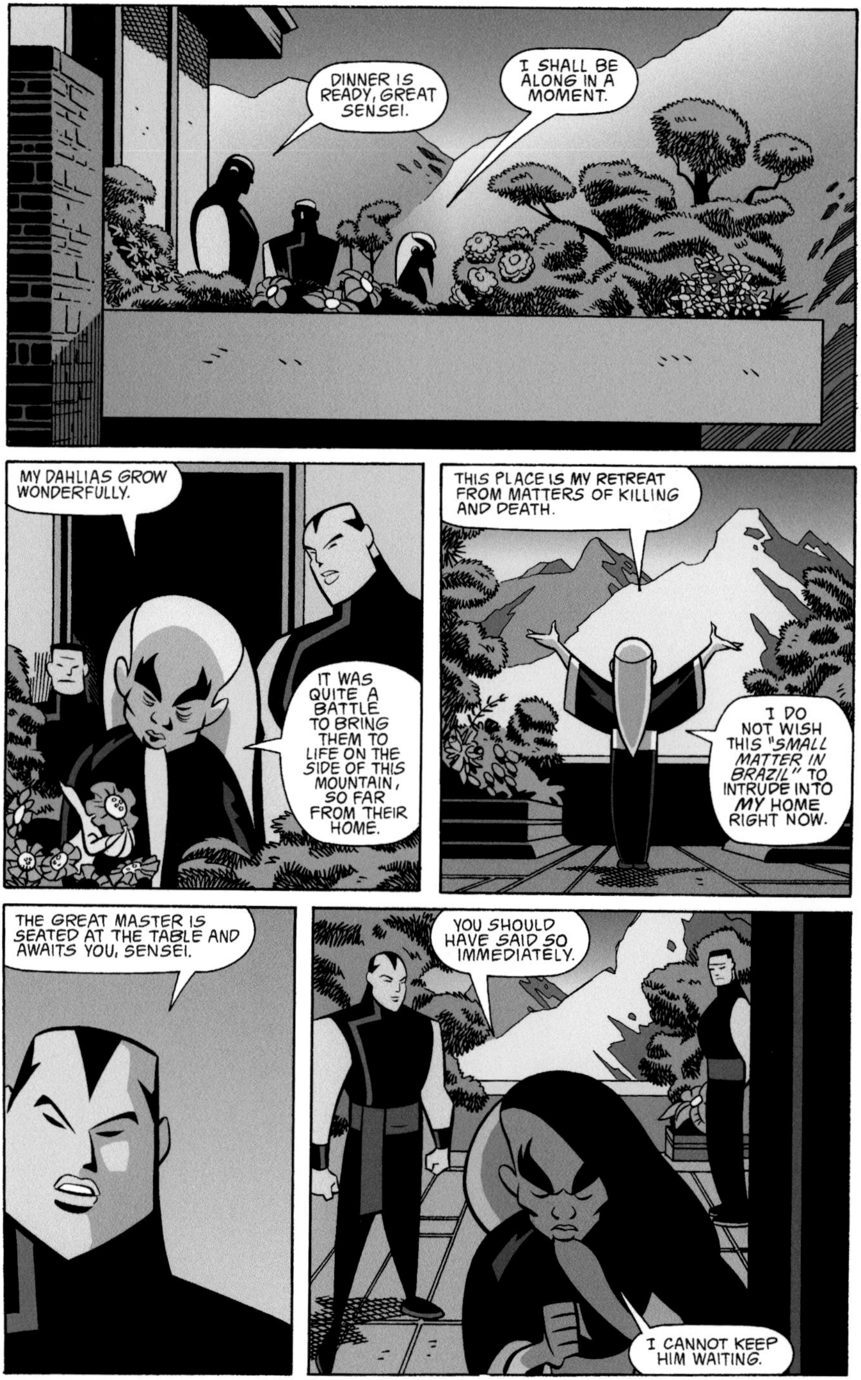
DINNER IS READY, GREAT SENSEI.
I SHALL BE ALONG IN A MOMENT.
MY DAHLIAS GROW WONDERFULLY.
IT WAS QUITE A BATTLE TO BRING THEM TO LIFE ON THE SIDE OF THIS MOUNTAIN, SO FAR FROM THEIR HOME.
THIS PLACE IS MY RETREAT FROM MATTERS OF KILLING AND DEATH.
I DO NOT WISH THIS *"SMALL MATTER IN BRAZIL"* TO INTRUDE INTO *MY* HOME RIGHT NOW.
THE GREAT MASTER IS SEATED AT THE TABLE AND AWAITS YOU, SENSEI.
YOU SHOULD HAVE SAID SO IMMEDIATELY.
I CANNOT KEEP HIM WAITING.

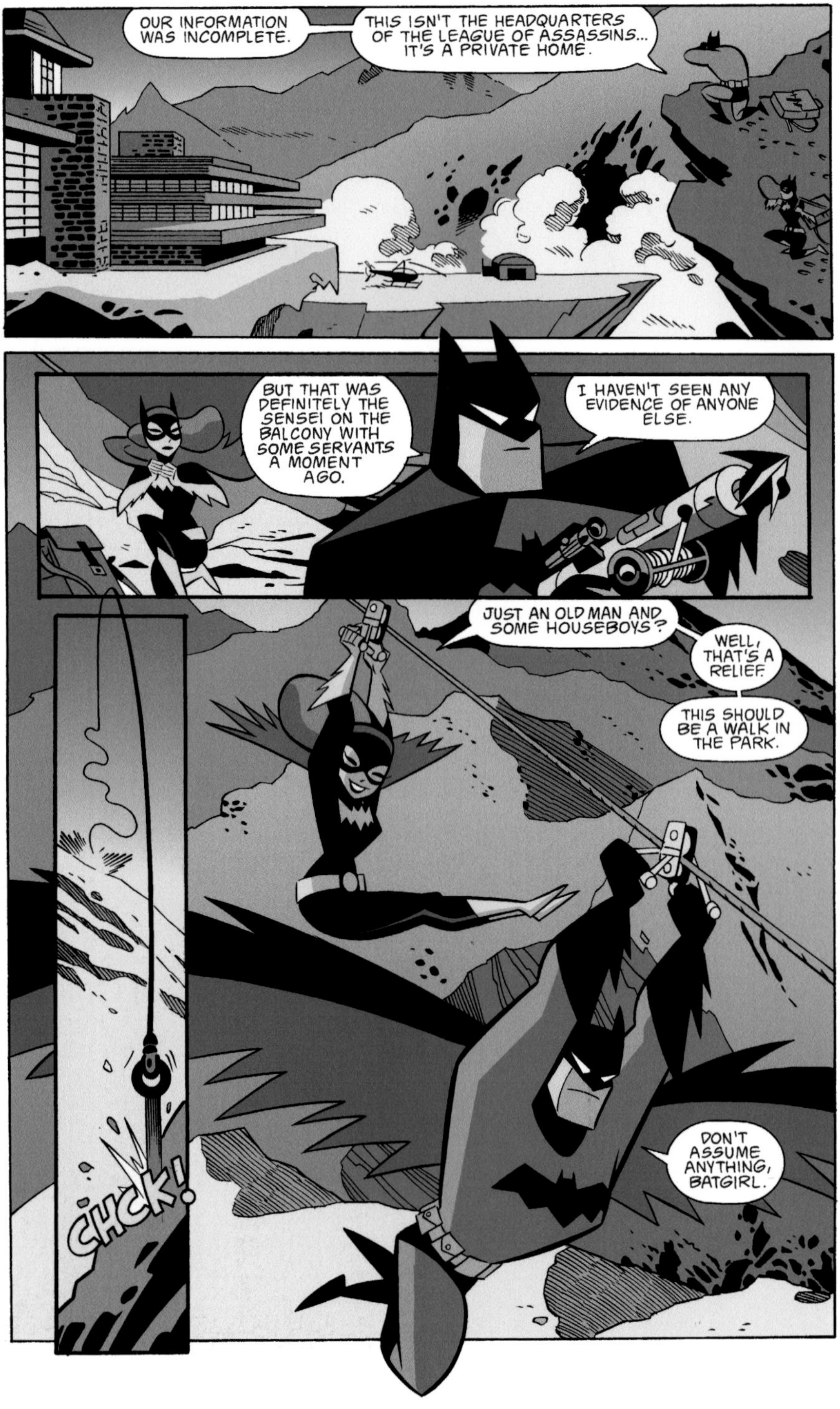

OUR INFORMATION WAS INCOMPLETE.
THIS ISN'T THE HEADQUARTERS OF THE LEAGUE OF ASSASSINS... IT'S A PRIVATE HOME.
BUT THAT WAS DEFINITELY THE SENSEI ON THE BALCONY WITH SOME SERVANTS A MOMENT AGO.
I HAVEN'T SEEN ANY EVIDENCE OF ANYONE ELSE.
JUST AN OLD MAN AND SOME HOUSEBOYS?
WELL, THAT'S A RELIEF.
THIS SHOULD BE A WALK IN THE PARK.
CHCK!
DON'T ASSUME ANYTHING, BATGIRL.

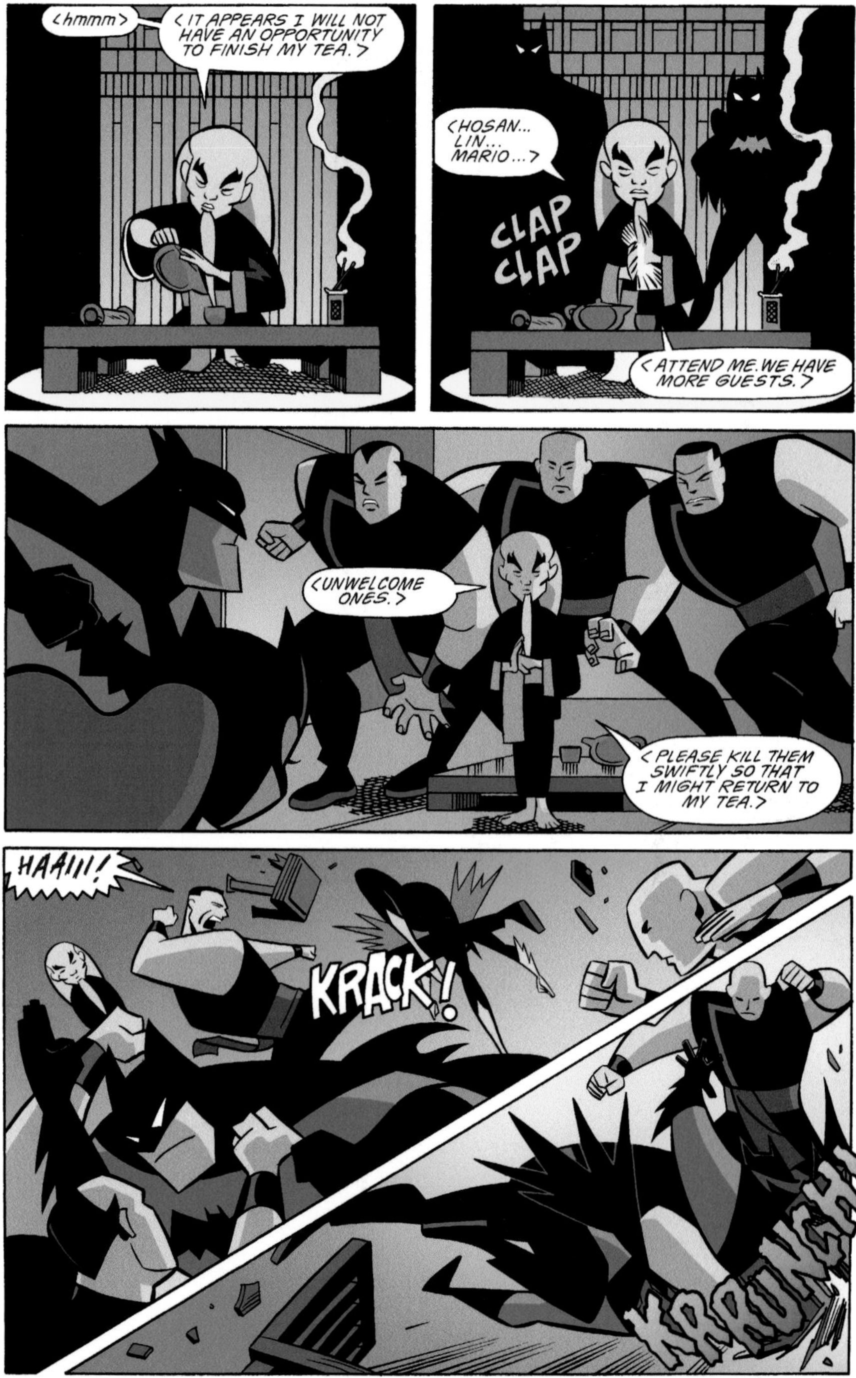
<hmmm>
<IT APPEARS I WILL NOT HAVE AN OPPORTUNITY TO FINISH MY TEA.>
<HOSAN... LIN... MARIO...>
CLAP CLAP
<ATTEND ME. WE HAVE MORE GUESTS.>
<UNWELCOME ONES.>
<PLEASE KILL THEM SWIFTLY SO THAT I MIGHT RETURN TO MY TEA.>
HAAIII!
KRACK!
KRRUNCH!

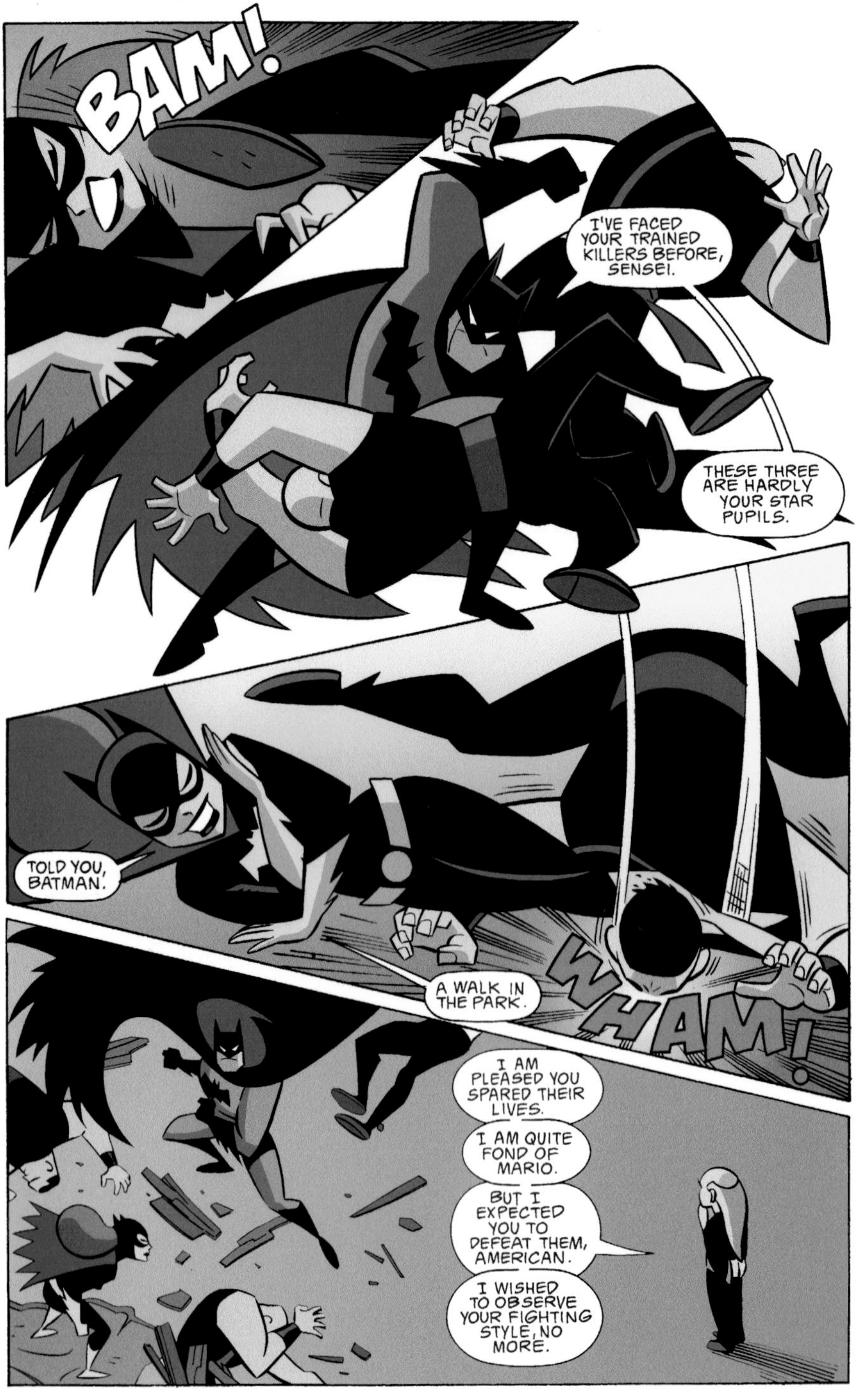
BAM!
I'VE FACED YOUR TRAINED KILLERS BEFORE, SENSEI.
THESE THREE ARE HARDLY YOUR STAR PUPILS.
TOLD YOU, BATMAN.
A WALK IN THE PARK.
WHAM!
I AM PLEASED YOU SPARED THEIR LIVES.
I AM QUITE FOND OF MARIO.
BUT I EXPECTED YOU TO DEFEAT THEM, AMERICAN.
I WISHED TO OBSERVE YOUR FIGHTING STYLE, NO MORE.

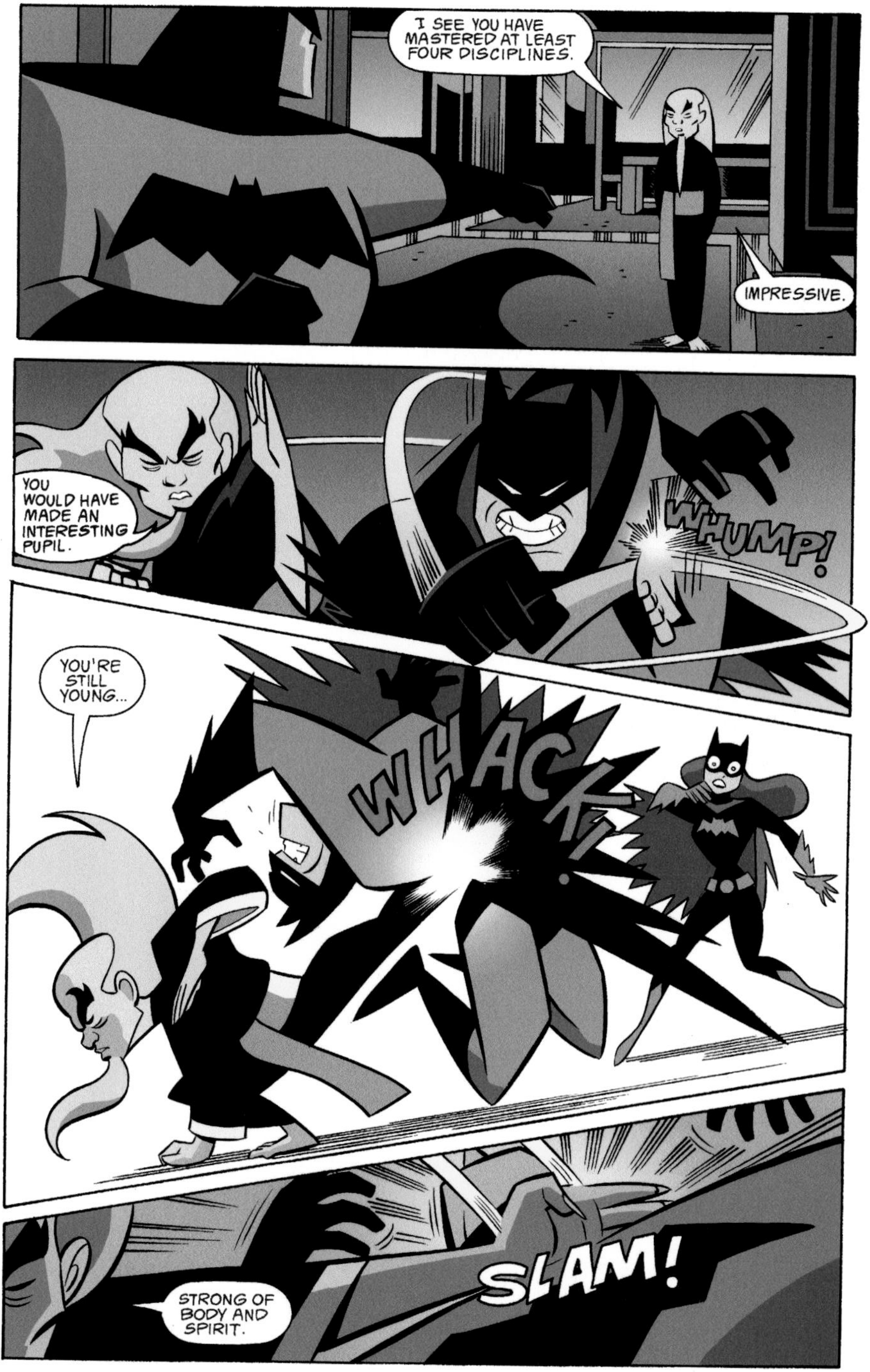
I SEE YOU HAVE MASTERED AT LEAST FOUR DISCIPLINES.
IMPRESSIVE.
YOU WOULD HAVE MADE AN INTERESTING PUPIL.
WHUMP!
YOU'RE STILL YOUNG...
WHACK!
SLAM!
STRONG OF BODY AND SPIRIT.

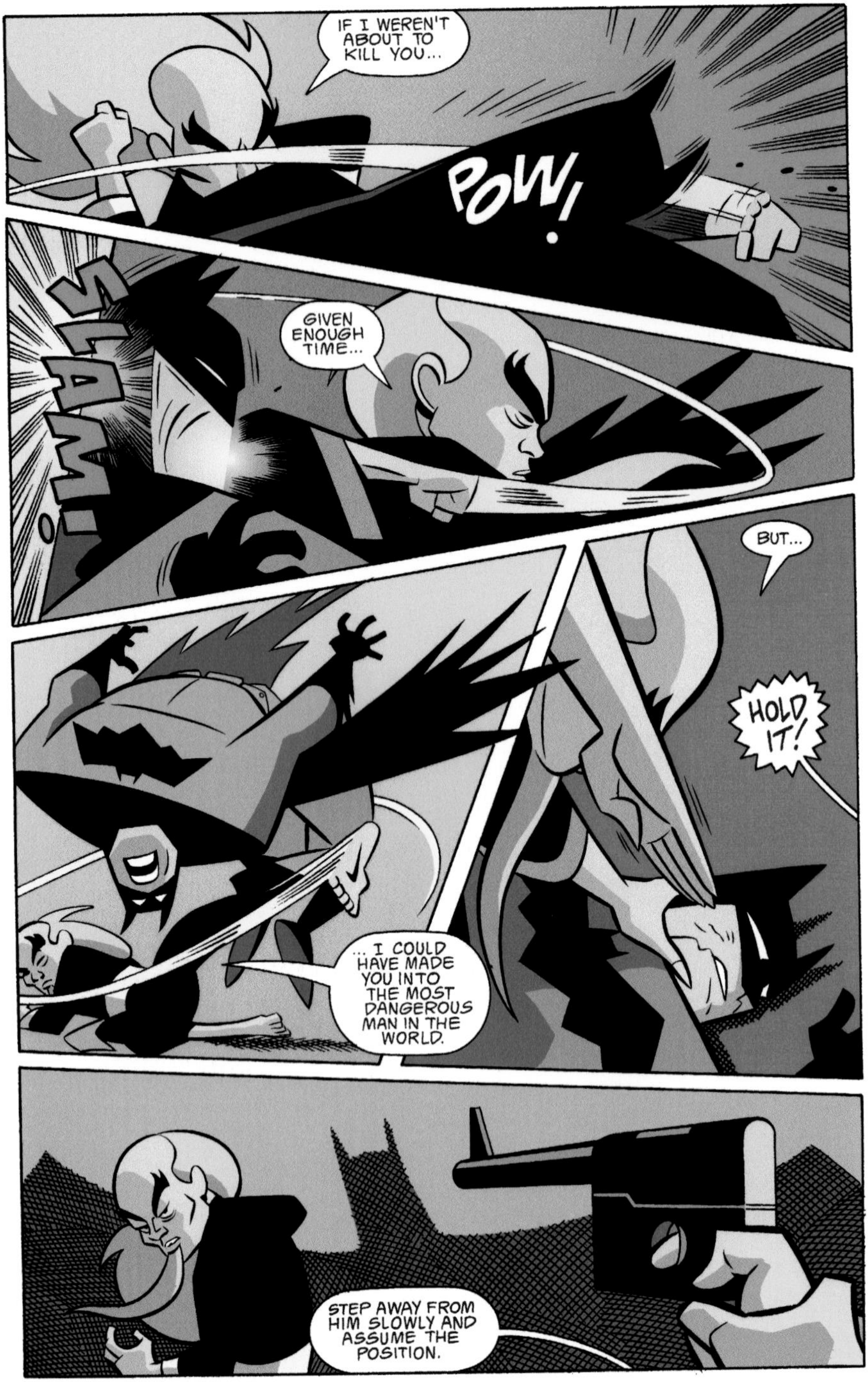
IF I WEREN'T ABOUT TO KILL YOU...
POW!
SLAM!
GIVEN ENOUGH TIME...
BUT...
HOLD IT!
...I COULD HAVE MADE YOU INTO THE MOST DANGEROUS MAN IN THE WORLD.
STEP AWAY FROM HIM SLOWLY AND ASSUME THE POSITION.

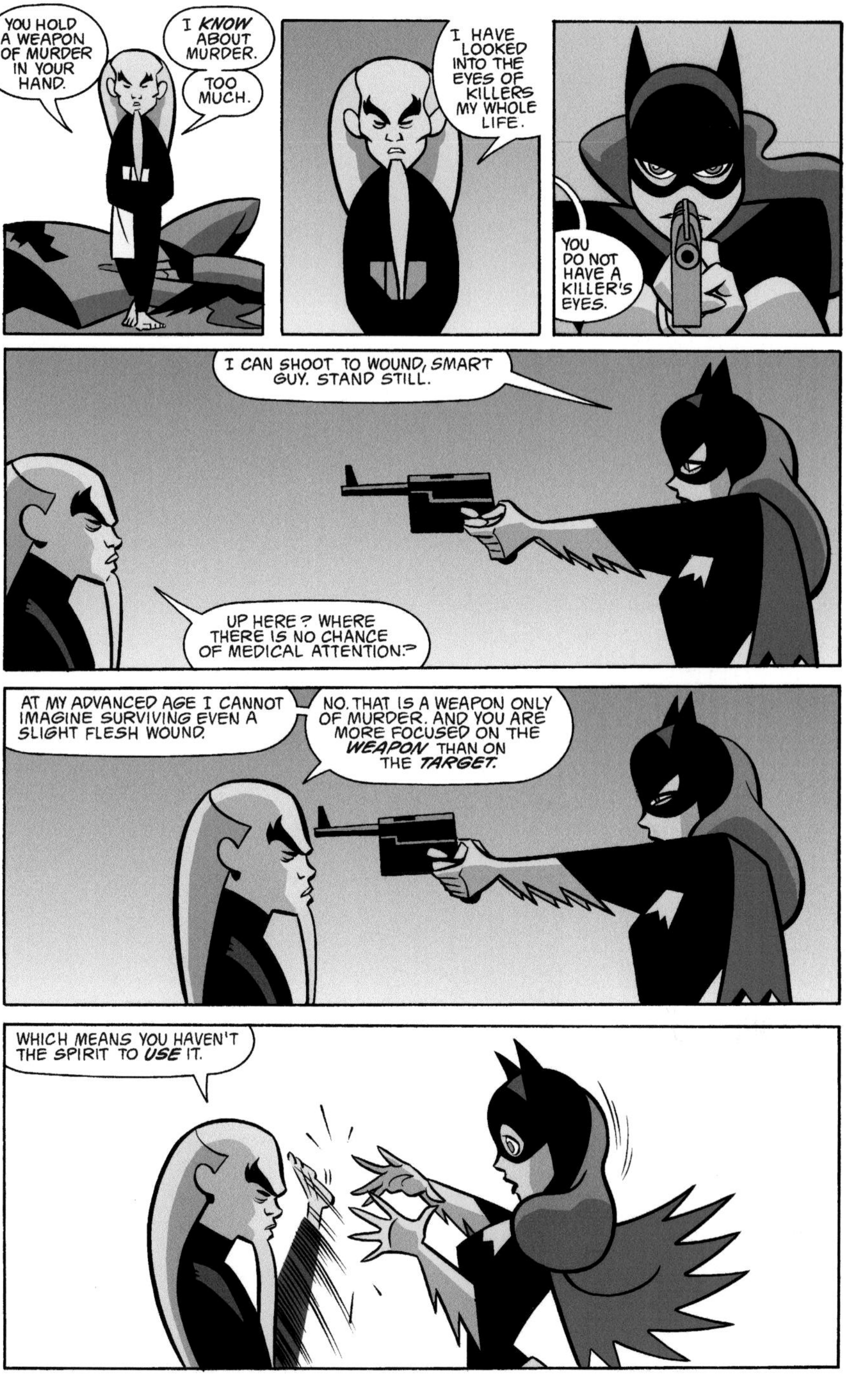
YOU HOLD A WEAPON OF MURDER IN YOUR HAND.
I *KNOW* ABOUT MURDER.
TOO MUCH.
I HAVE LOOKED INTO THE EYES OF KILLERS MY WHOLE LIFE.
YOU DO NOT HAVE A KILLER'S EYES.
I CAN SHOOT TO WOUND, SMART GUY. STAND STILL.
UP HERE? WHERE THERE IS NO CHANCE OF MEDICAL ATTENTION?
AT MY ADVANCED AGE I CANNOT IMAGINE SURVIVING EVEN A SLIGHT FLESH WOUND.
NO. THAT IS A WEAPON ONLY OF MURDER. AND YOU ARE MORE FOCUSED ON THE *WEAPON* THAN ON THE *TARGET.*
WHICH MEANS YOU HAVEN'T THE SPIRIT TO *USE* IT.

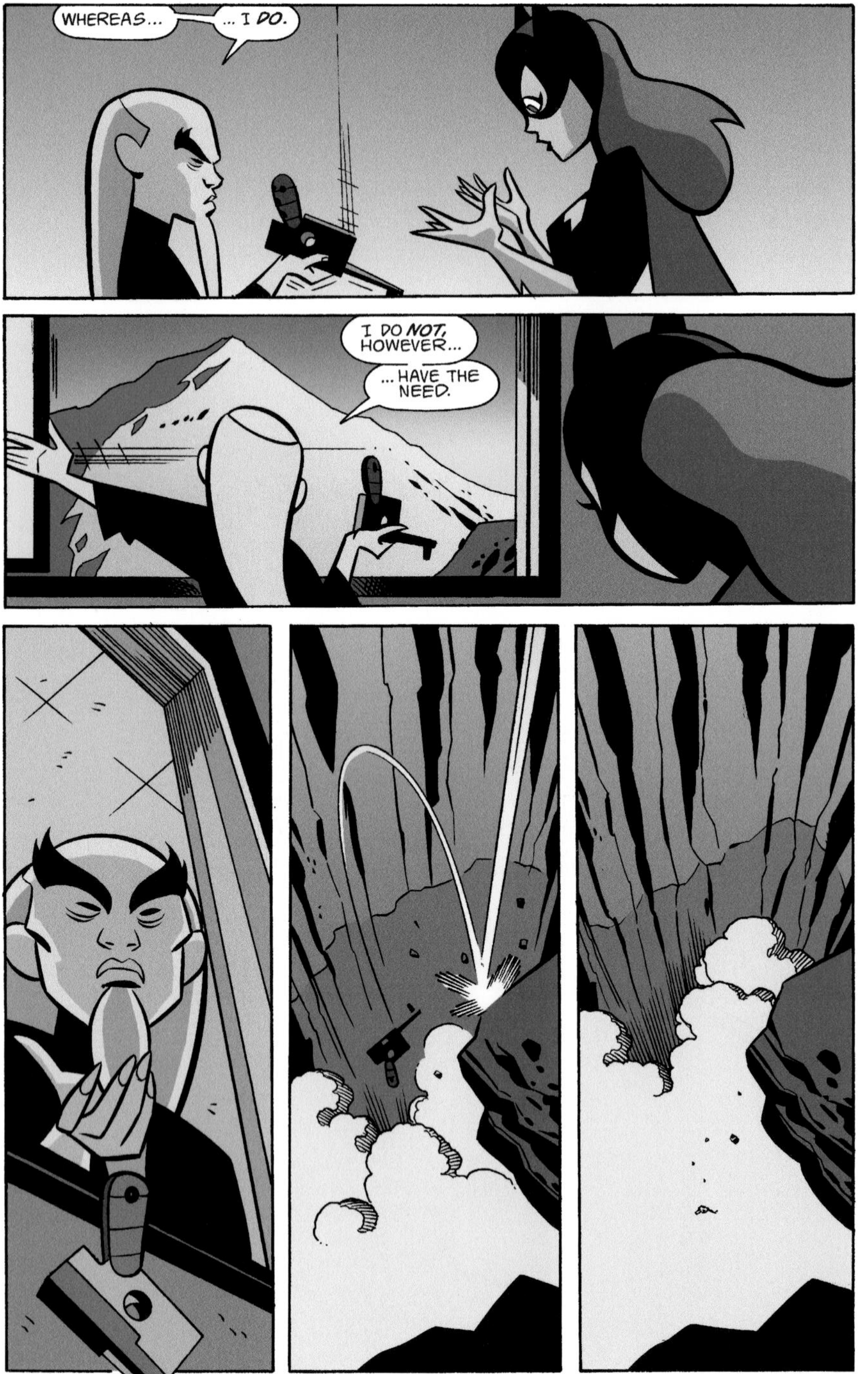
WHEREAS...
... I DO.
I DO NOT, HOWEVER...
... HAVE THE NEED.

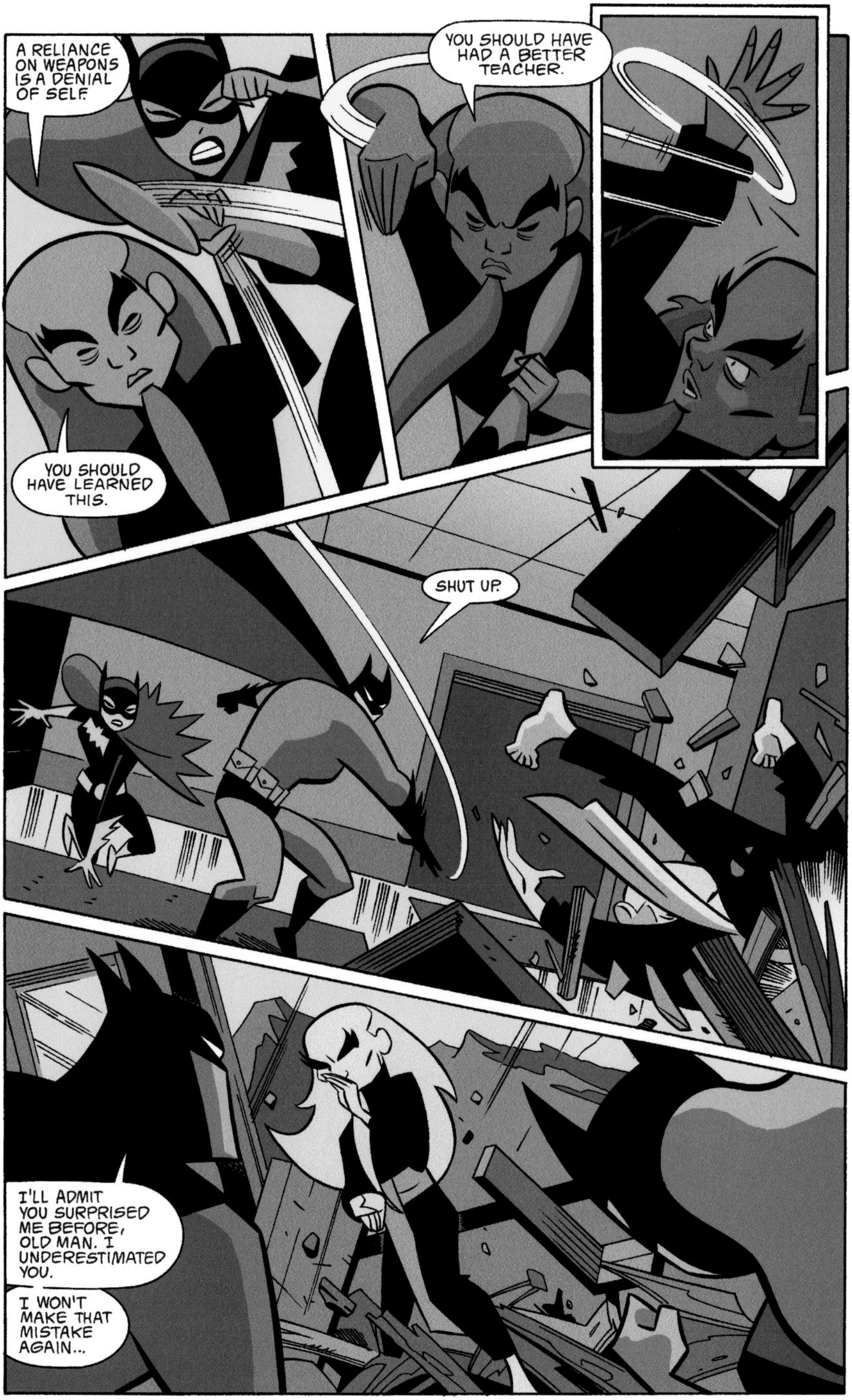
A RELIANCE ON WEAPONS IS A DENIAL OF SELF.
YOU SHOULD HAVE LEARNED THIS.
YOU SHOULD HAVE HAD A BETTER TEACHER.
SHUT UP.
I'LL ADMIT YOU SURPRISED ME BEFORE, OLD MAN. I UNDERESTIMATED YOU.
I WON'T MAKE THAT MISTAKE AGAIN...

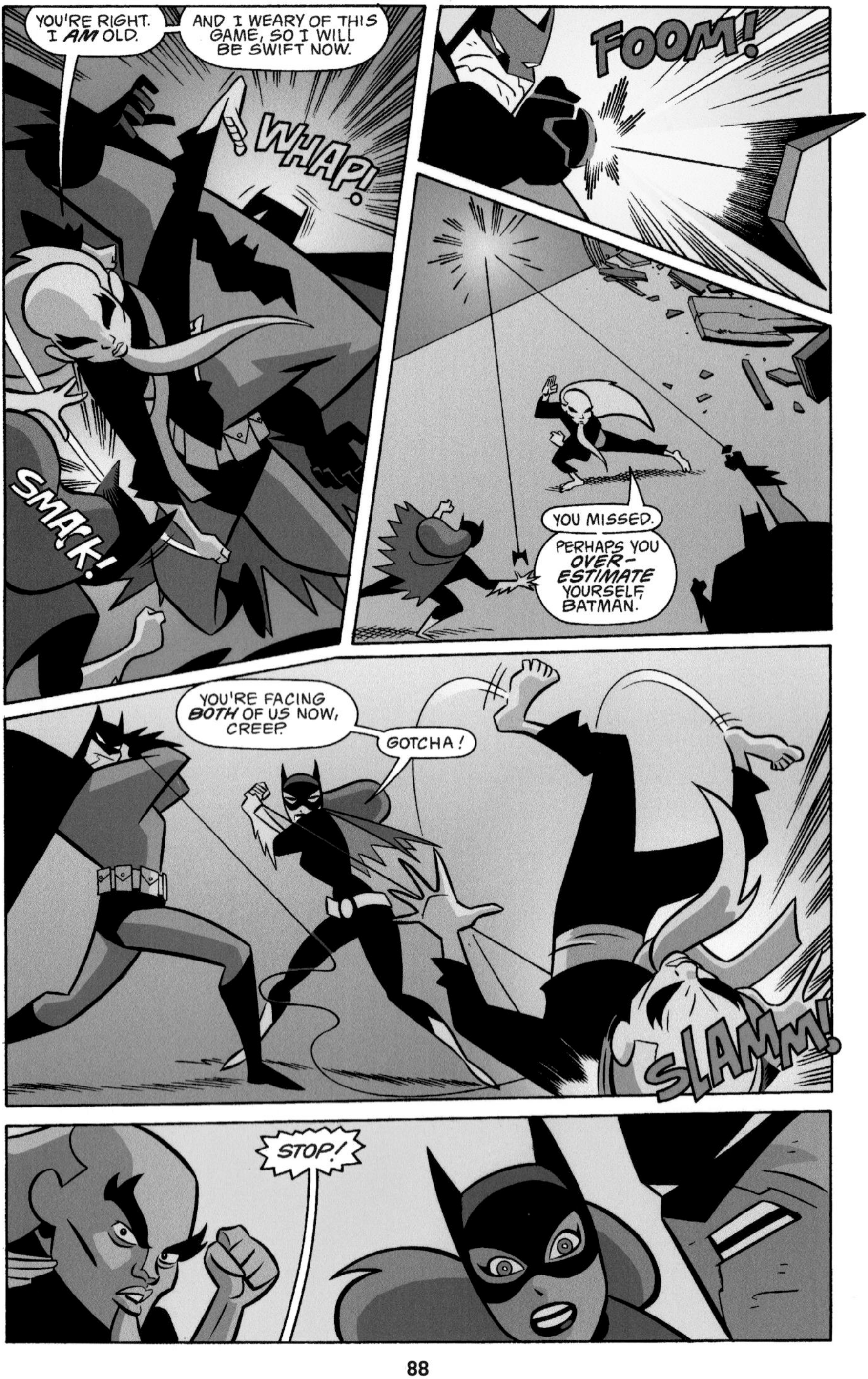
YOU'RE RIGHT. I AM OLD.
AND I WEARY OF THIS GAME, SO I WILL BE SWIFT NOW.
WHAP!
SMACK!
FOOM!
YOU MISSED.
PERHAPS YOU OVER-ESTIMATE YOURSELF, BATMAN.
YOU'RE FACING BOTH OF US NOW, CREEP.
GOTCHA!
SLAMM!
STOP!

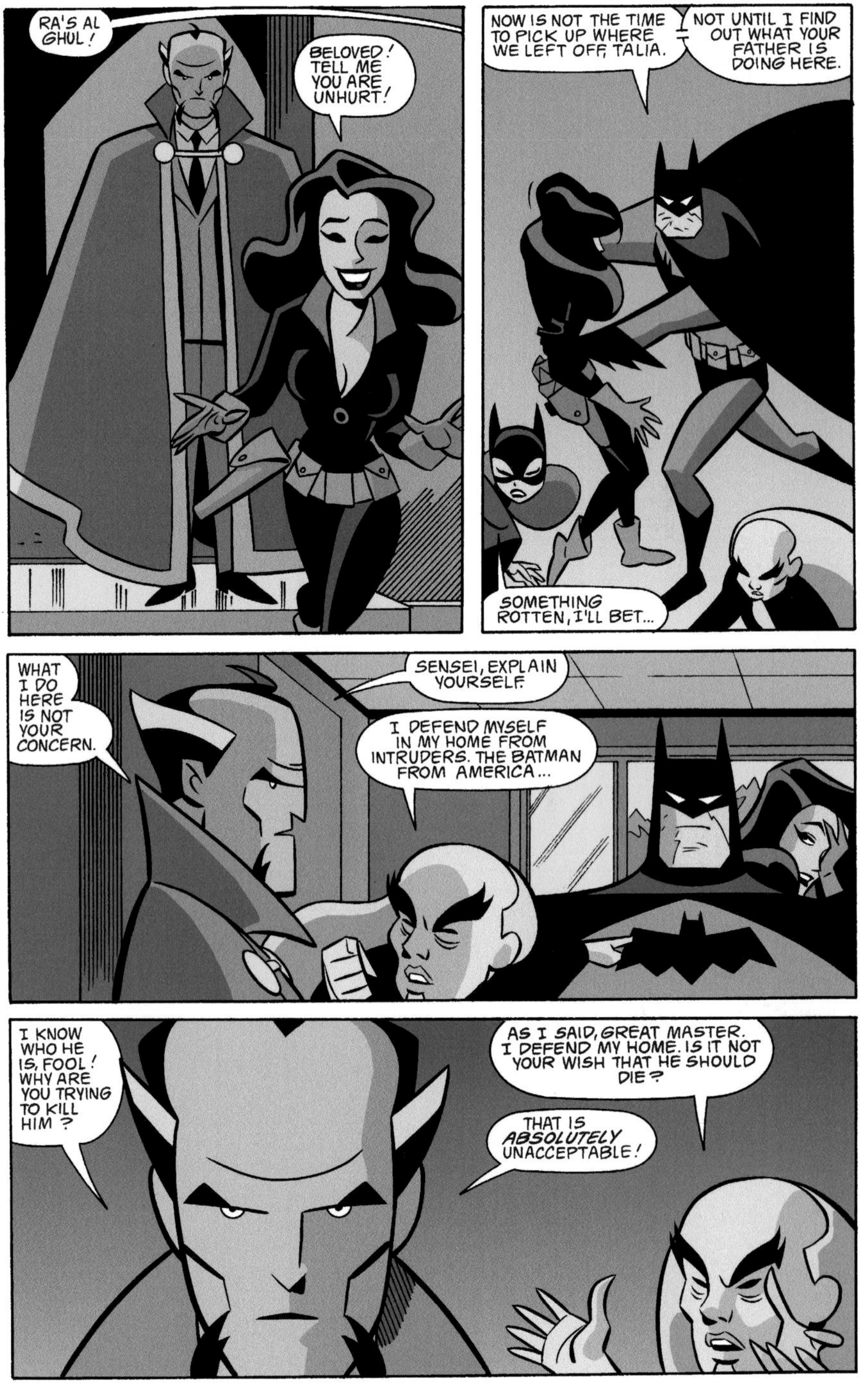
RA'S AL GHUL!
BELOVED! TELL ME YOU ARE UNHURT!
NOW IS NOT THE TIME TO PICK UP WHERE WE LEFT OFF, TALIA.
NOT UNTIL I FIND OUT WHAT YOUR FATHER IS DOING HERE.
SOMETHING ROTTEN, I'LL BET...
WHAT I DO HERE IS NOT YOUR CONCERN.
SENSEI, EXPLAIN YOURSELF.
I DEFEND MYSELF IN MY HOME FROM INTRUDERS. THE BATMAN FROM AMERICA...
I KNOW WHO HE IS, FOOL! WHY ARE YOU TRYING TO KILL HIM?
AS I SAID, GREAT MASTER. I DEFEND MY HOME. IS IT NOT YOUR WISH THAT HE SHOULD DIE?
THAT IS *ABSOLUTELY* UNACCEPTABLE!

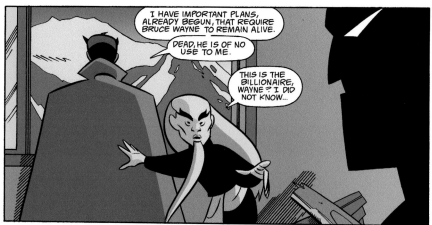

I HAVE IMPORTANT PLANS, ALREADY BEGUN, THAT REQUIRE BRUCE WAYNE TO REMAIN ALIVE.

DEAD, HE IS OF NO USE TO ME.

THIS IS THE BILLIONAIRE, WAYNE? I DID NOT KNOW...

IT WAS NOT IMPORTANT THAT YOU KNOW THIS MAN'S SECRET. BUT YOU MUST LET HIM GO.

I NEED HIM ALIVE.

I DON'T NEED YOUR HELP, RA'S...

ON THE CONTRARY, BATMAN. THE SENSEI WAS MOMENTS AWAY FROM KILLING YOU AND YOUR PARTNER...

HE WOULD HAVE *TRIED!*

NO MATTER. SENSEI, ALLOW THEM TO GO UNHARMED.

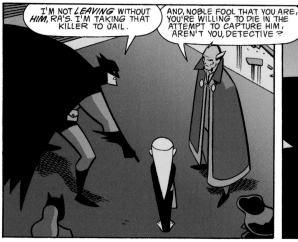

I'M NOT *LEAVING* WITHOUT *HIM*, RA'S. I'M TAKING THAT KILLER TO JAIL.

AND, NOBLE FOOL THAT YOU ARE, YOU'RE WILLING TO DIE IN THE ATTEMPT TO CAPTURE HIM, AREN'T YOU, DETECTIVE?

HE COMES WITH ME.

NO MATTER WHAT.

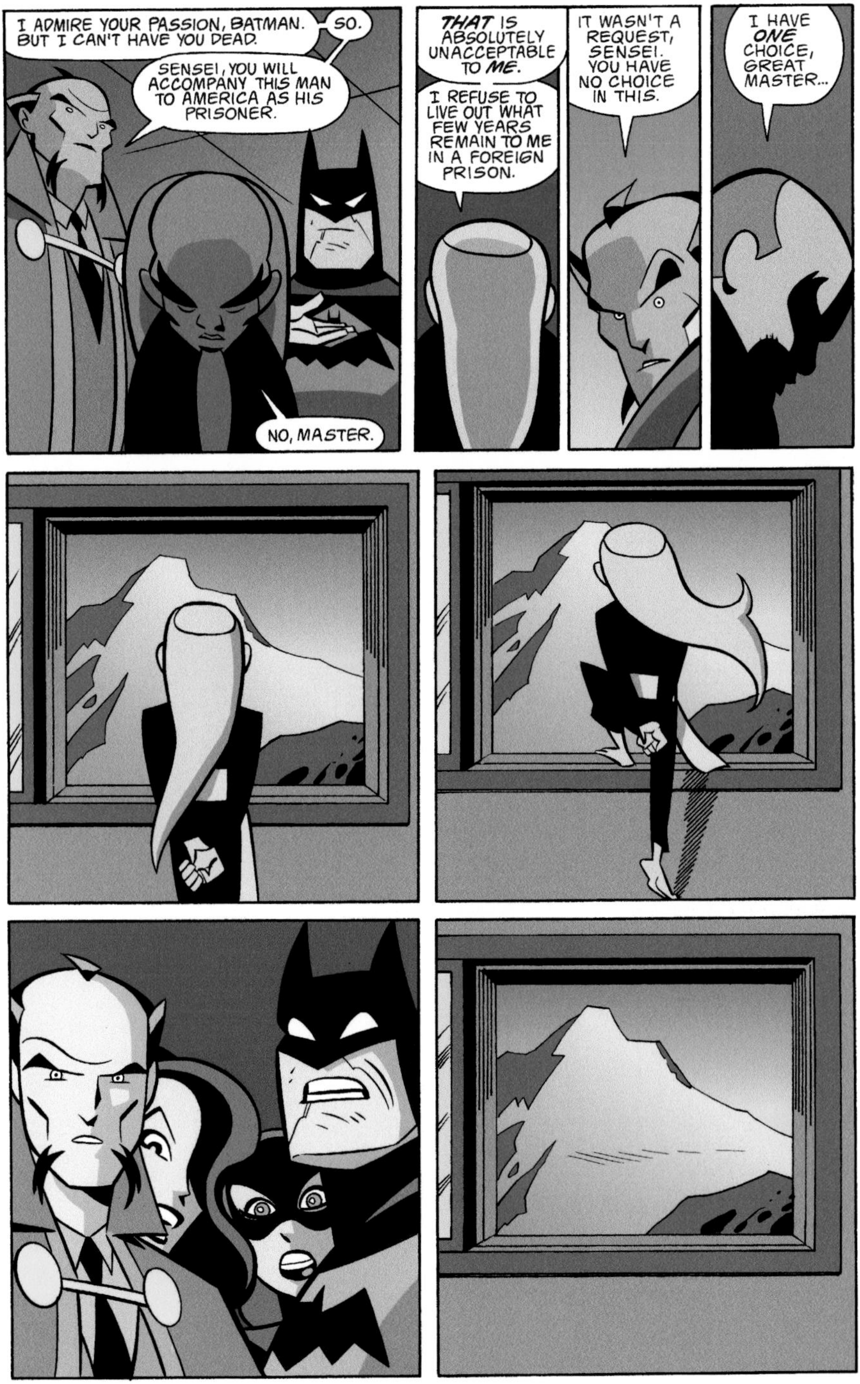
I ADMIRE YOUR PASSION, BATMAN. BUT I CAN'T HAVE YOU DEAD.
SO.
SENSEI, YOU WILL ACCOMPANY THIS MAN TO AMERICA AS HIS PRISONER.
NO, MASTER.
THAT IS ABSOLUTELY UNACCEPTABLE TO ME.
I REFUSE TO LIVE OUT WHAT FEW YEARS REMAIN TO ME IN A FOREIGN PRISON.
IT WASN'T A REQUEST, SENSEI. YOU HAVE NO CHOICE IN THIS.
I HAVE ONE CHOICE, GREAT MASTER...

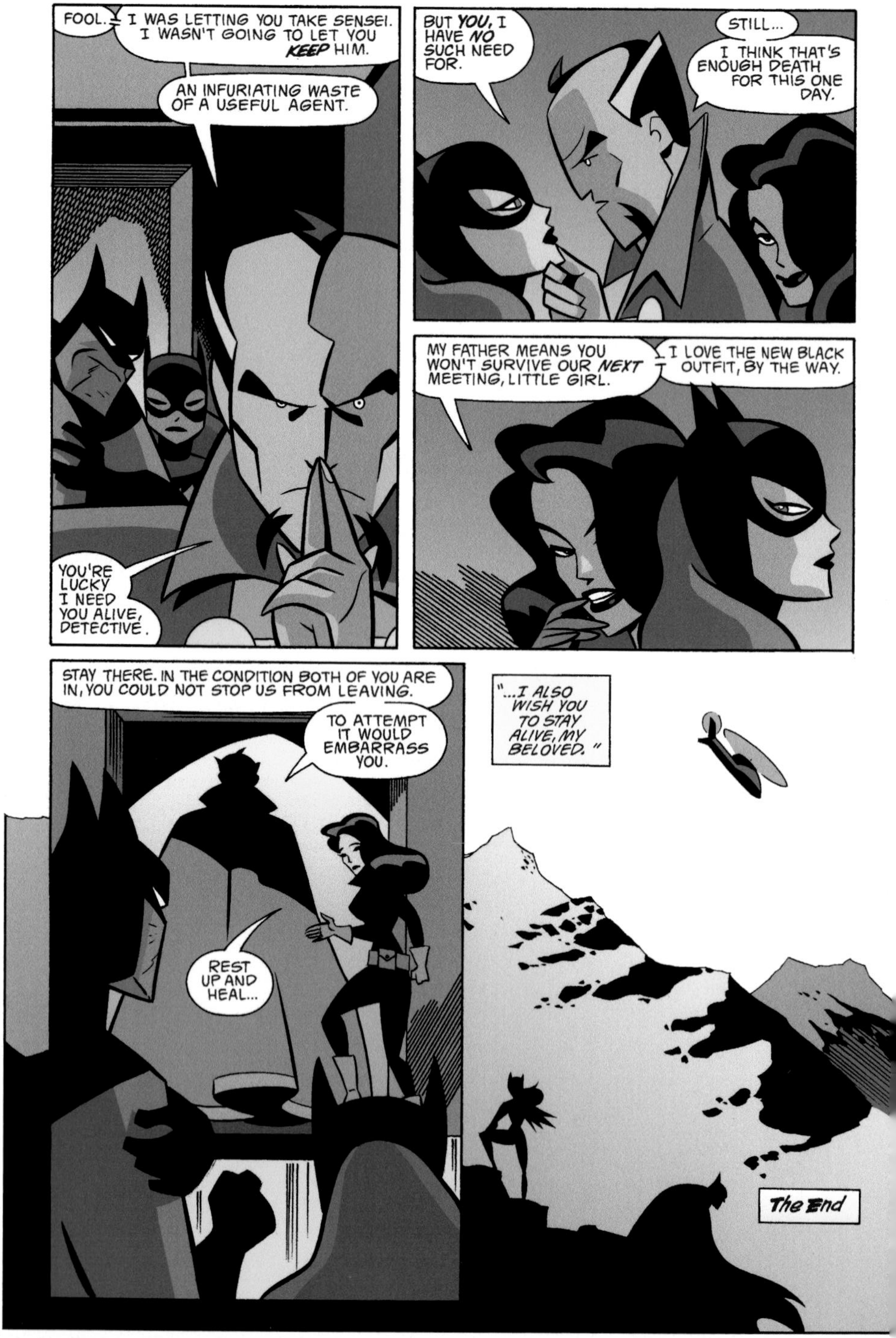
FOOL.
I WAS LETTING YOU TAKE SENSEI. I WASN'T GOING TO LET YOU *KEEP* HIM.
AN INFURIATING WASTE OF A USEFUL AGENT.
YOU'RE LUCKY I NEED YOU ALIVE, DETECTIVE.
BUT *YOU*, I HAVE *NO* SUCH NEED FOR.
STILL...
I THINK THAT'S ENOUGH DEATH FOR THIS ONE DAY.
MY FATHER MEANS YOU WON'T SURVIVE OUR *NEXT* MEETING, LITTLE GIRL.
I LOVE THE NEW BLACK OUTFIT, BY THE WAY.
STAY THERE. IN THE CONDITION BOTH OF YOU ARE IN, YOU COULD NOT STOP US FROM LEAVING.
TO ATTEMPT IT WOULD EMBARRASS YOU.
REST UP AND HEAL...
"...I ALSO WISH YOU TO STAY ALIVE, MY BELOVED."
The End

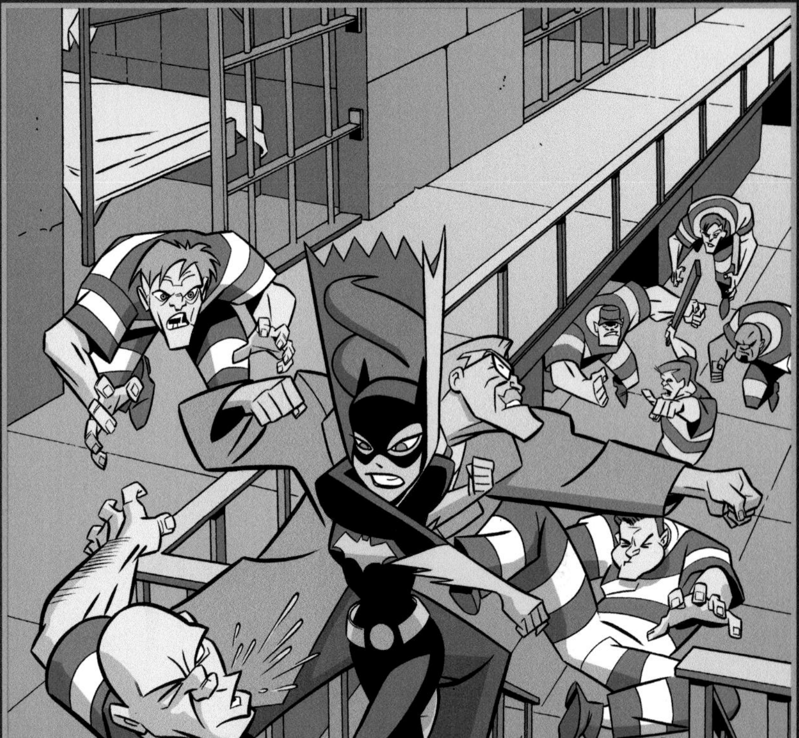
1246
B Smith
T Beatty

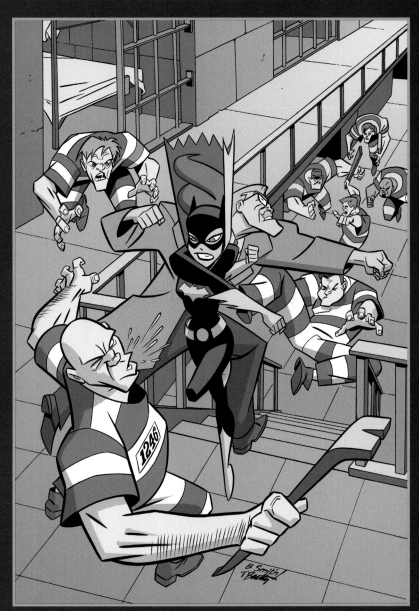

CHAPTER 4: MINUTE DIFFERENCES

BATGIRL

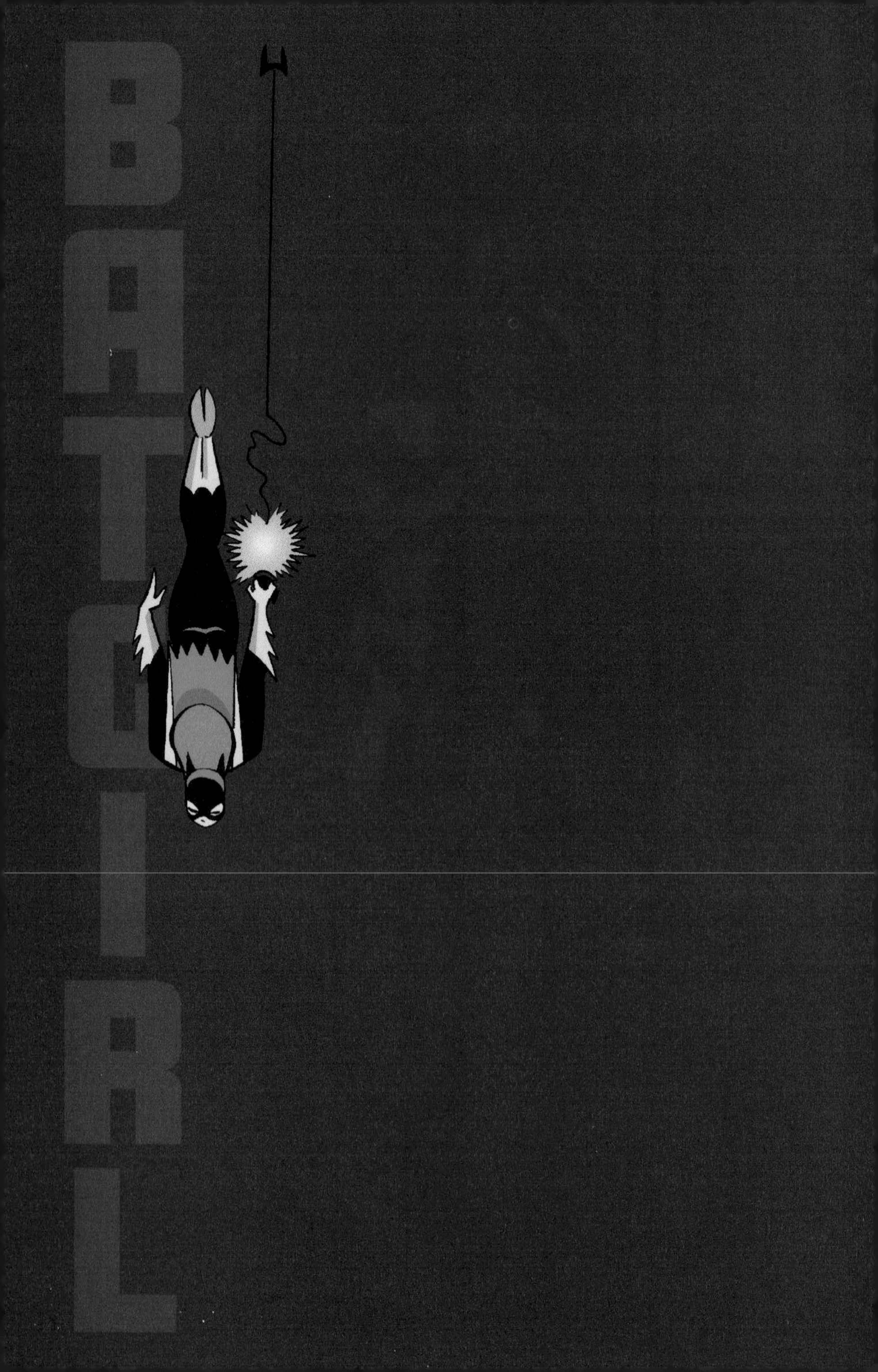
BATGIRL

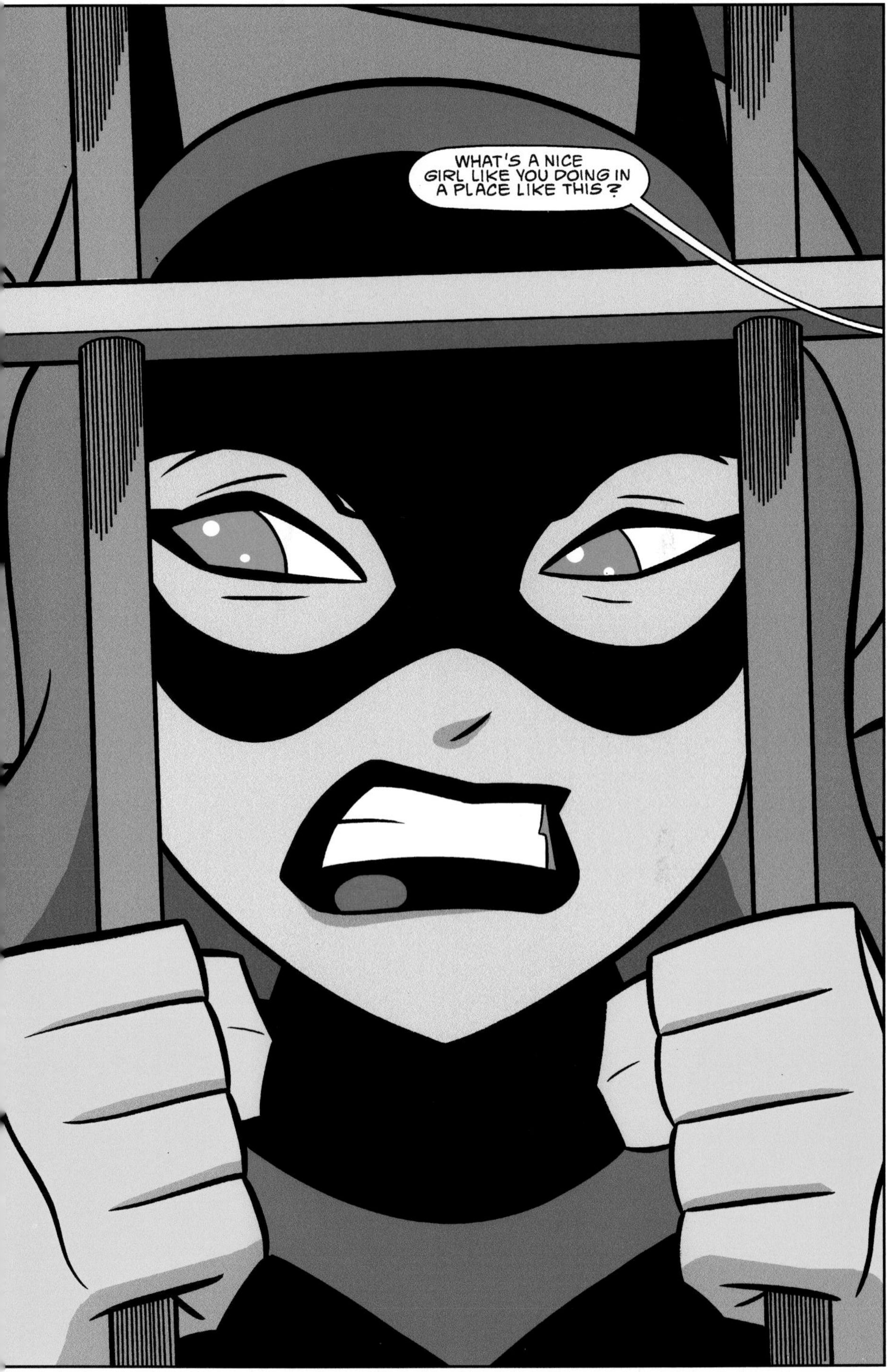
WHAT'S A NICE GIRL LIKE YOU DOING IN A PLACE LIKE THIS?

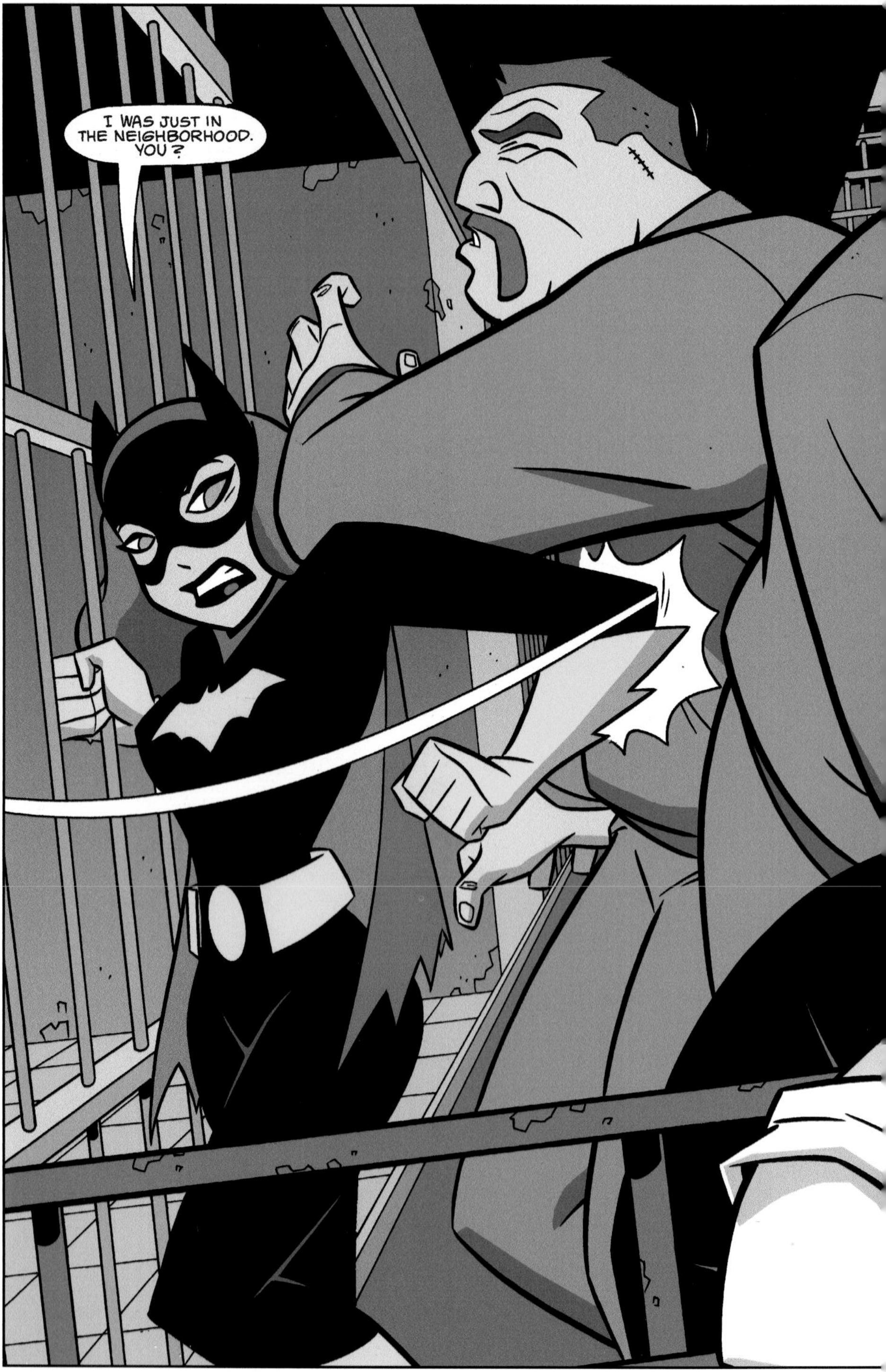
I WAS JUST IN THE NEIGHBORHOOD. YOU?

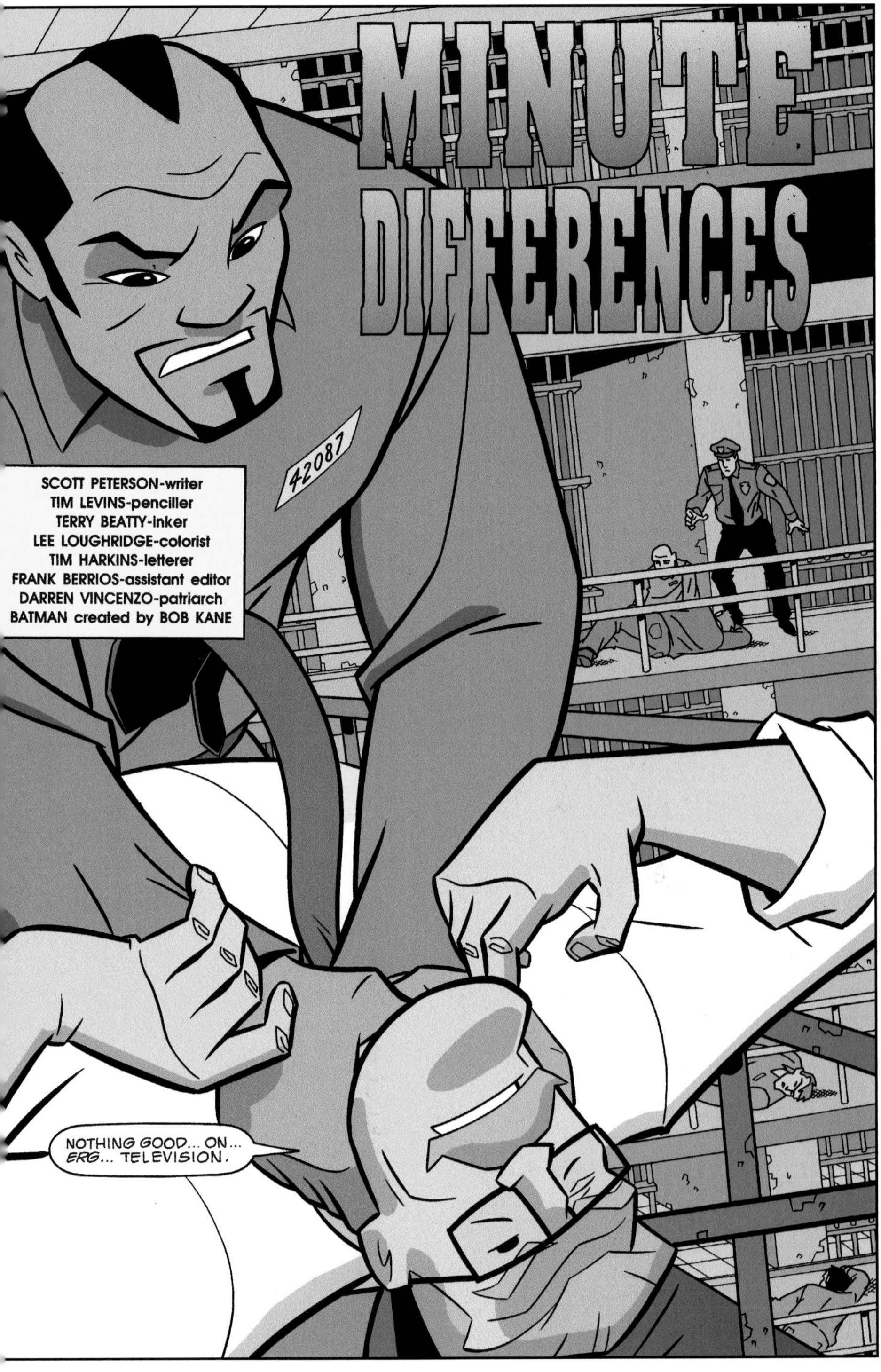
MINUTE DIFFERENCES
42087
SCOTT PETERSON-writer
TIM LEVINS-penciller
TERRY BEATTY-inker
LEE LOUGHRIDGE-colorist
TIM HARKINS-letterer
FRANK BERRIOS-assistant editor
DARREN VINCENZO-patriarch
BATMAN created by BOB KANE
NOTHING GOOD... ON... ERG... TELEVISION.

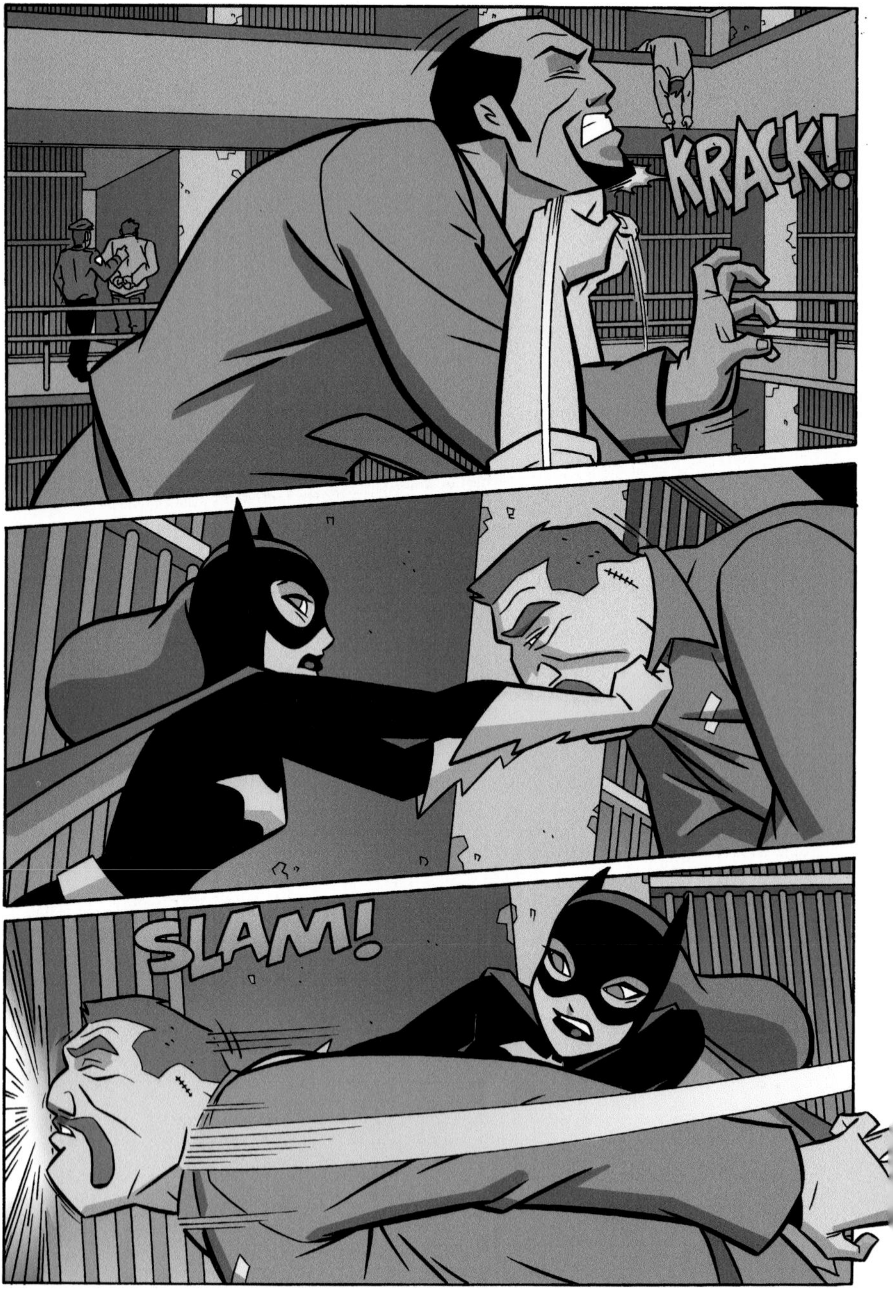
KRACK!
SLAM!

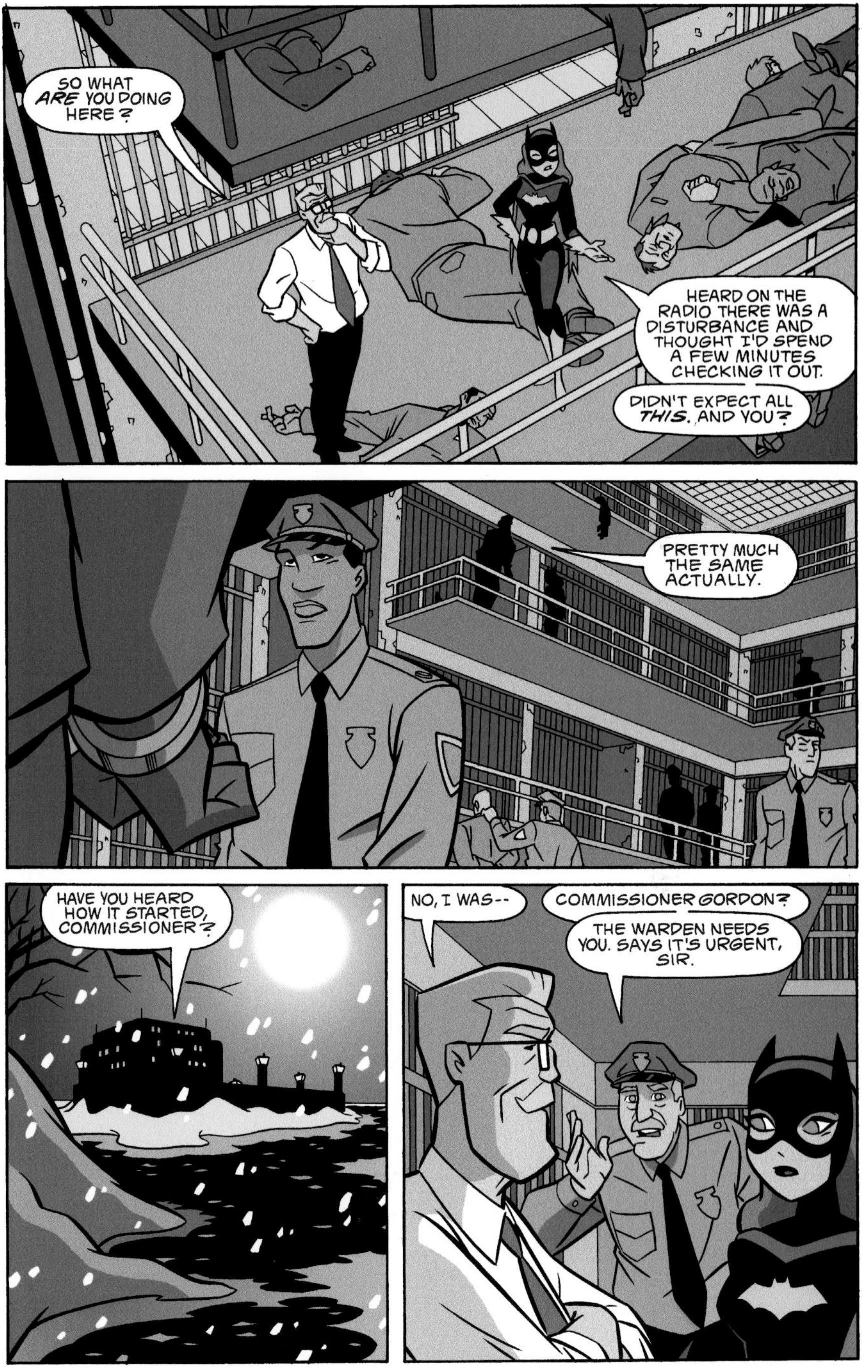
SO WHAT ARE YOU DOING HERE?
HEARD ON THE RADIO THERE WAS A DISTURBANCE AND THOUGHT I'D SPEND A FEW MINUTES CHECKING IT OUT.
DIDN'T EXPECT ALL THIS. AND YOU?
PRETTY MUCH THE SAME ACTUALLY.
HAVE YOU HEARD HOW IT STARTED, COMMISSIONER?
NO, I WAS--
COMMISSIONER GORDON?
THE WARDEN NEEDS YOU. SAYS IT'S URGENT, SIR.

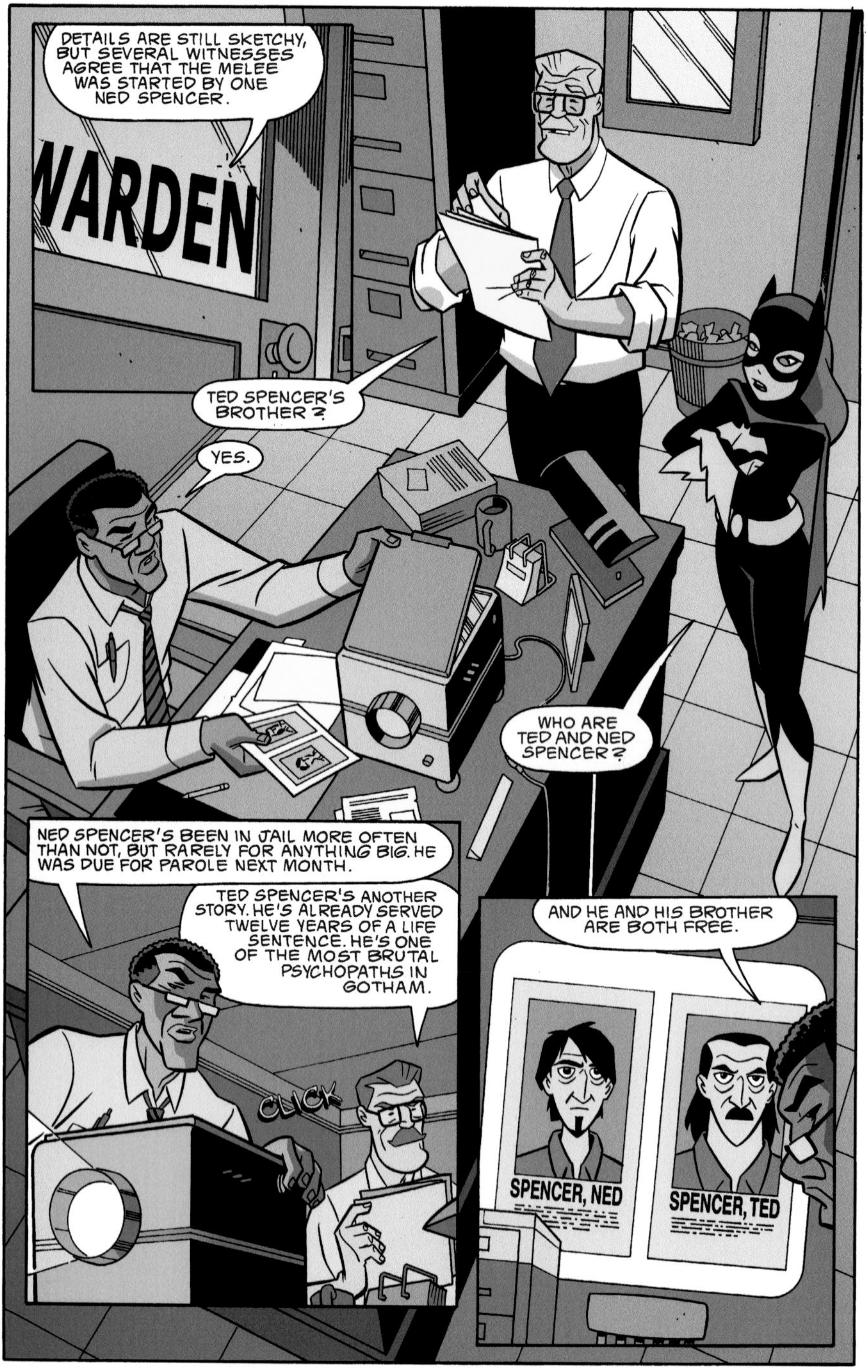
DETAILS ARE STILL SKETCHY, BUT SEVERAL WITNESSES AGREE THAT THE MELEE WAS STARTED BY ONE NED SPENCER.
WARDEN
TED SPENCER'S BROTHER?
YES.
WHO ARE TED AND NED SPENCER?
NED SPENCER'S BEEN IN JAIL MORE OFTEN THAN NOT, BUT RARELY FOR ANYTHING BIG. HE WAS DUE FOR PAROLE NEXT MONTH.
TED SPENCER'S ANOTHER STORY. HE'S ALREADY SERVED TWELVE YEARS OF A LIFE SENTENCE. HE'S ONE OF THE MOST BRUTAL PSYCHOPATHS IN GOTHAM.
CLICK
AND HE AND HIS BROTHER ARE BOTH FREE.
SPENCER, NED
SPENCER, TED

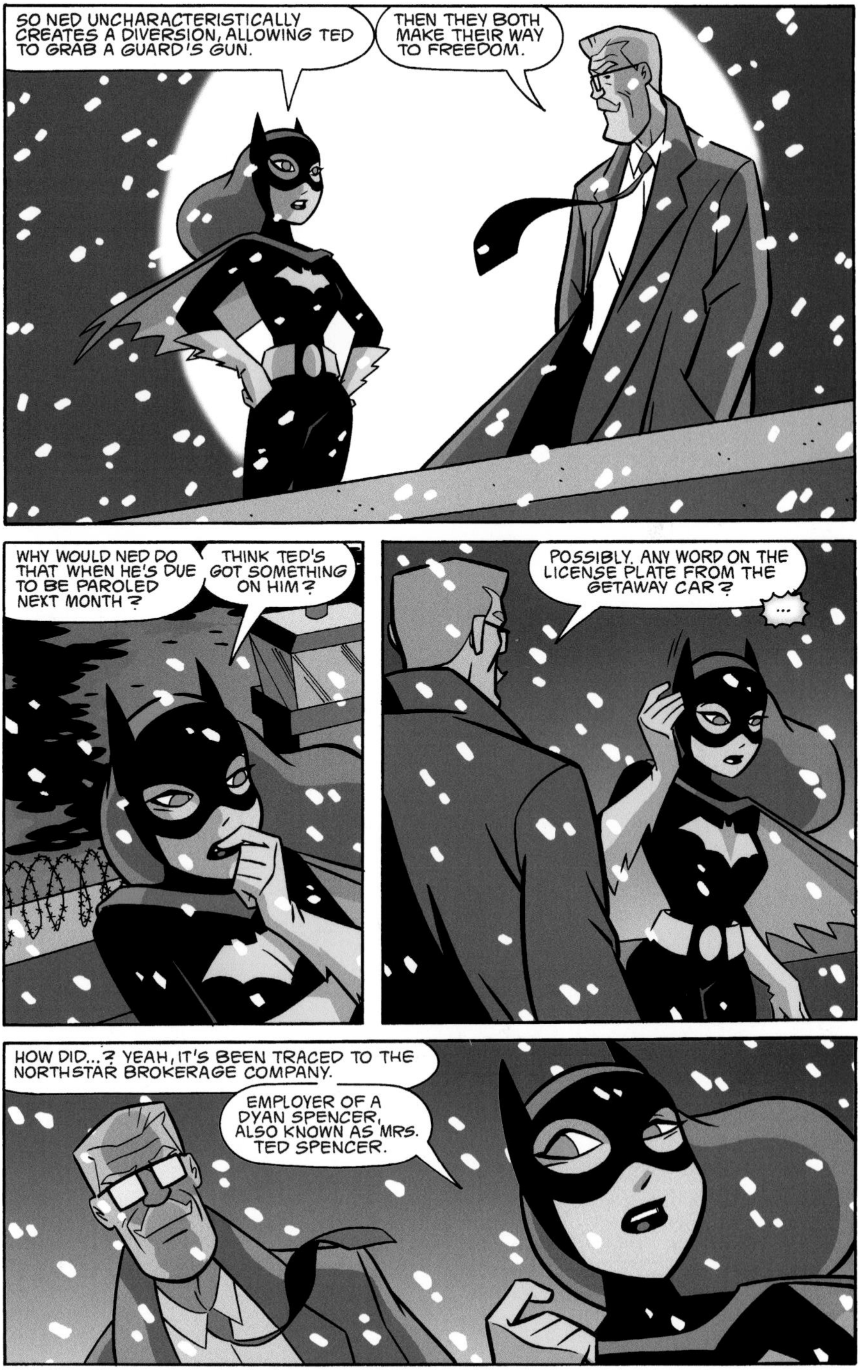
SO NED UNCHARACTERISTICALLY CREATES A DIVERSION, ALLOWING TED TO GRAB A GUARD'S GUN.
THEN THEY BOTH MAKE THEIR WAY TO FREEDOM.
WHY WOULD NED DO THAT WHEN HE'S DUE TO BE PAROLED NEXT MONTH?
THINK TED'S GOT SOMETHING ON HIM?
POSSIBLY. ANY WORD ON THE LICENSE PLATE FROM THE GETAWAY CAR?
...
HOW DID...? YEAH, IT'S BEEN TRACED TO THE NORTHSTAR BROKERAGE COMPANY.
EMPLOYER OF A DYAN SPENCER, ALSO KNOWN AS MRS. TED SPENCER.

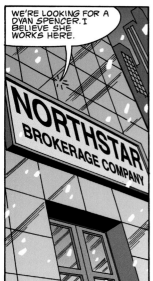

WE'RE LOOKING FOR A DYAN SPENCER. I BELIEVE SHE WORKS HERE.

NORTHSTAR BROKERAGE COMPANY

SHE DOES, BUT I'M AFRAID EVERYONE'S GONE FOR THE DAY.

I SEE. A COMPANY CAR WAS INVOLVED IN A BREAKOUT AT THE PRISON TONIGHT.

OH, DYAN WOULD NEVER HAVE ANYTHING TO DO WITH THAT.

OF COURSE NOT. I COULDN'T HELP BUT NOTICE THAT YOU APPARENTLY HAVE ACCESS TO A COMPANY CAR.

WHERE WERE YOU AT--

BETTY WELSH

SPLSH!

102

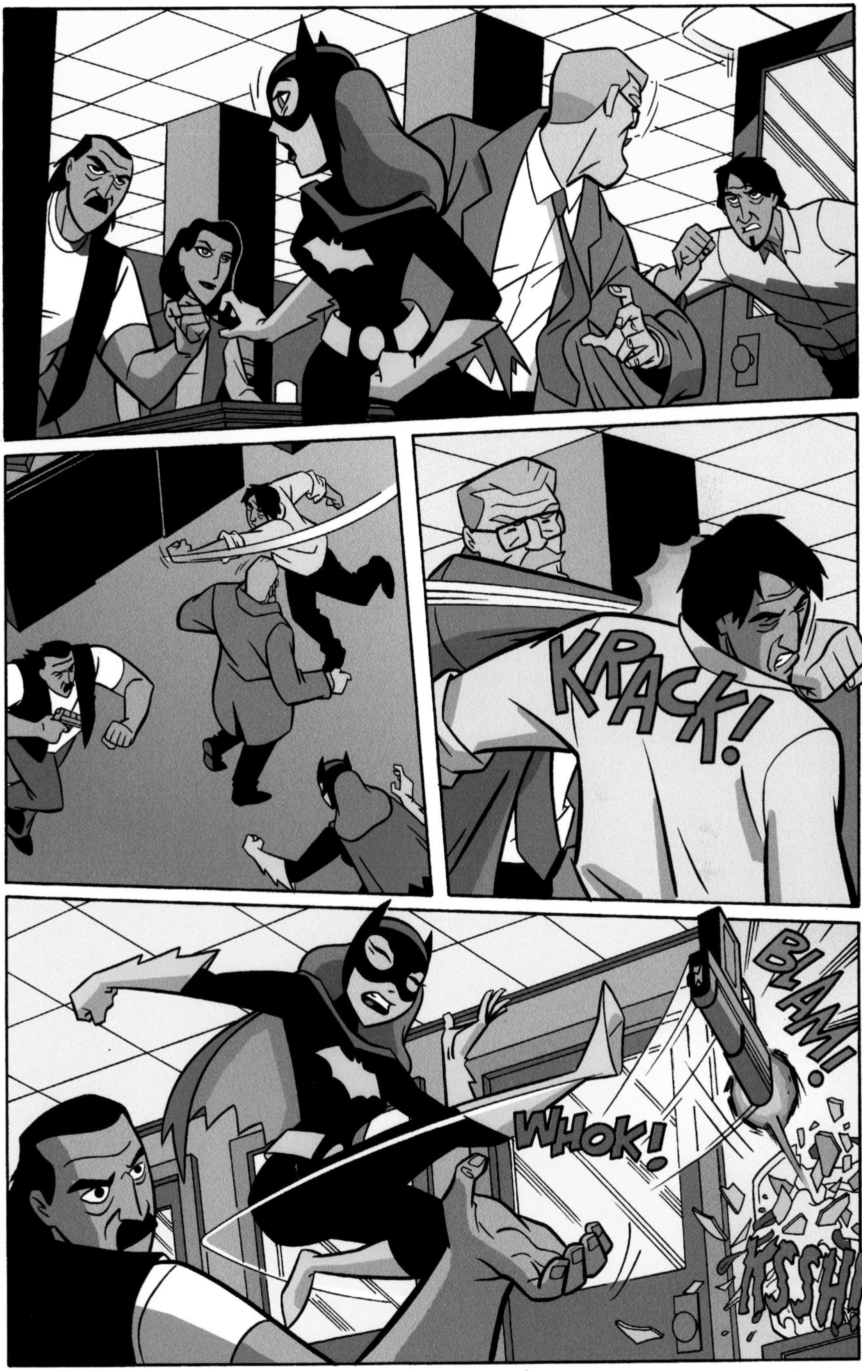
KRACK!
BLAM!
WHOK!
KSSH!

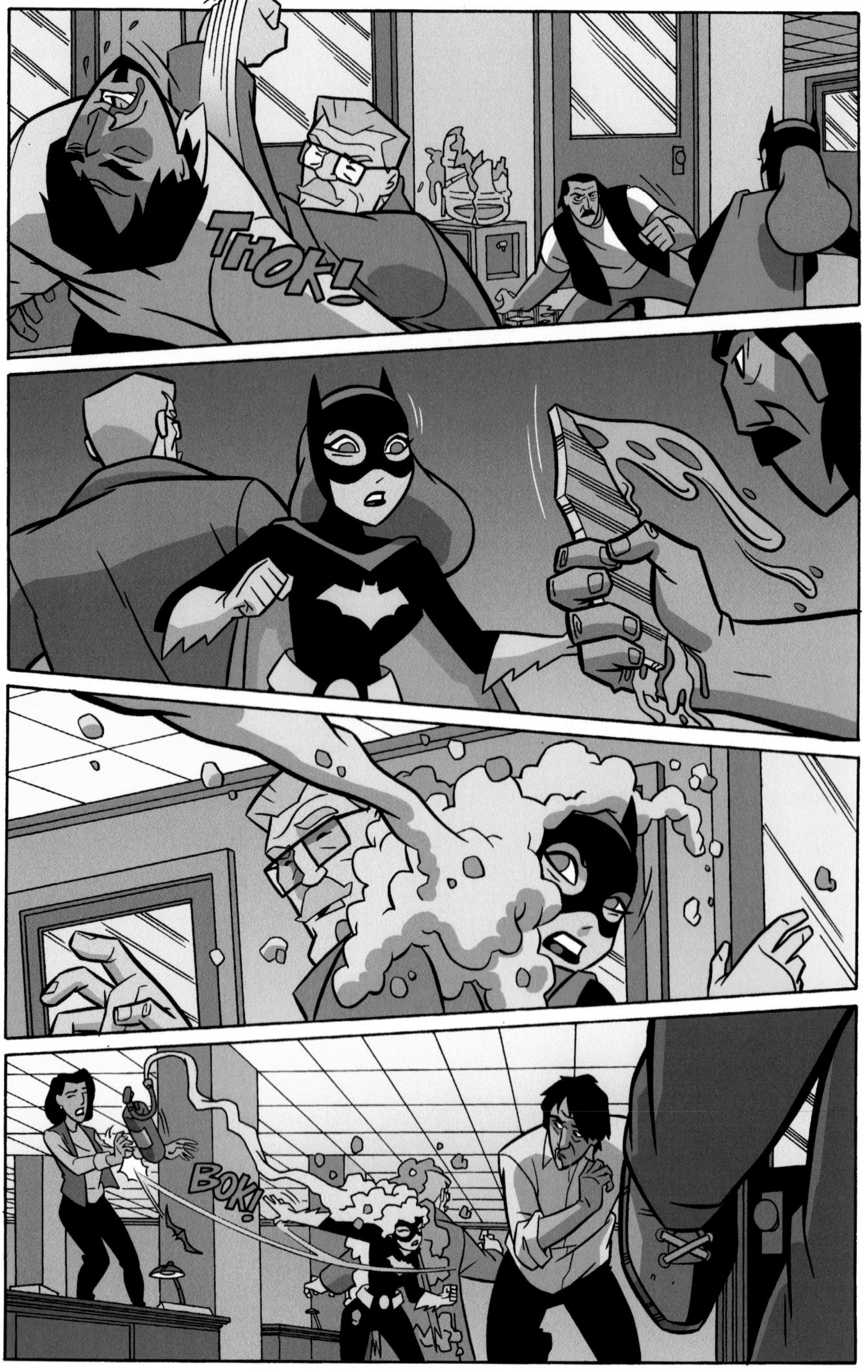
THOK!
BOK!

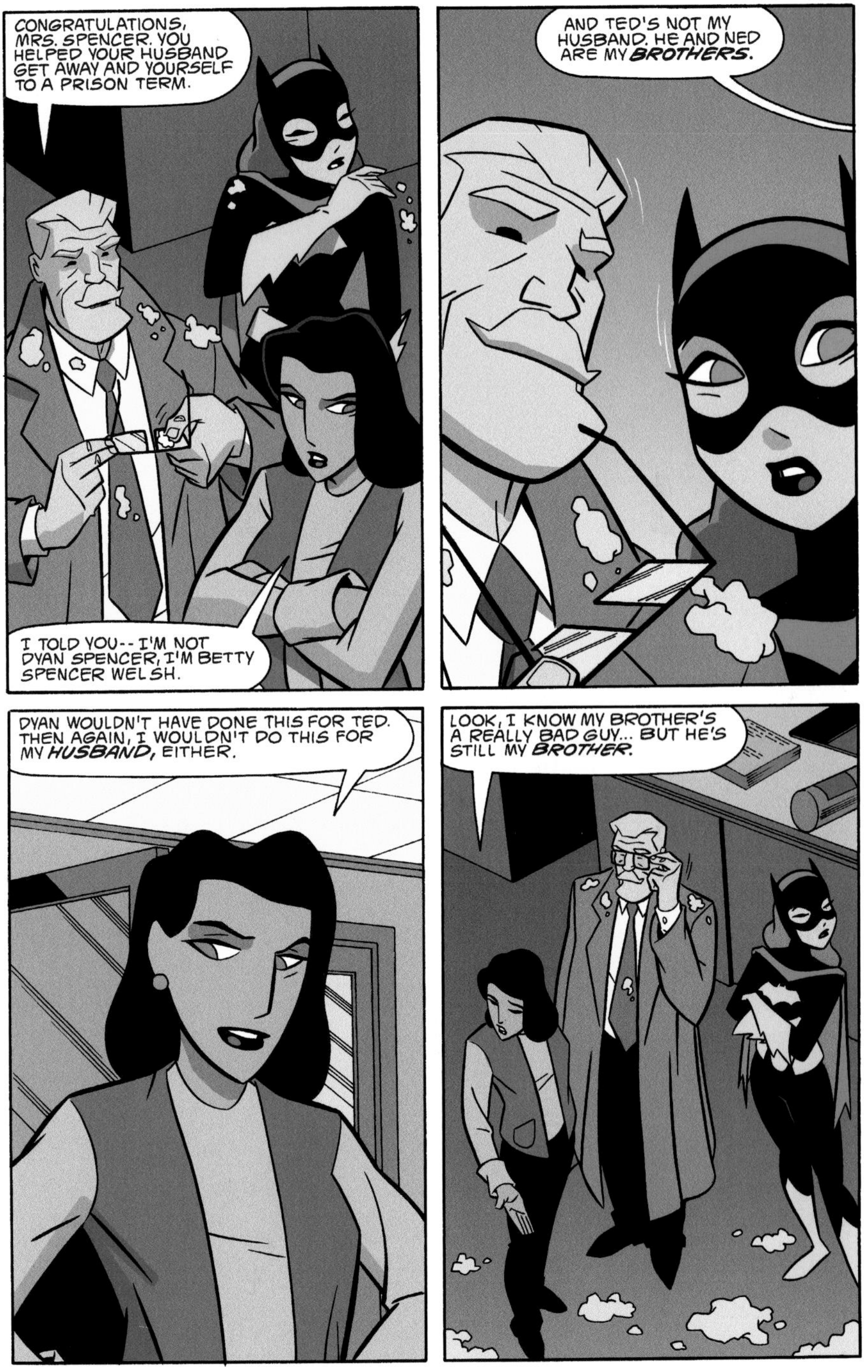
CONGRATULATIONS, MRS. SPENCER. YOU HELPED YOUR HUSBAND GET AWAY AND YOURSELF TO A PRISON TERM.
I TOLD YOU-- I'M NOT DYAN SPENCER, I'M BETTY SPENCER WELSH.
AND TED'S NOT MY HUSBAND. HE AND NED ARE MY BROTHERS.
DYAN WOULDN'T HAVE DONE THIS FOR TED. THEN AGAIN, I WOULDN'T DO THIS FOR MY HUSBAND, EITHER.
LOOK, I KNOW MY BROTHER'S A REALLY BAD GUY... BUT HE'S STILL MY BROTHER.

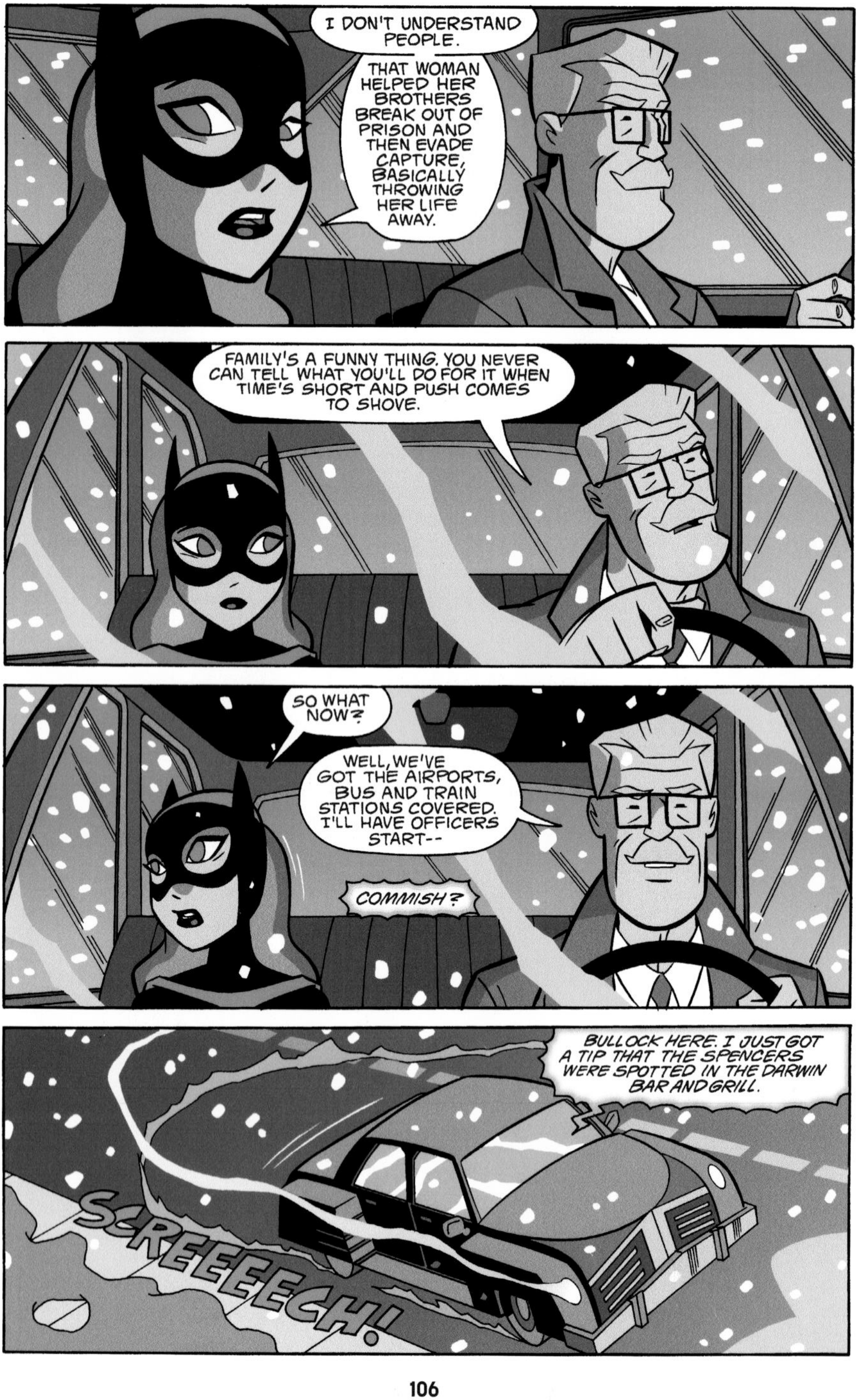
I DON'T UNDERSTAND PEOPLE.
THAT WOMAN HELPED HER BROTHERS BREAK OUT OF PRISON AND THEN EVADE CAPTURE, BASICALLY THROWING HER LIFE AWAY.
FAMILY'S A FUNNY THING. YOU NEVER CAN TELL WHAT YOU'LL DO FOR IT WHEN TIME'S SHORT AND PUSH COMES TO SHOVE.
SO WHAT NOW?
WELL, WE'VE GOT THE AIRPORTS, BUS AND TRAIN STATIONS COVERED. I'LL HAVE OFFICERS START--
COMMISH?
BULLOCK HERE. I JUST GOT A TIP THAT THE SPENCERS WERE SPOTTED IN THE DARWIN BAR AND GRILL.
SCREEEEECH!

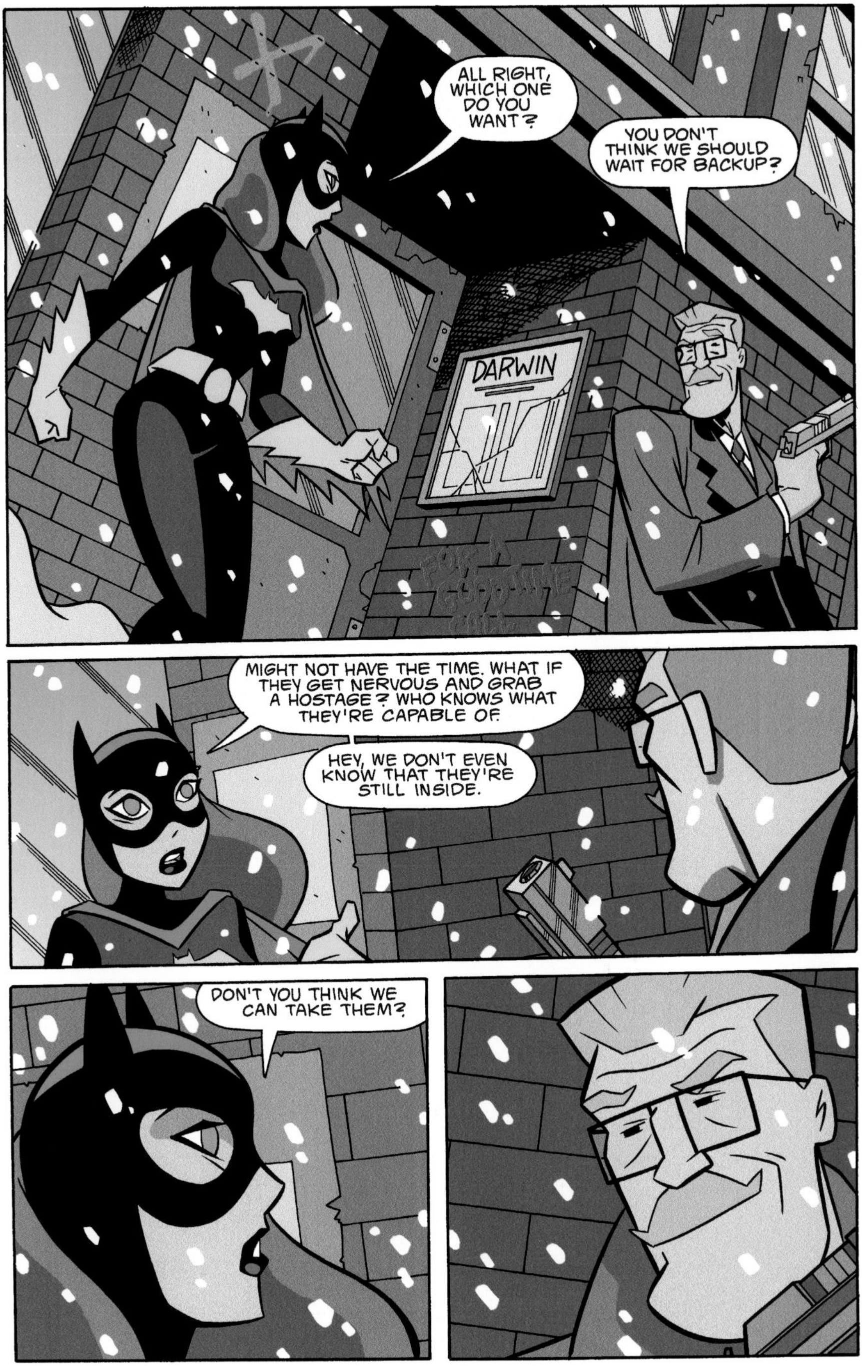

ALL RIGHT, WHICH ONE DO YOU WANT?
YOU DON'T THINK WE SHOULD WAIT FOR BACKUP?
DARWIN
MIGHT NOT HAVE THE TIME. WHAT IF THEY GET NERVOUS AND GRAB A HOSTAGE? WHO KNOWS WHAT THEY'RE CAPABLE OF.
HEY, WE DON'T EVEN KNOW THAT THEY'RE STILL INSIDE.
DON'T YOU THINK WE CAN TAKE THEM?

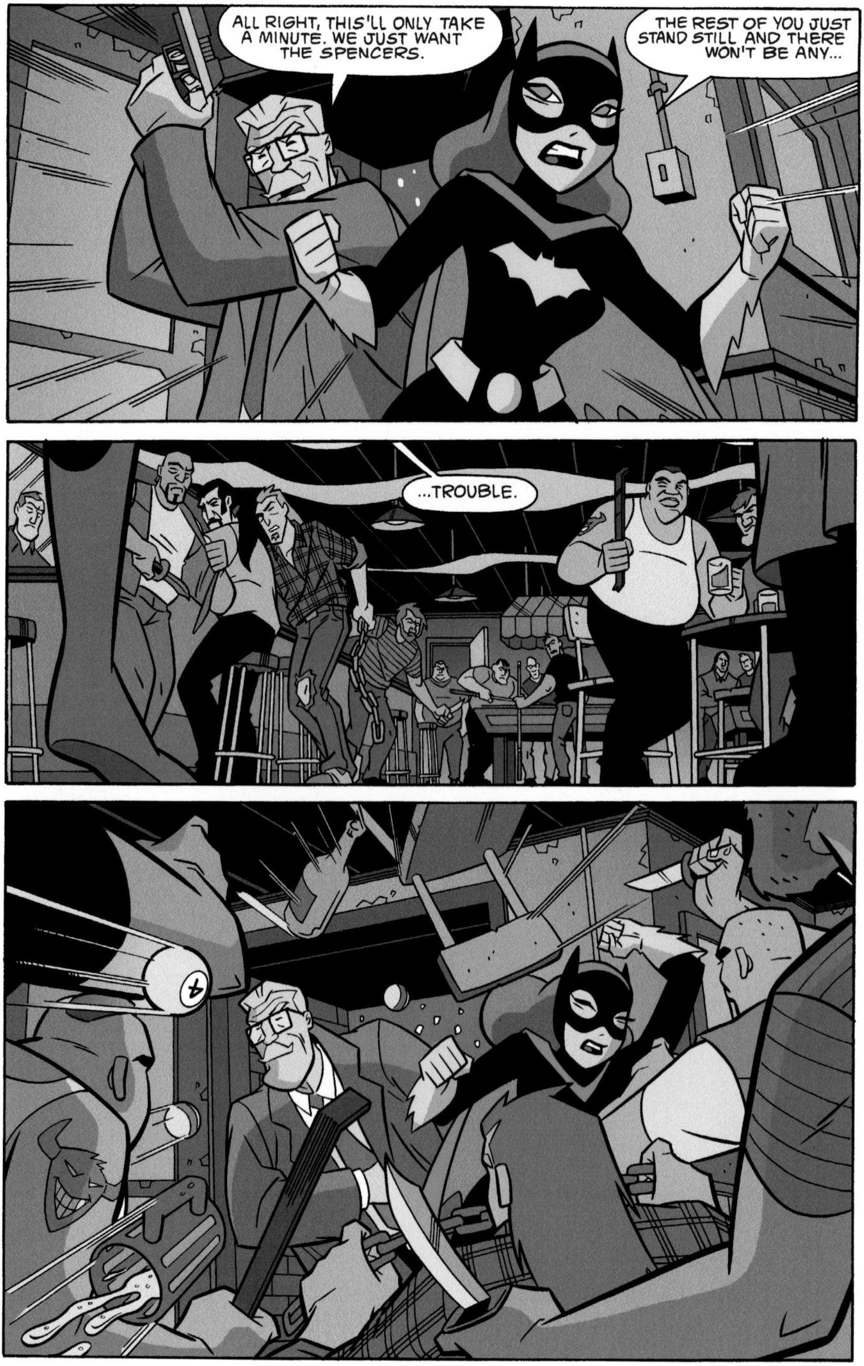
ALL RIGHT, THIS'LL ONLY TAKE A MINUTE. WE JUST WANT THE SPENCERS.
THE REST OF YOU JUST STAND STILL AND THERE WON'T BE ANY...
...TROUBLE.

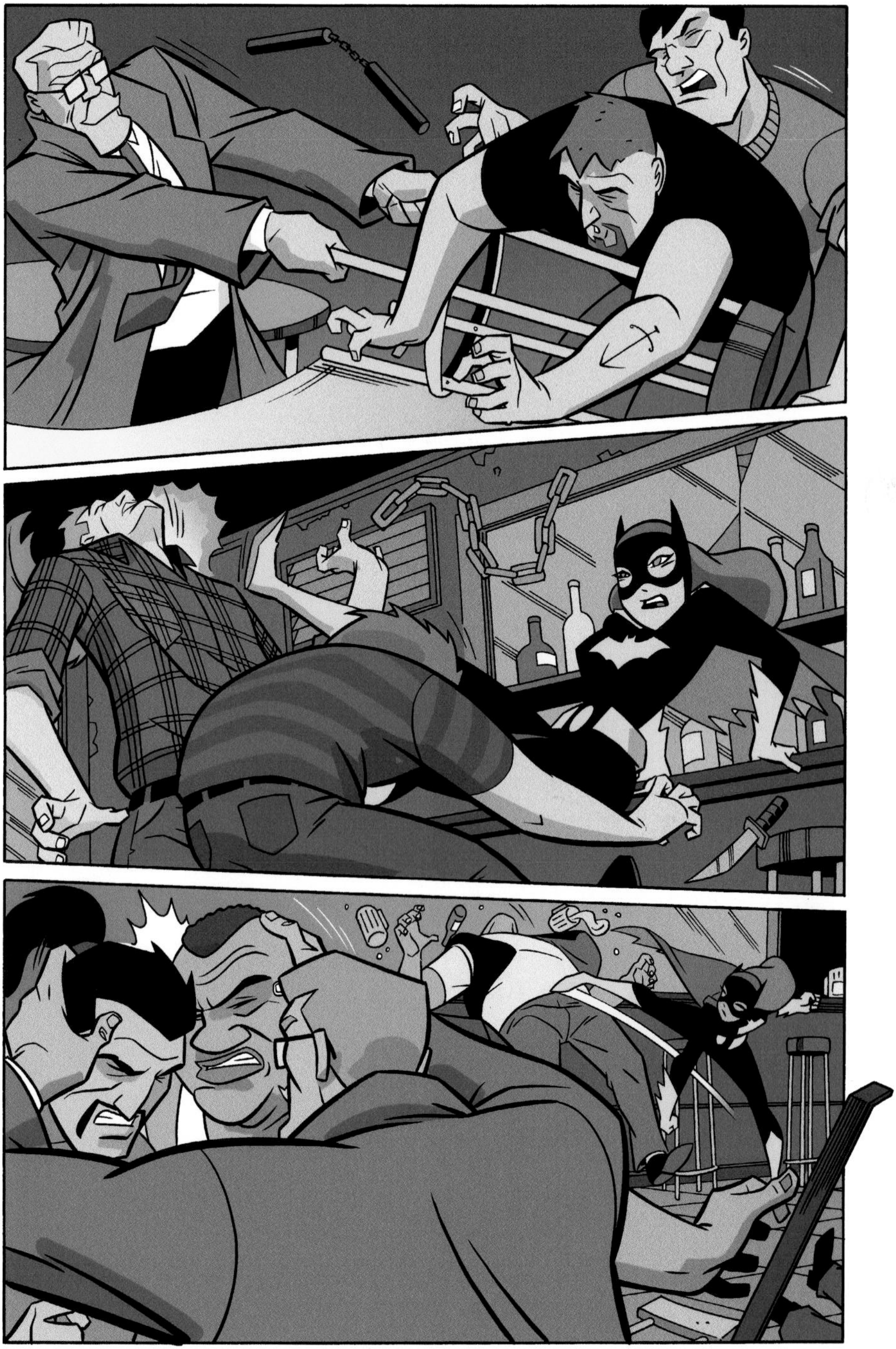

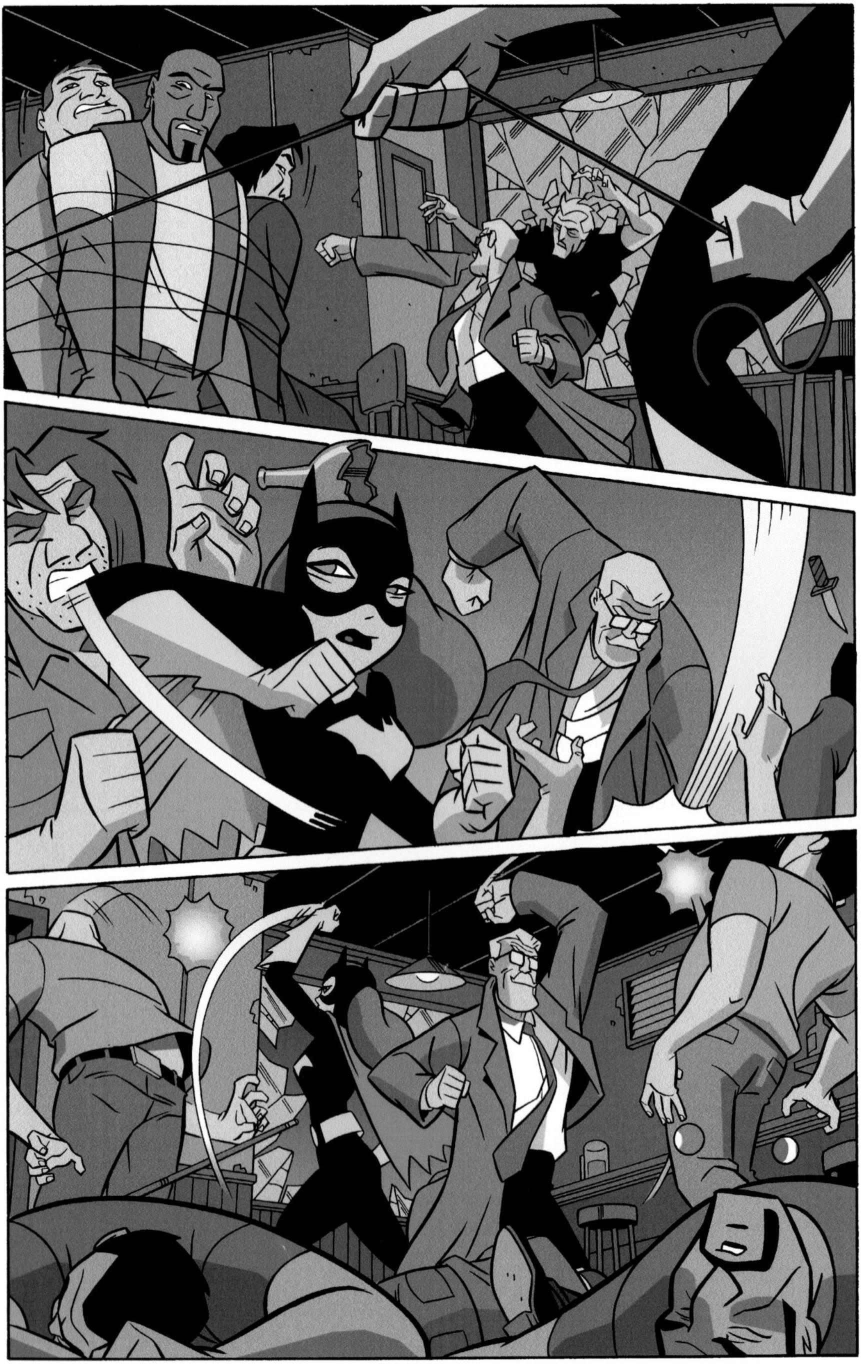

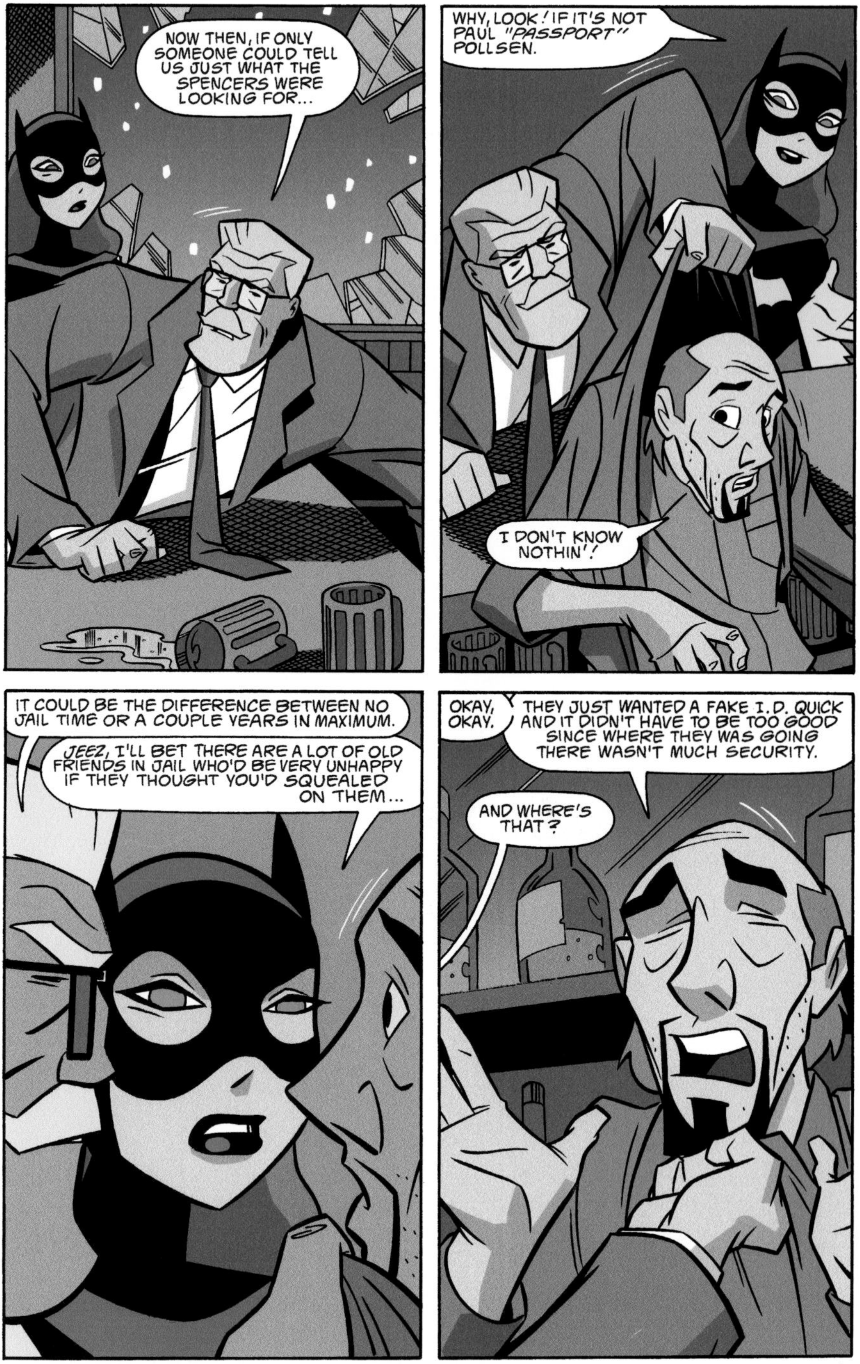
NOW THEN, IF ONLY SOMEONE COULD TELL US JUST WHAT THE SPENCERS WERE LOOKING FOR...
WHY, LOOK! IF IT'S NOT PAUL "PASSPORT" POLLSEN.
I DON'T KNOW NOTHIN'!
IT COULD BE THE DIFFERENCE BETWEEN NO JAIL TIME OR A COUPLE YEARS IN MAXIMUM.
JEEZ, I'LL BET THERE ARE A LOT OF OLD FRIENDS IN JAIL WHO'D BE VERY UNHAPPY IF THEY THOUGHT YOU'D SQUEALED ON THEM...
OKAY, OKAY.
THEY JUST WANTED A FAKE I.D. QUICK AND IT DIDN'T HAVE TO BE TOO GOOD SINCE WHERE THEY WAS GOING THERE WASN'T MUCH SECURITY.
AND WHERE'S THAT?

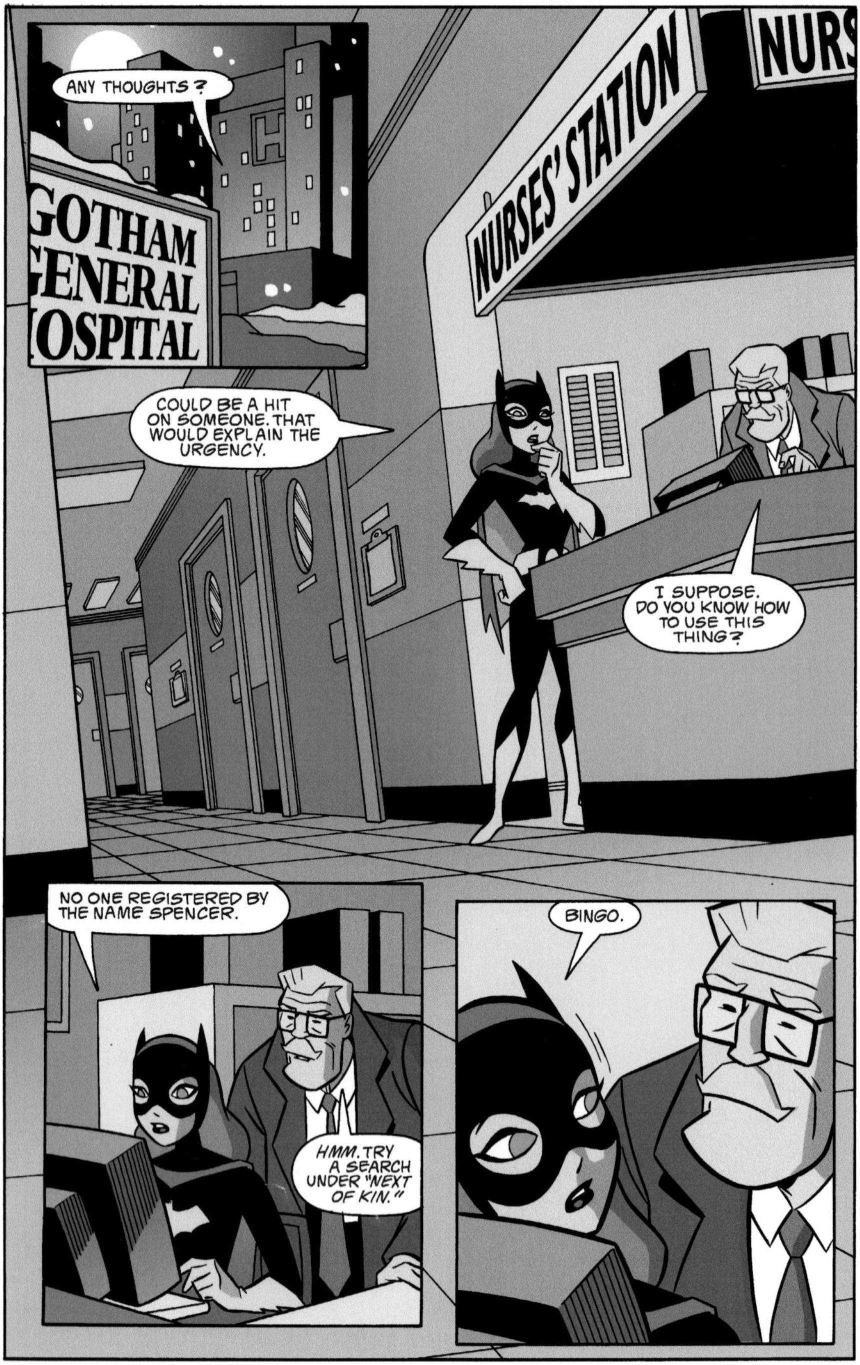
ANY THOUGHTS?
GOTHAM GENERAL HOSPITAL
NURSES' STATION
COULD BE A HIT ON SOMEONE. THAT WOULD EXPLAIN THE URGENCY.
I SUPPOSE. DO YOU KNOW HOW TO USE THIS THING?
NO ONE REGISTERED BY THE NAME SPENCER.
HMM. TRY A SEARCH UNDER "NEXT OF KIN."
BINGO.

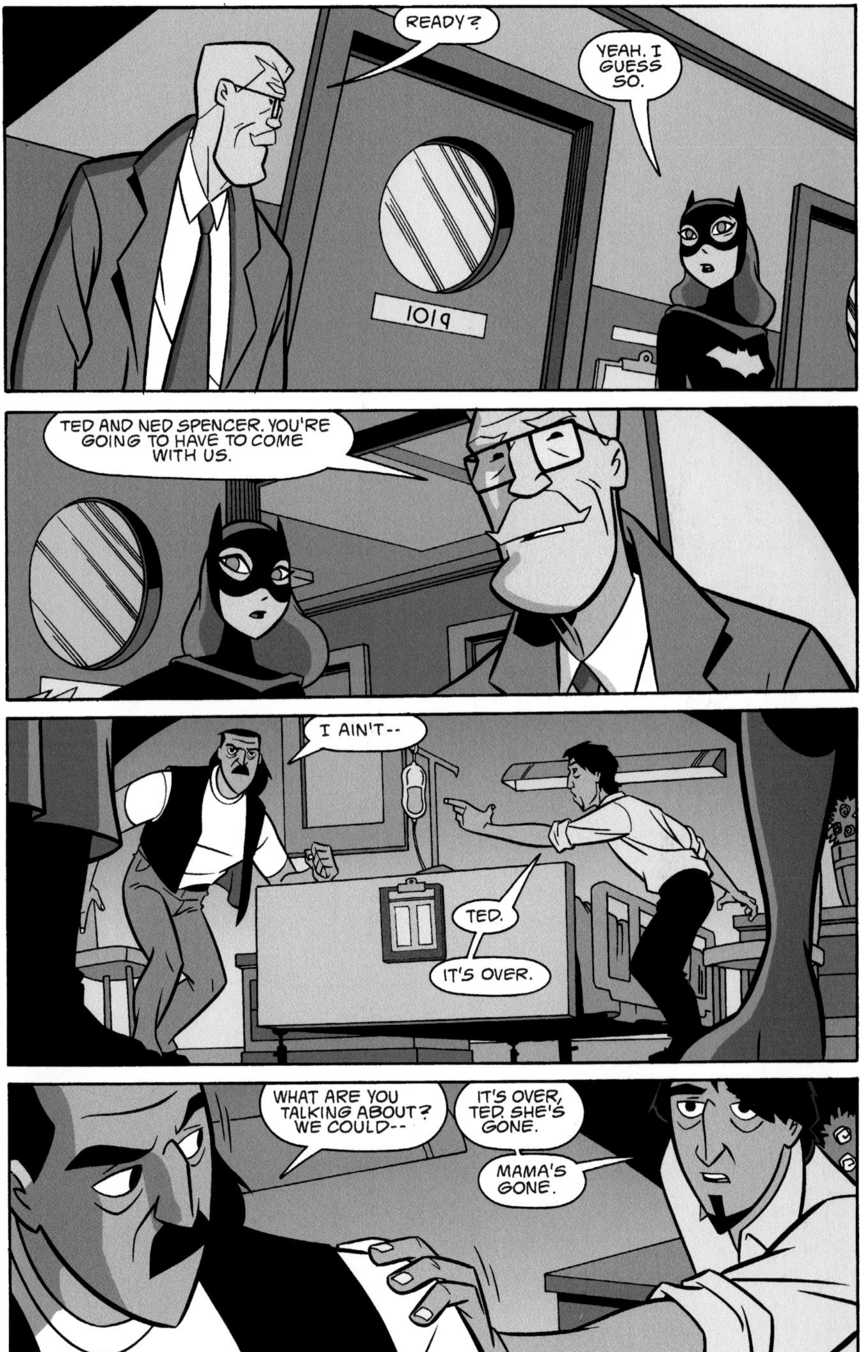
READY?
YEAH. I GUESS SO.
1019
TED AND NED SPENCER. YOU'RE GOING TO HAVE TO COME WITH US.
I AIN'T--
TED.
IT'S OVER.
WHAT ARE YOU TALKING ABOUT? WE COULD--
IT'S OVER, TED. SHE'S GONE.
MAMA'S GONE.

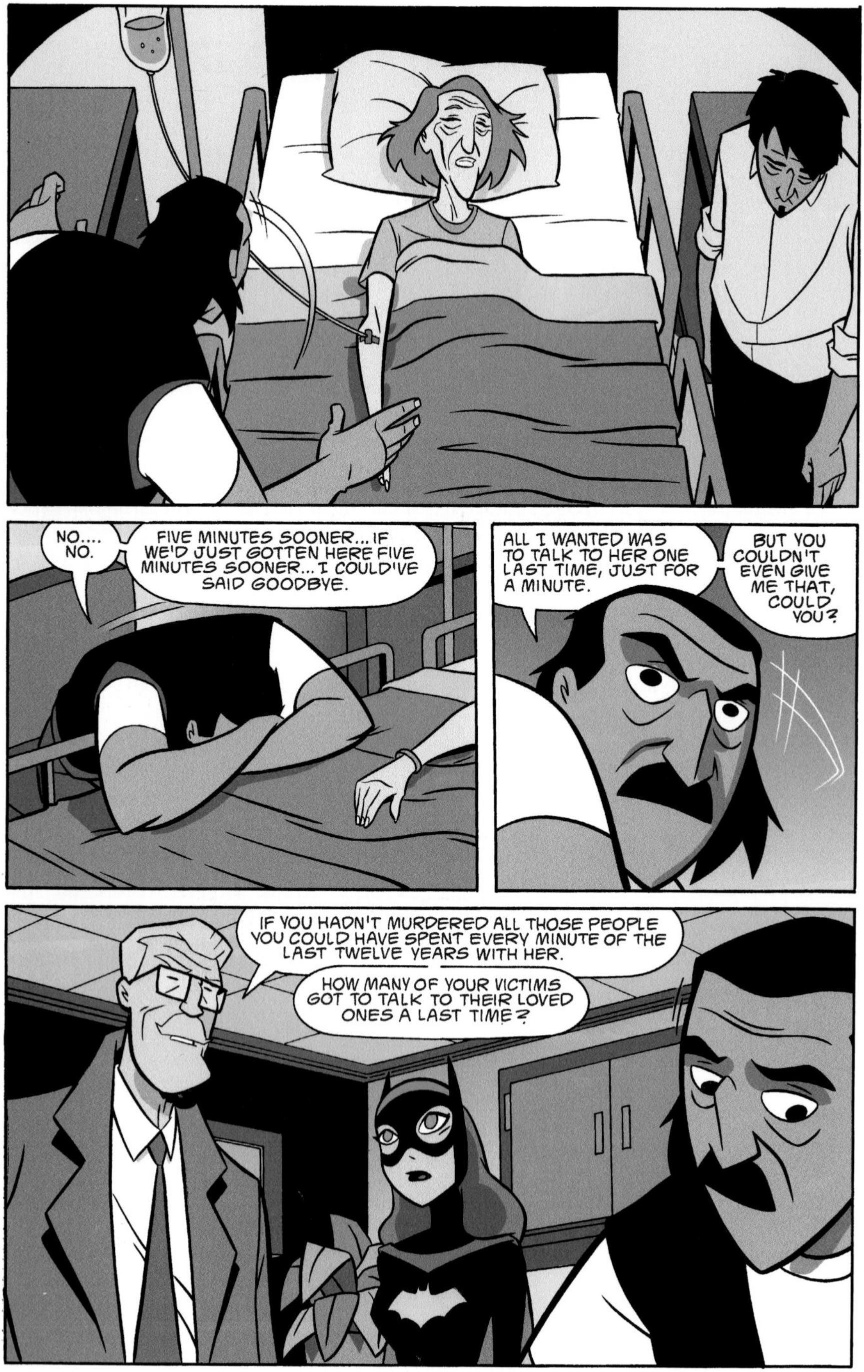
NO.... NO.
FIVE MINUTES SOONER... IF WE'D JUST GOTTEN HERE FIVE MINUTES SOONER... I COULD'VE SAID GOODBYE.
ALL I WANTED WAS TO TALK TO HER ONE LAST TIME, JUST FOR A MINUTE.
BUT YOU COULDN'T EVEN GIVE ME THAT, COULD YOU?
IF YOU HADN'T MURDERED ALL THOSE PEOPLE YOU COULD HAVE SPENT EVERY MINUTE OF THE LAST TWELVE YEARS WITH HER.
HOW MANY OF YOUR VICTIMS GOT TO TALK TO THEIR LOVED ONES A LAST TIME?

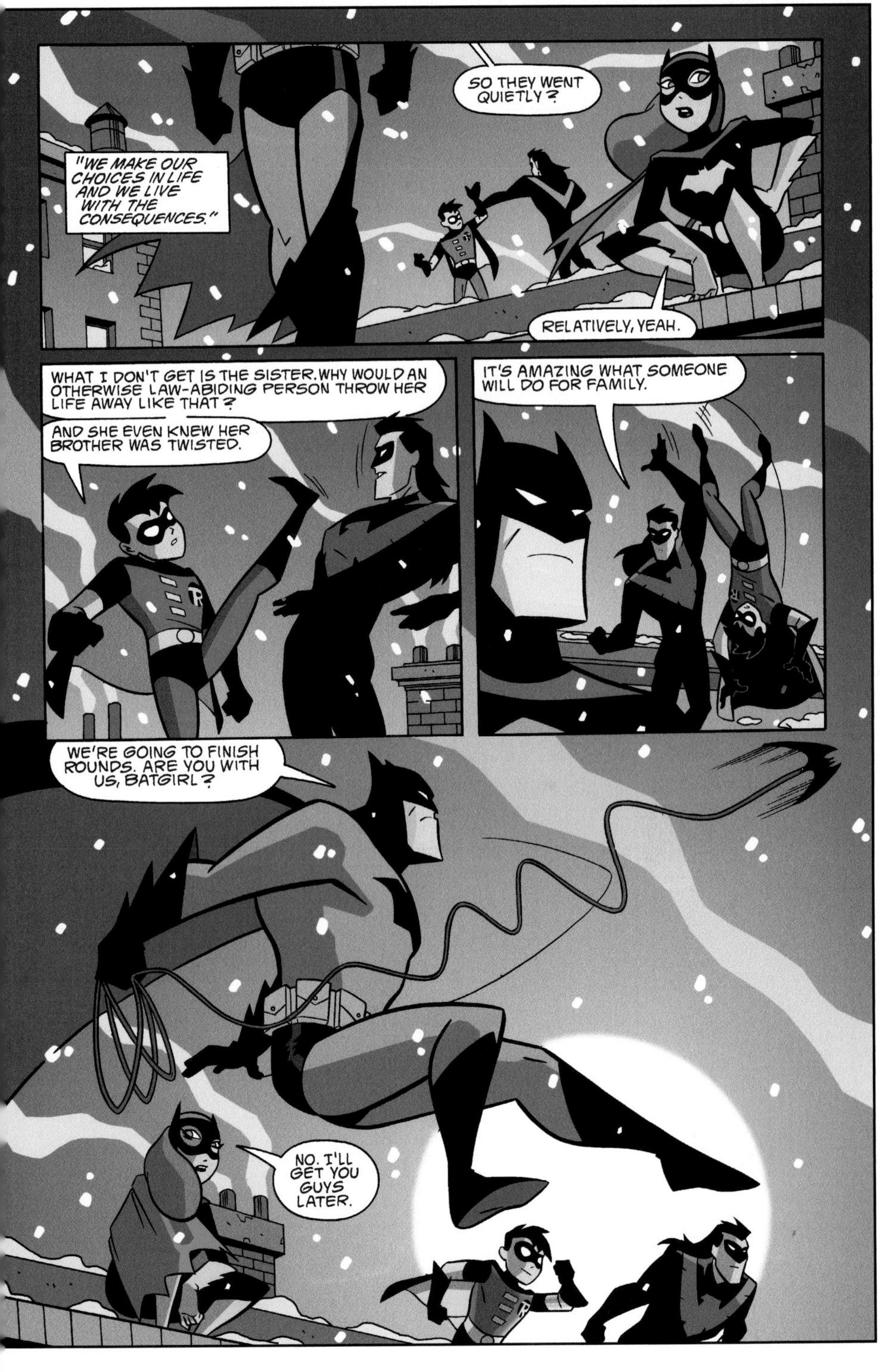
"WE MAKE OUR CHOICES IN LIFE AND WE LIVE WITH THE CONSEQUENCES."
SO THEY WENT QUIETLY?
RELATIVELY, YEAH.
WHAT I DON'T GET IS THE SISTER. WHY WOULD AN OTHERWISE LAW-ABIDING PERSON THROW HER LIFE AWAY LIKE THAT?
AND SHE EVEN KNEW HER BROTHER WAS TWISTED.
IT'S AMAZING WHAT SOMEONE WILL DO FOR FAMILY.
WE'RE GOING TO FINISH ROUNDS. ARE YOU WITH US, BATGIRL?
NO. I'LL GET YOU GUYS LATER.

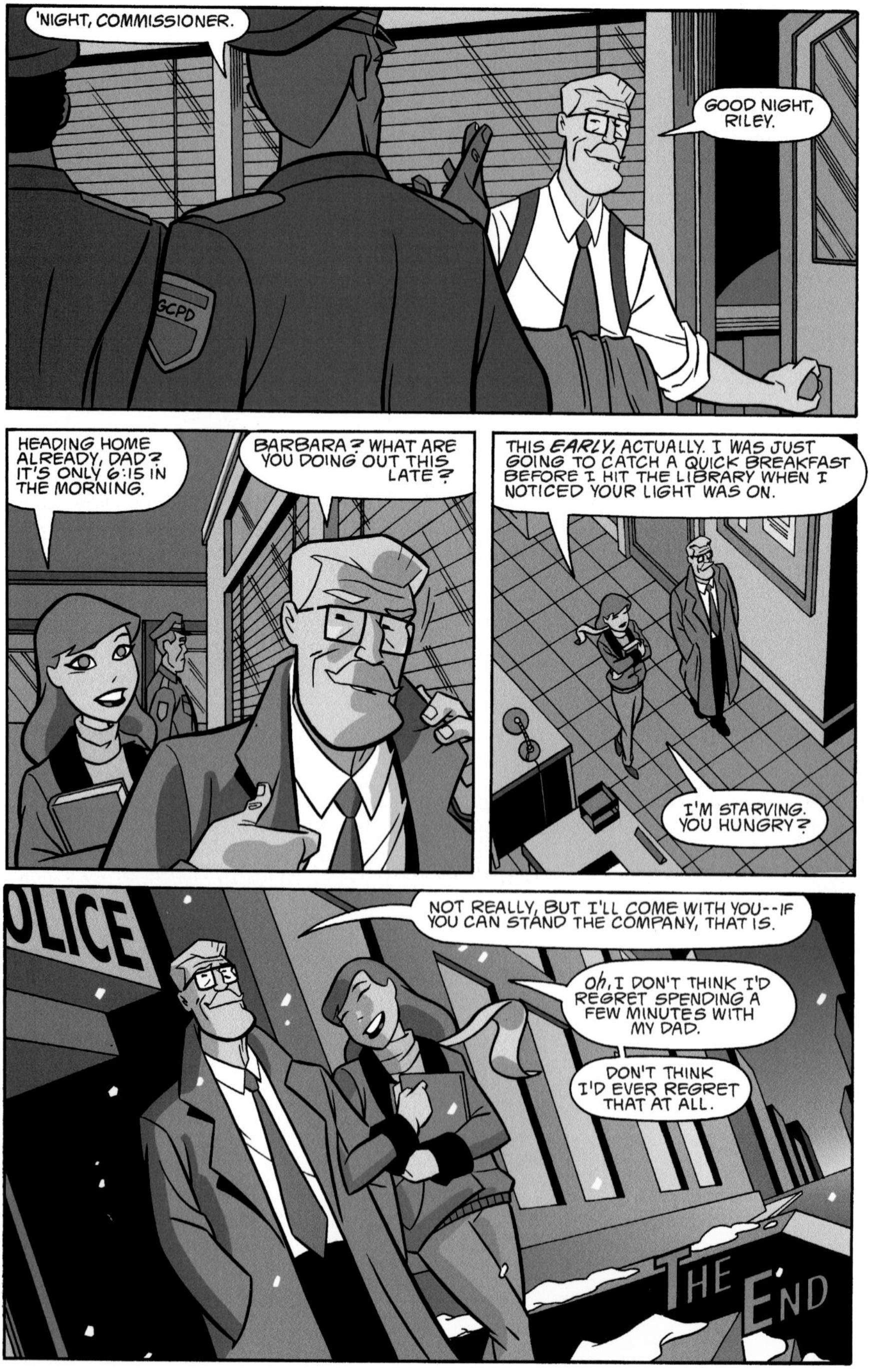
'NIGHT, COMMISSIONER.
GOOD NIGHT, RILEY.
GCPD
HEADING HOME ALREADY, DAD? IT'S ONLY 6:15 IN THE MORNING.
BARBARA? WHAT ARE YOU DOING OUT THIS LATE?
THIS *EARLY*, ACTUALLY. I WAS JUST GOING TO CATCH A QUICK BREAKFAST BEFORE I HIT THE LIBRARY WHEN I NOTICED YOUR LIGHT WAS ON.
I'M STARVING. YOU HUNGRY?
OLICE
NOT REALLY, BUT I'LL COME WITH YOU--IF YOU CAN STAND THE COMPANY, THAT IS.
OH, I DON'T THINK I'D REGRET SPENDING A FEW MINUTES WITH MY DAD.
DON'T THINK I'D EVER REGRET THAT AT ALL.
THE END

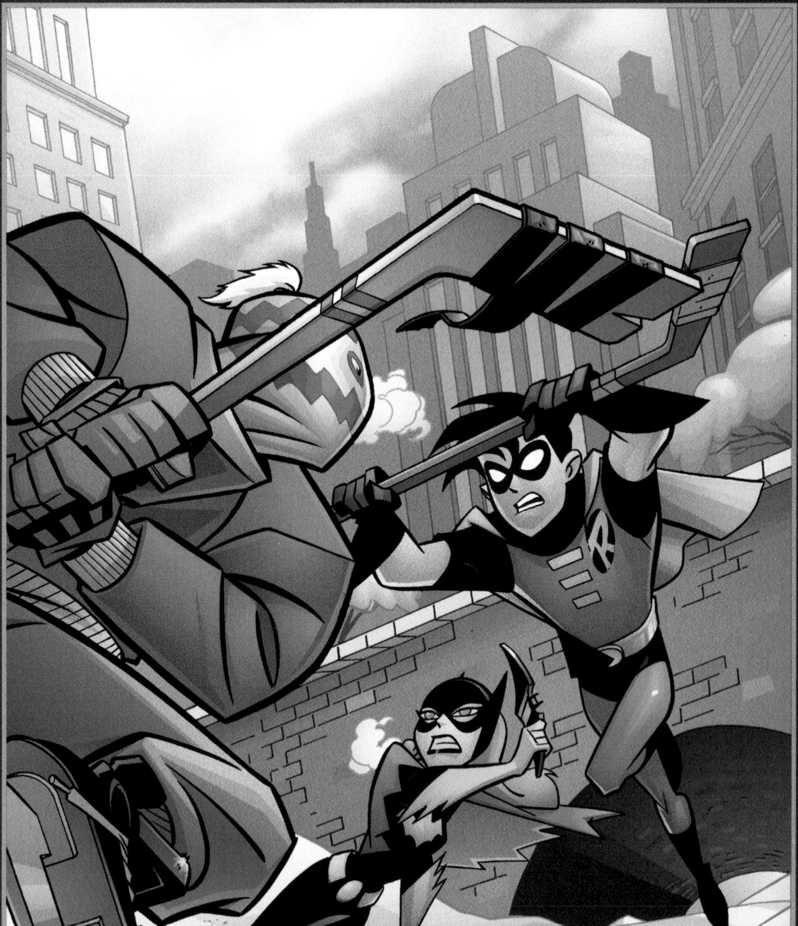
B. Smith/T. Beatty

CHAPTER 5: STICKING

BATGIRL

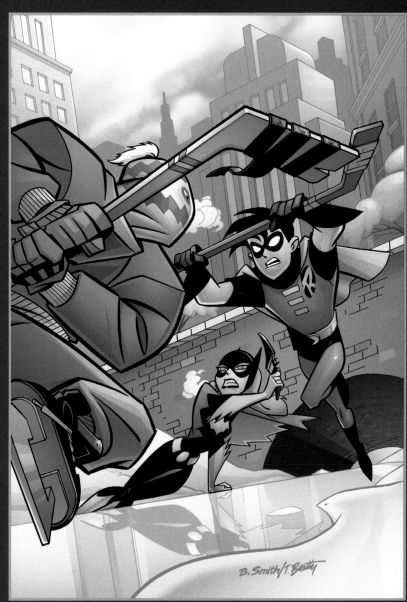

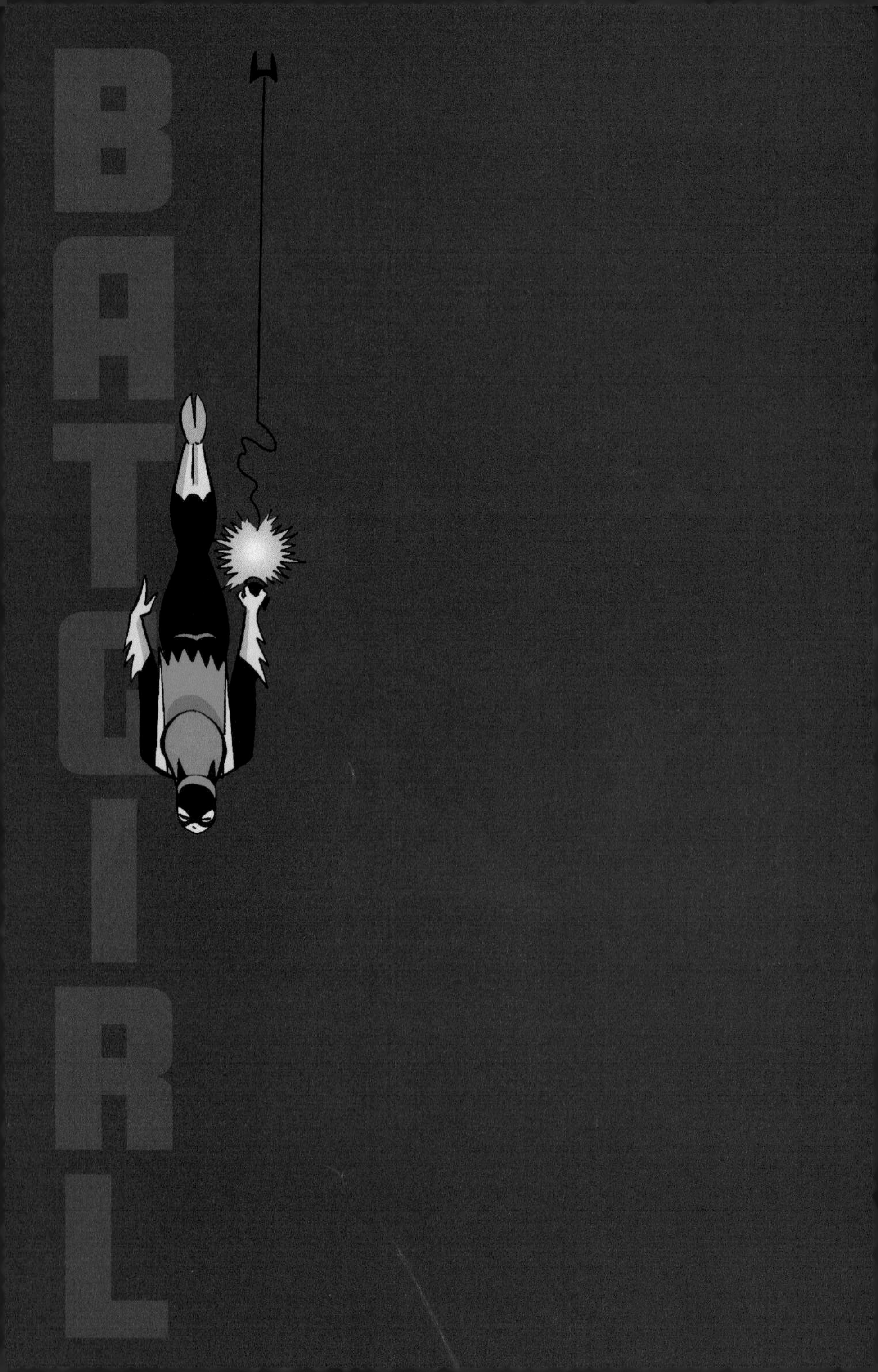
BATGIRL

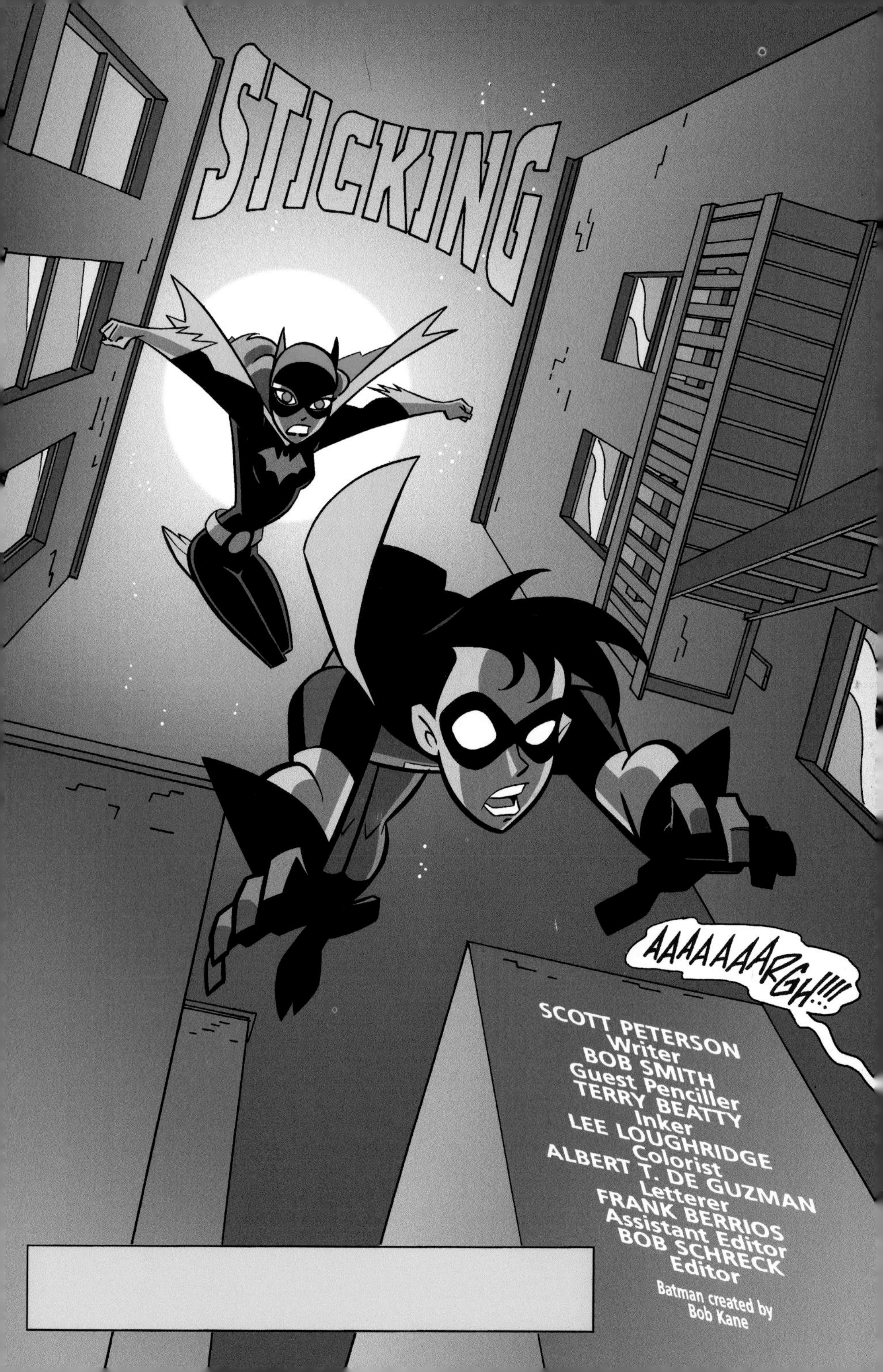
STICKING
AAAAAAARGH!!!!
SCOTT PETERSON
Writer
BOB SMITH
Guest Penciller
TERRY BEATTY
Inker
LEE LOUGHRIDGE
Colorist
ALBERT T. DE GUZMAN
Letterer
FRANK BERRIOS
Assistant Editor
BOB SCHRECK
Editor
Batman created by
Bob Kane

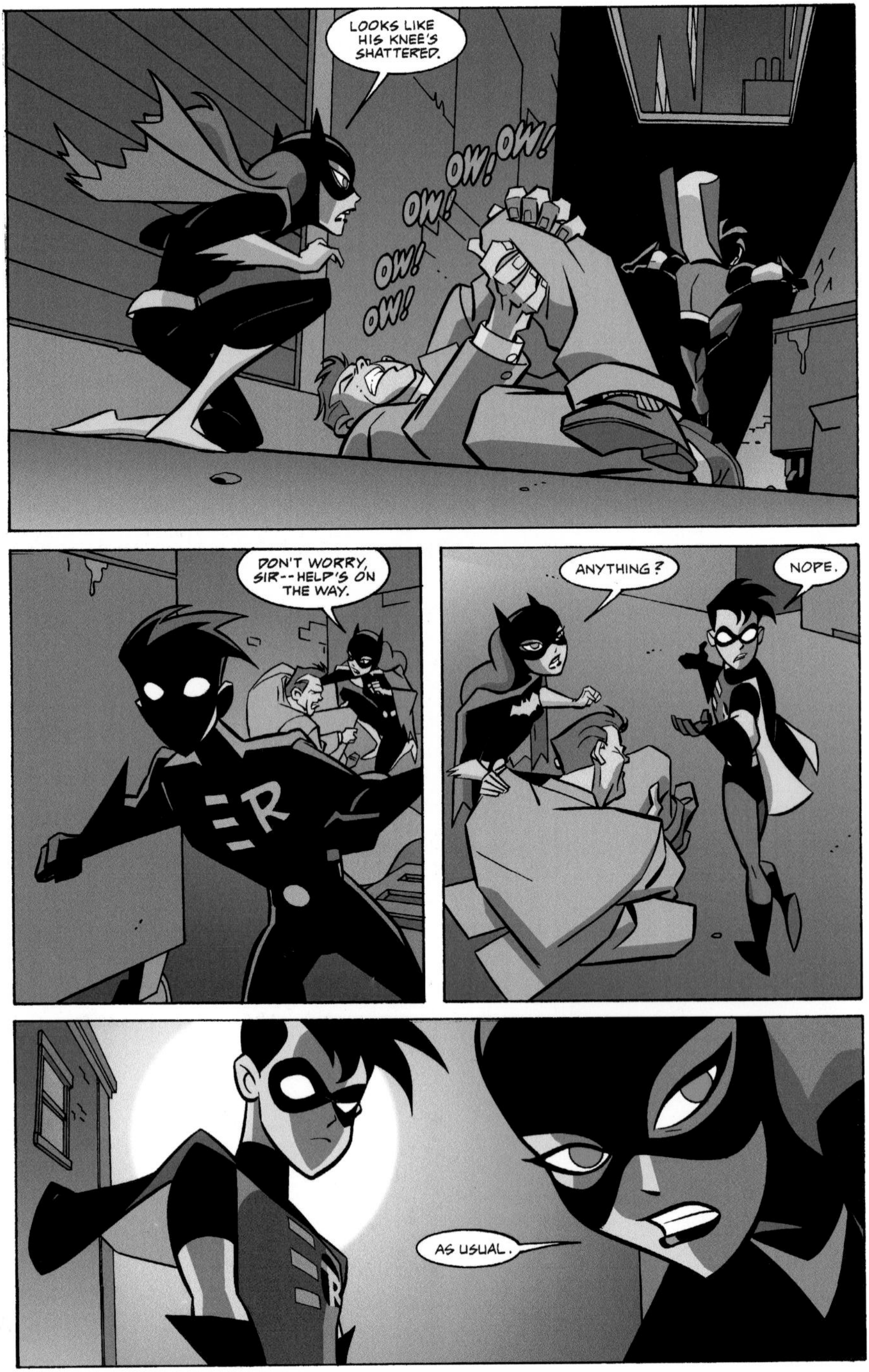
LOOKS LIKE HIS KNEE'S SHATTERED.
OW! OW! OW! OW! OW!
DON'T WORRY, SIR--HELP'S ON THE WAY.
ANYTHING?
NOPE.
AS USUAL.

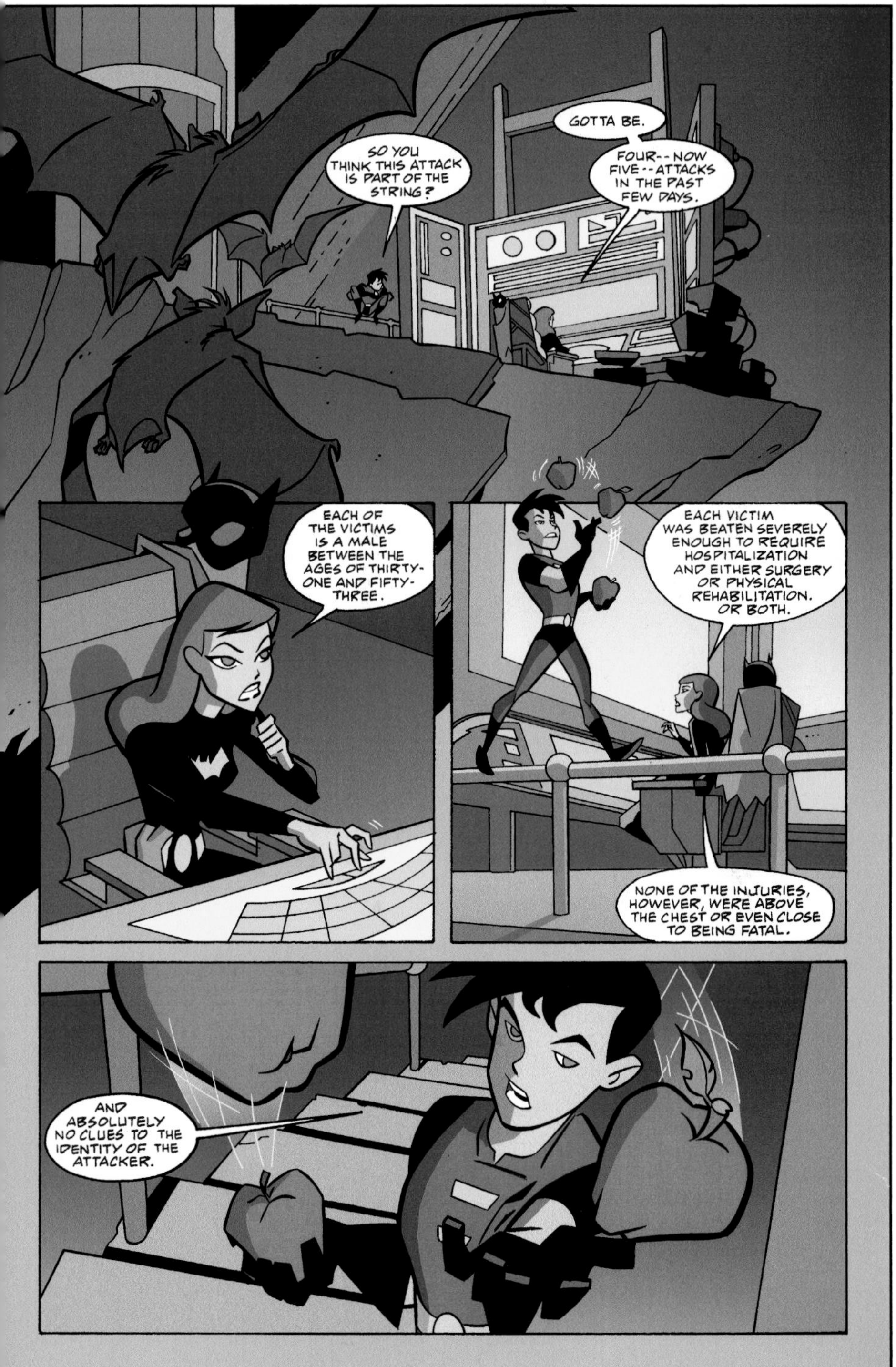
SO YOU THINK THIS ATTACK IS PART OF THE STRING?
GOTTA BE.
FOUR--NOW FIVE--ATTACKS IN THE PAST FEW DAYS.
EACH OF THE VICTIMS IS A MALE BETWEEN THE AGES OF THIRTY-ONE AND FIFTY-THREE.
EACH VICTIM WAS BEATEN SEVERELY ENOUGH TO REQUIRE HOSPITALIZATION AND EITHER SURGERY OR PHYSICAL REHABILITATION. OR BOTH.
NONE OF THE INJURIES, HOWEVER, WERE ABOVE THE CHEST OR EVEN CLOSE TO BEING FATAL.
AND ABSOLUTELY NO CLUES TO THE IDENTITY OF THE ATTACKER.

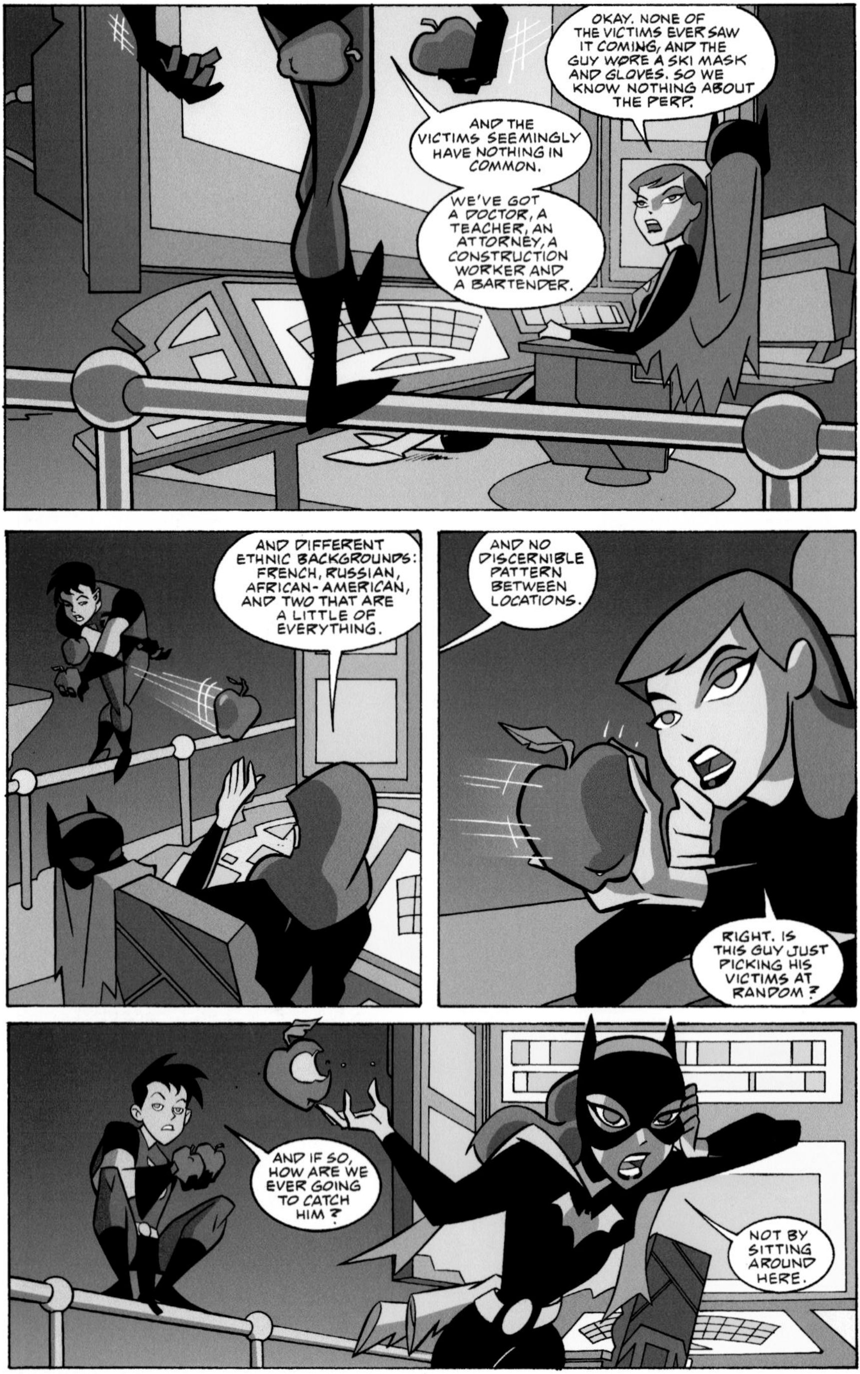
OKAY. NONE OF THE VICTIMS EVER SAW IT COMING, AND THE GUY WORE A SKI MASK AND GLOVES. SO WE KNOW NOTHING ABOUT THE PERP.
AND THE VICTIMS SEEMINGLY HAVE NOTHING IN COMMON.
WE'VE GOT A DOCTOR, A TEACHER, AN ATTORNEY, A CONSTRUCTION WORKER AND A BARTENDER.
AND DIFFERENT ETHNIC BACKGROUNDS: FRENCH, RUSSIAN, AFRICAN-AMERICAN, AND TWO THAT ARE A LITTLE OF EVERYTHING.
AND NO DISCERNIBLE PATTERN BETWEEN LOCATIONS.
RIGHT. IS THIS GUY JUST PICKING HIS VICTIMS AT RANDOM?
AND IF SO, HOW ARE WE EVER GOING TO CATCH HIM?
NOT BY SITTING AROUND HERE.

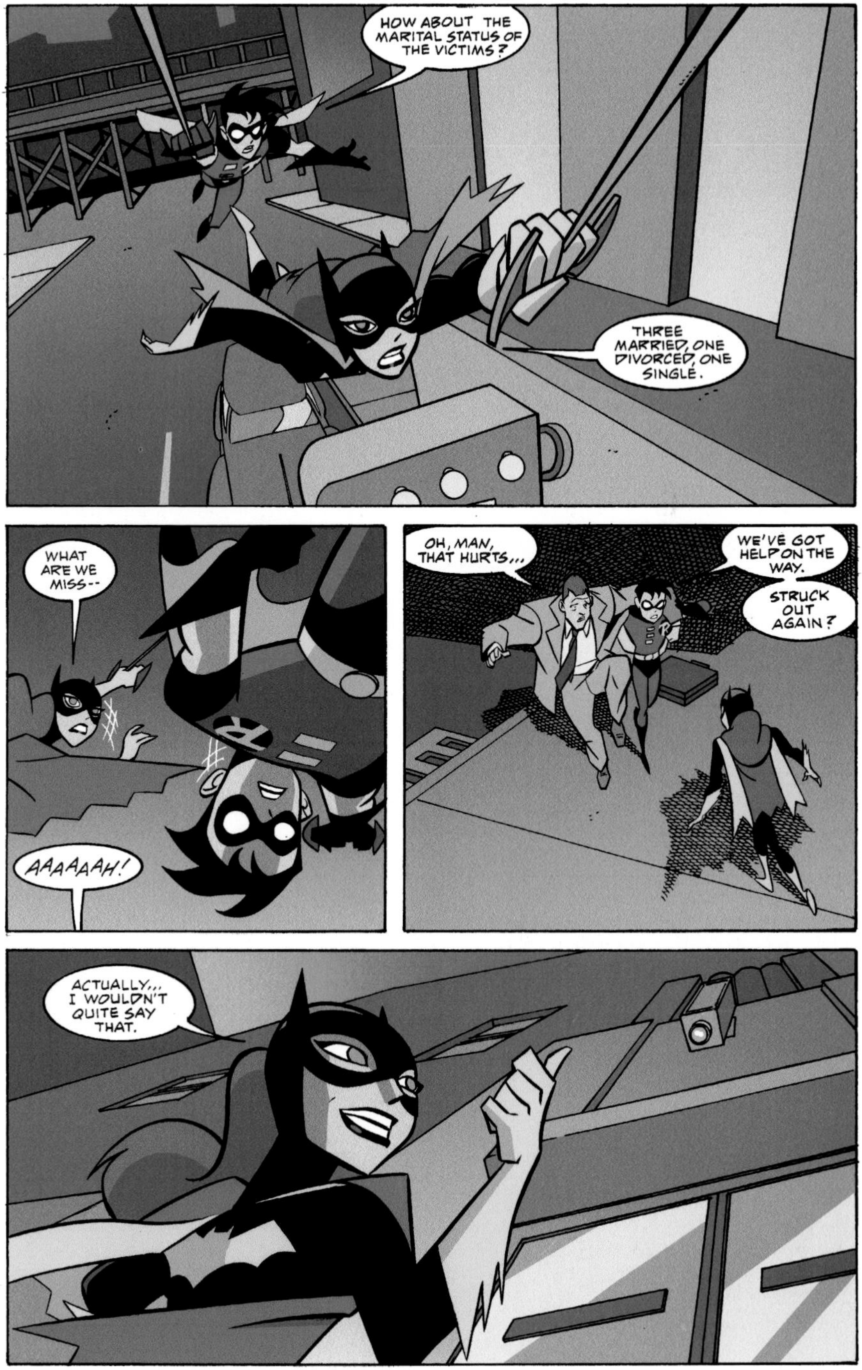
HOW ABOUT THE MARITAL STATUS OF THE VICTIMS?
THREE MARRIED, ONE DIVORCED, ONE SINGLE.
WHAT ARE WE MISS--
AAAAAAH!
OH, MAN, THAT HURTS...
WE'VE GOT HELP ON THE WAY.
STRUCK OUT AGAIN?
ACTUALLY... I WOULDN'T QUITE SAY THAT.

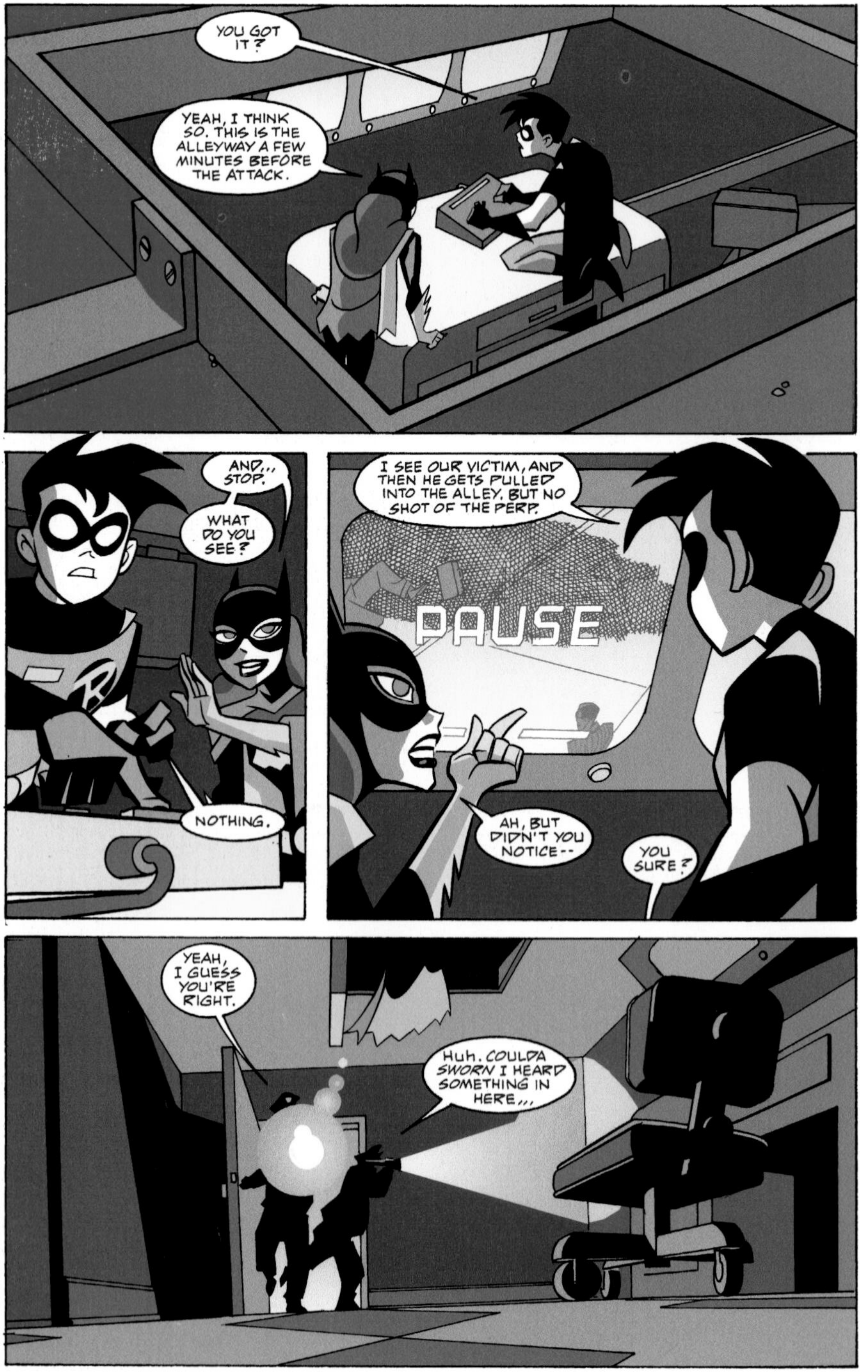
YOU GOT IT?
YEAH, I THINK SO. THIS IS THE ALLEYWAY A FEW MINUTES BEFORE THE ATTACK.
AND... STOP.
WHAT DO YOU SEE?
NOTHING.
I SEE OUR VICTIM, AND THEN HE GETS PULLED INTO THE ALLEY. BUT NO SHOT OF THE PERP.
PAUSE
AH, BUT DIDN'T YOU NOTICE--
YOU SURE?
YEAH, I GUESS YOU'RE RIGHT.
Huh. COULDA SWORN I HEARD SOMETHING IN HERE...

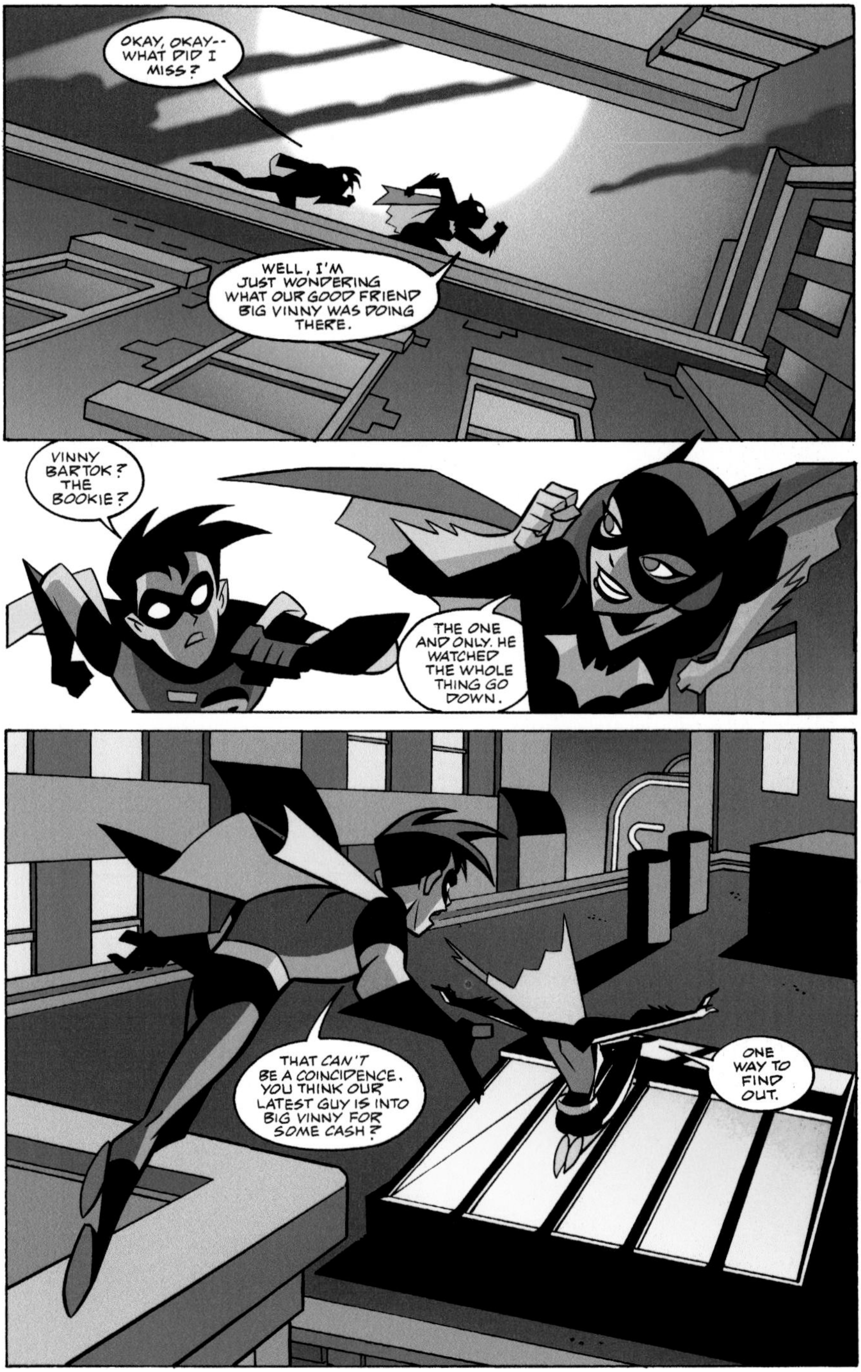
OKAY, OKAY-- WHAT DID I MISS?
WELL, I'M JUST WONDERING WHAT OUR GOOD FRIEND BIG VINNY WAS DOING THERE.
VINNY BARTOK? THE BOOKIE?
THE ONE AND ONLY. HE WATCHED THE WHOLE THING GO DOWN.
THAT CAN'T BE A COINCIDENCE. YOU THINK OUR LATEST GUY IS INTO BIG VINNY FOR SOME CASH?
ONE WAY TO FIND OUT.

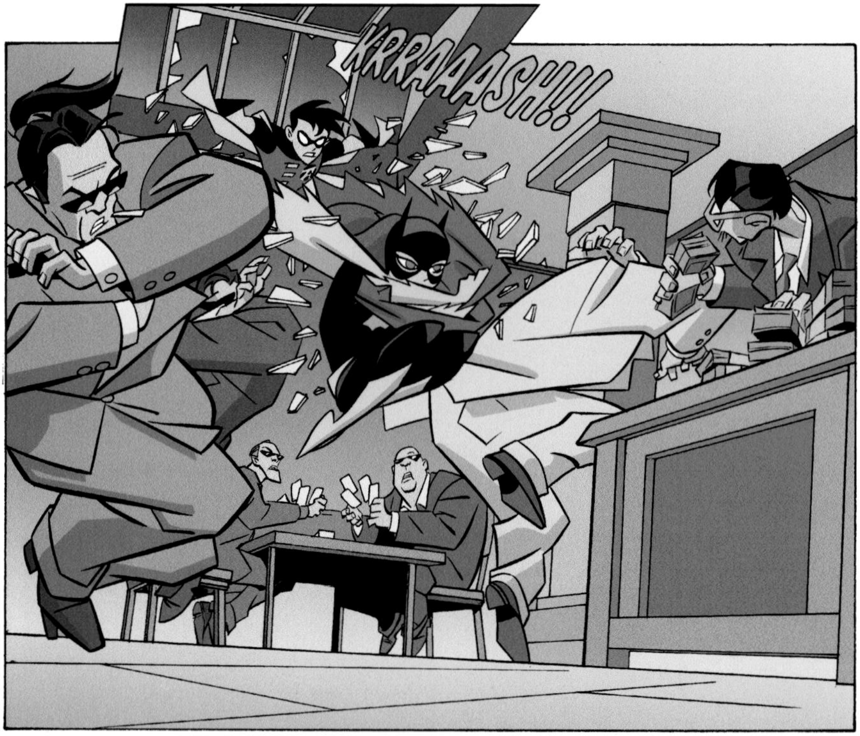
KRRAAASH!!!

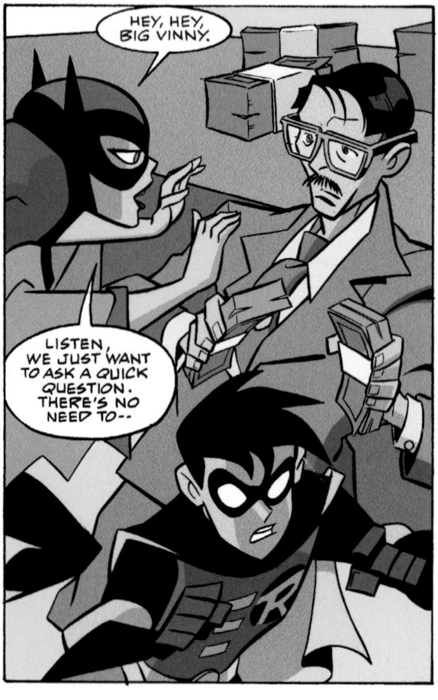
HEY, HEY, BIG VINNY.
LISTEN, WE JUST WANT TO ASK A QUICK QUESTION. THERE'S NO NEED TO--

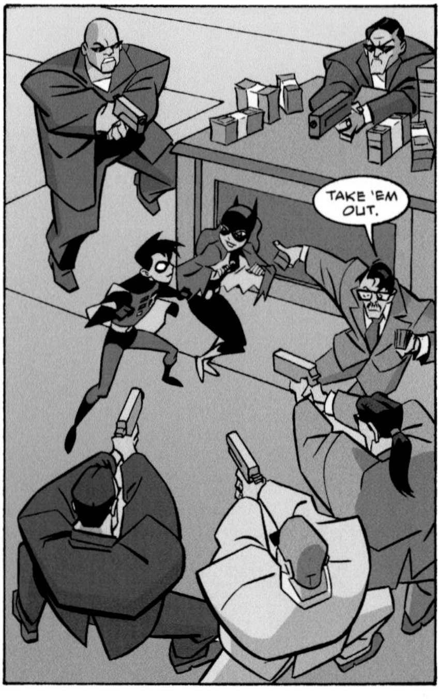
TAKE 'EM OUT.

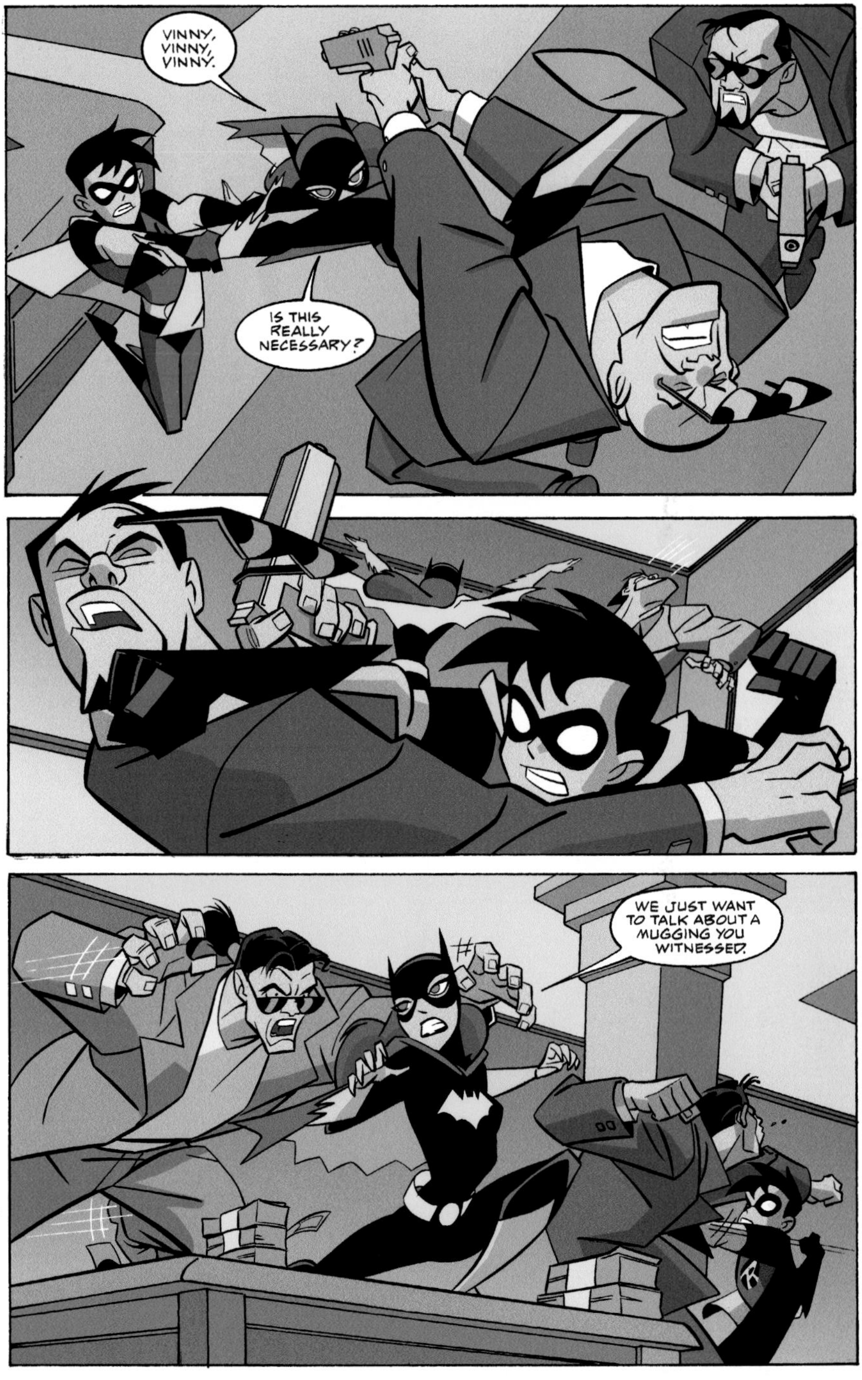
VINNY, VINNY, VINNY.
IS THIS REALLY NECESSARY?
WE JUST WANT TO TALK ABOUT A MUGGING YOU WITNESSED.

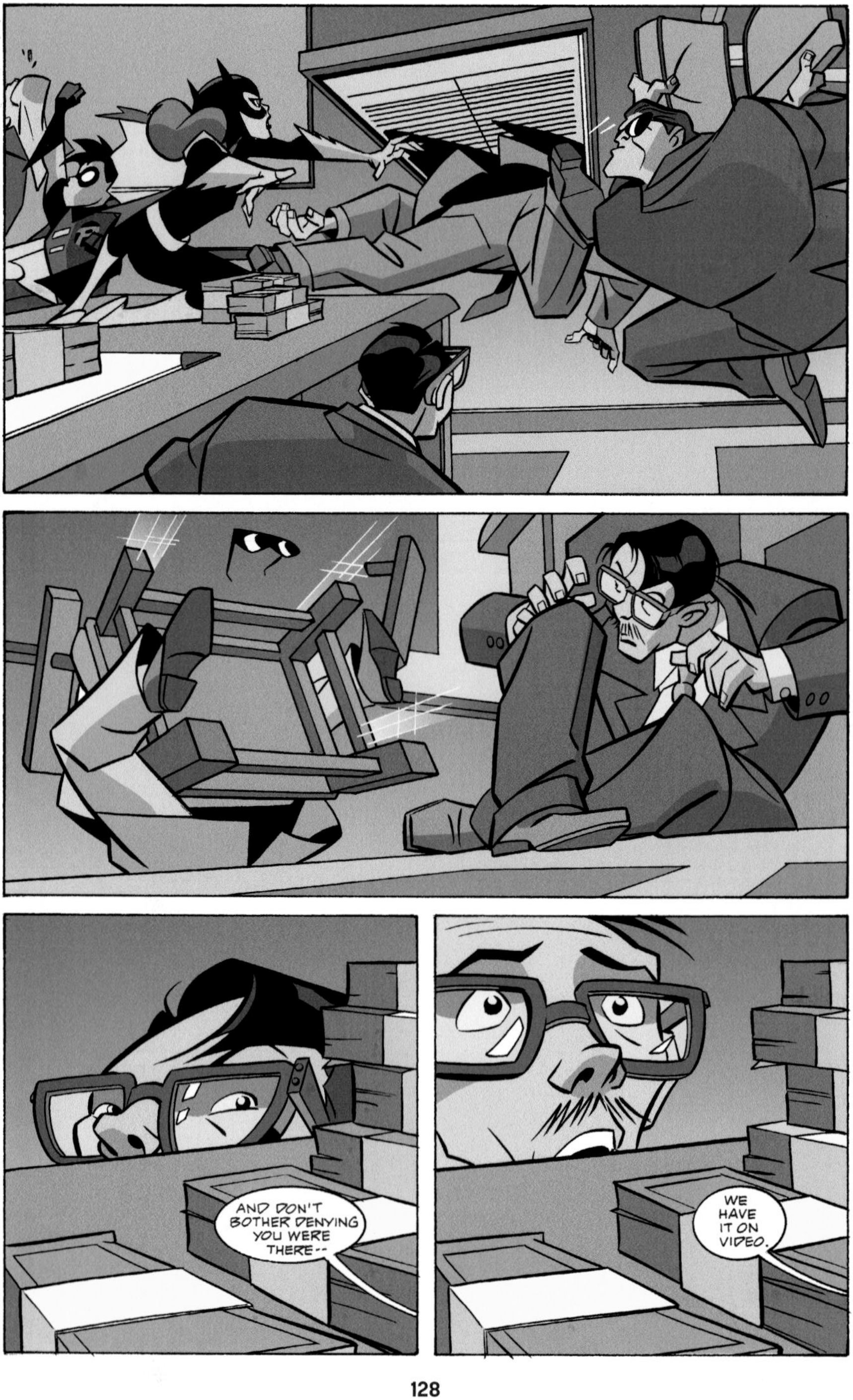
AND DON'T BOTHER DENYING YOU WERE THERE--
WE HAVE IT ON VIDEO.

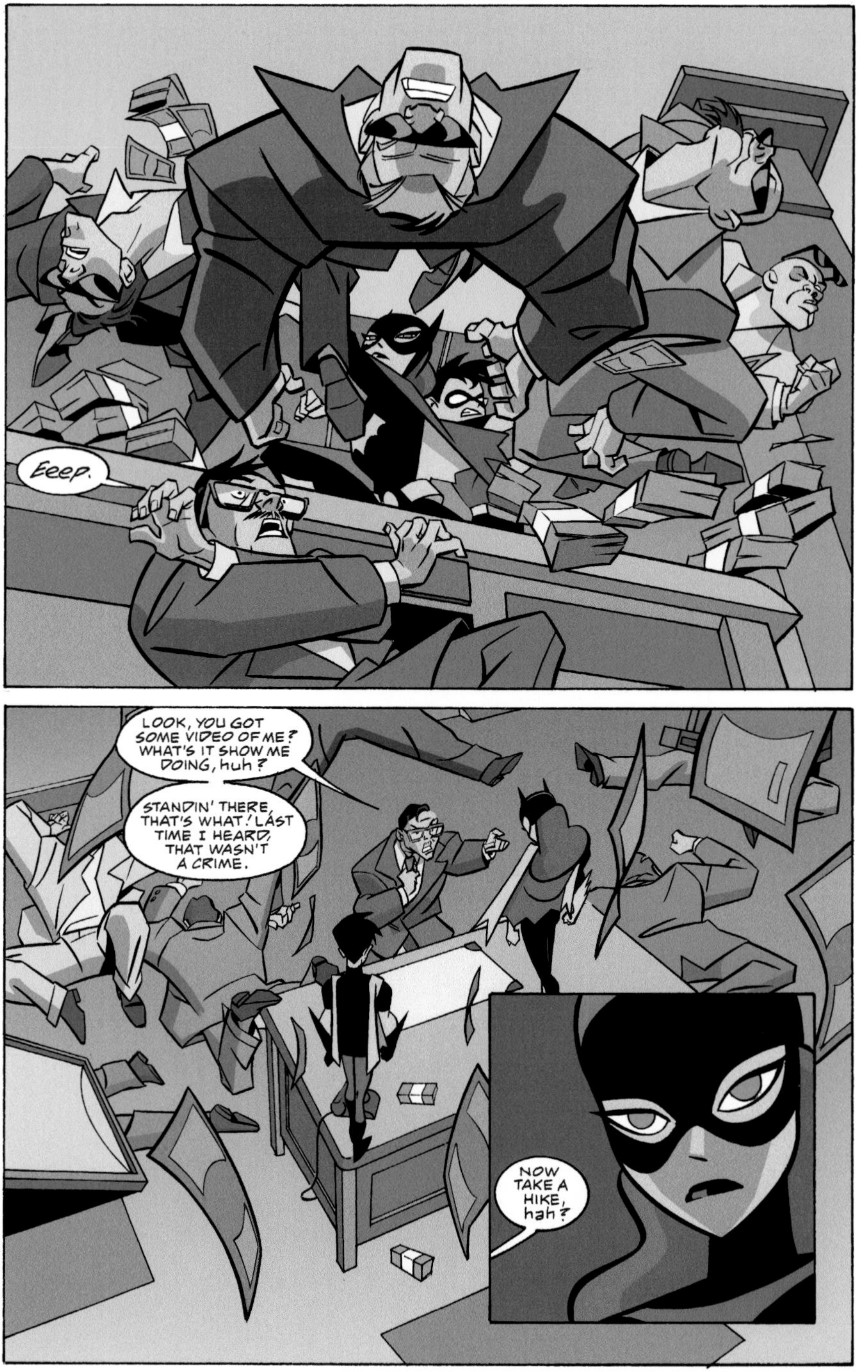
Eeep.
LOOK, YOU GOT SOME VIDEO OF ME? WHAT'S IT SHOW ME DOING, huh?
STANDIN' THERE, THAT'S WHAT! LAST TIME I HEARD, THAT WASN'T A CRIME.
NOW TAKE A HIKE, hah?

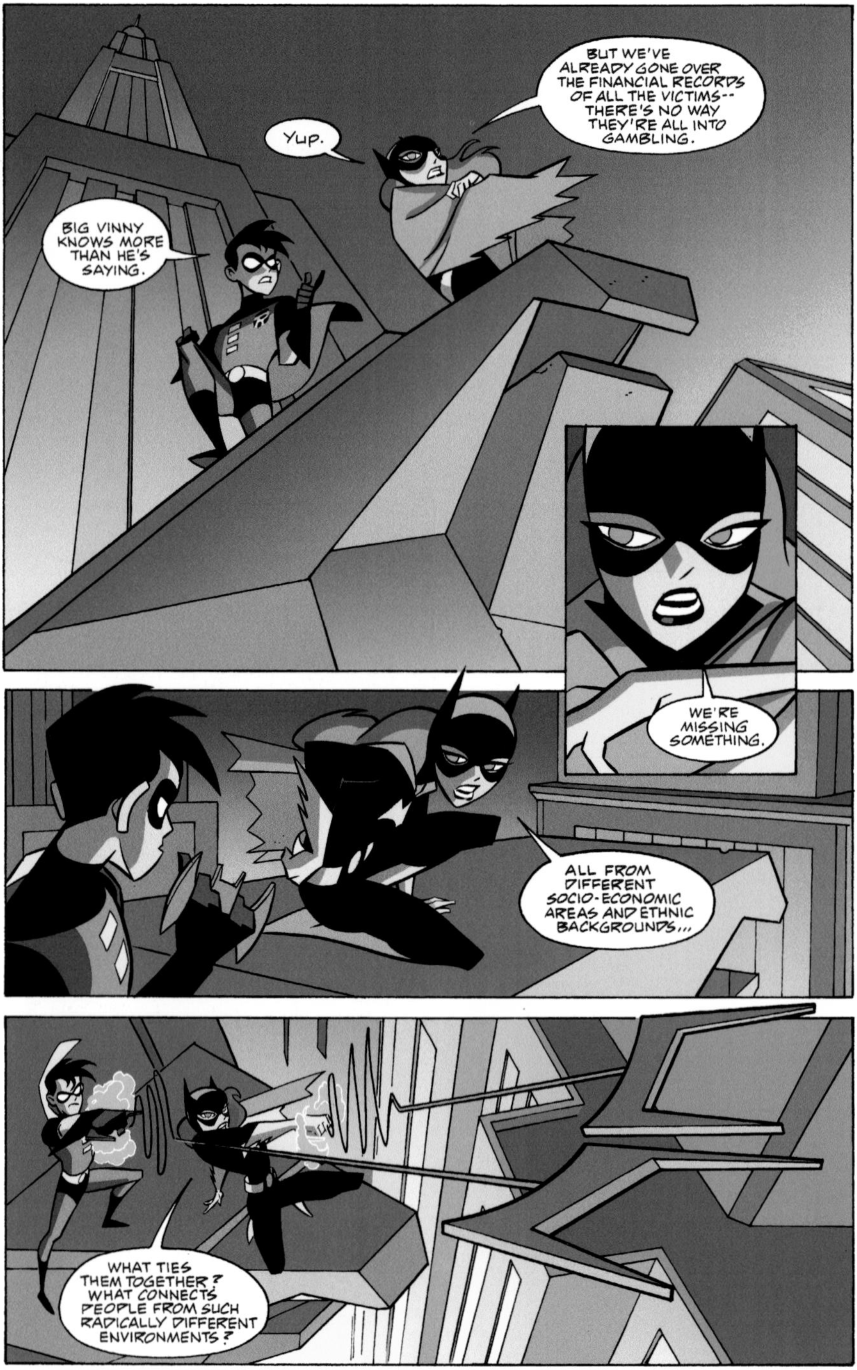
BUT WE'VE ALREADY GONE OVER THE FINANCIAL RECORDS OF ALL THE VICTIMS-- THERE'S NO WAY THEY'RE ALL INTO GAMBLING.
Yup.
BIG VINNY KNOWS MORE THAN HE'S SAYING.
WE'RE MISSING SOMETHING.
ALL FROM DIFFERENT SOCIO-ECONOMIC AREAS AND ETHNIC BACKGROUNDS...
WHAT TIES THEM TOGETHER? WHAT CONNECTS PEOPLE FROM SUCH RADICALLY DIFFERENT ENVIRONMENTS?

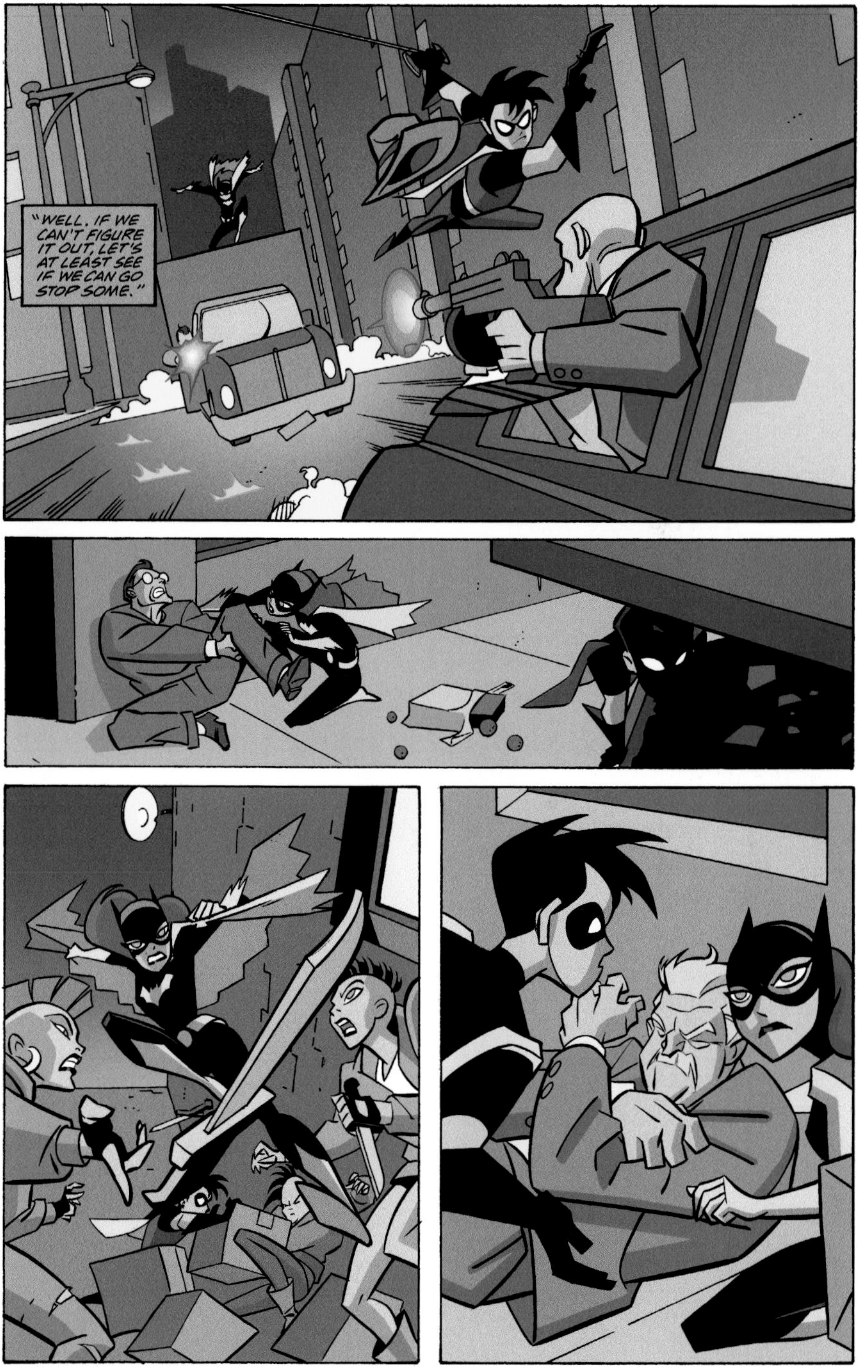
"WELL. IF WE CAN'T FIGURE IT OUT, LET'S AT LEAST SEE IF WE CAN GO STOP SOME."

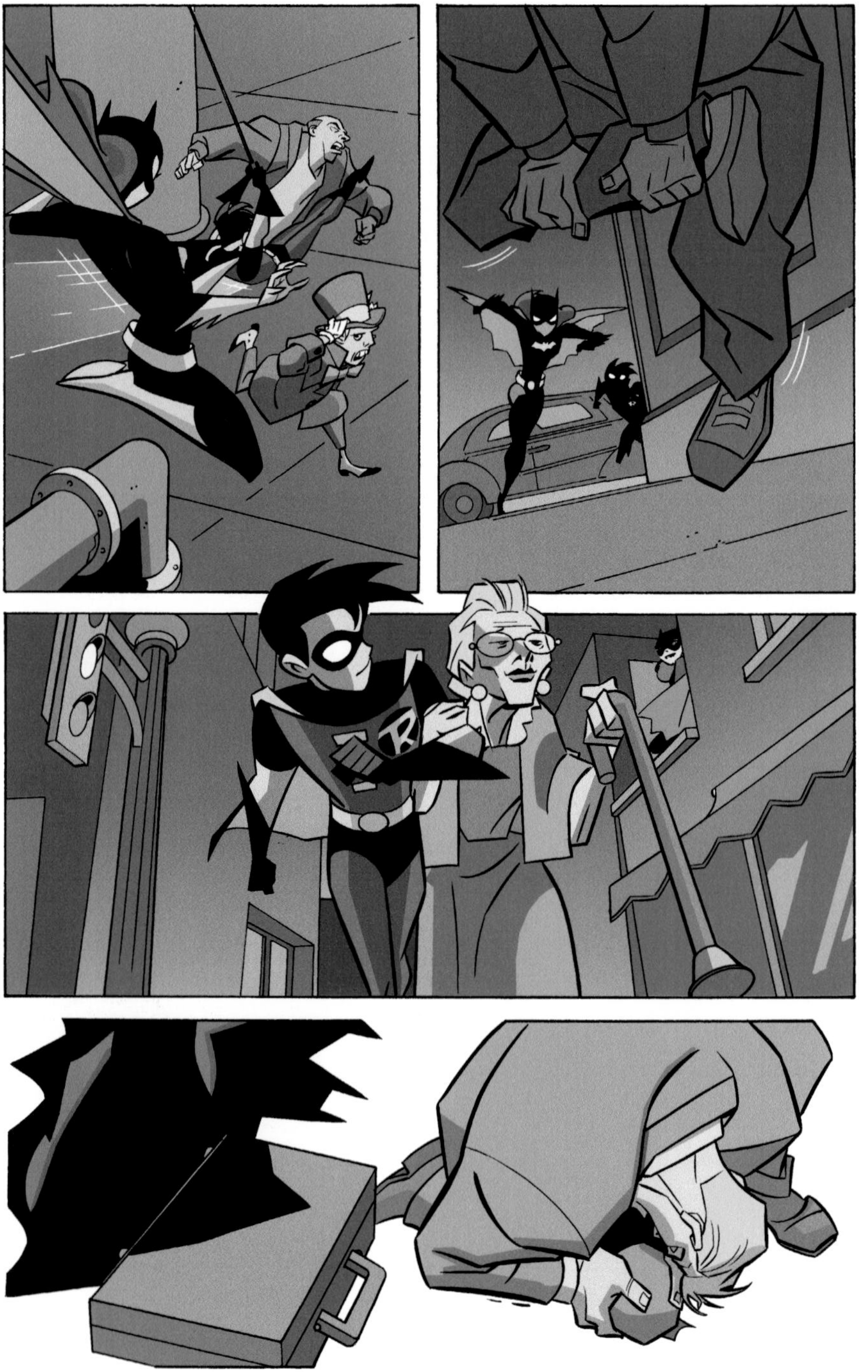

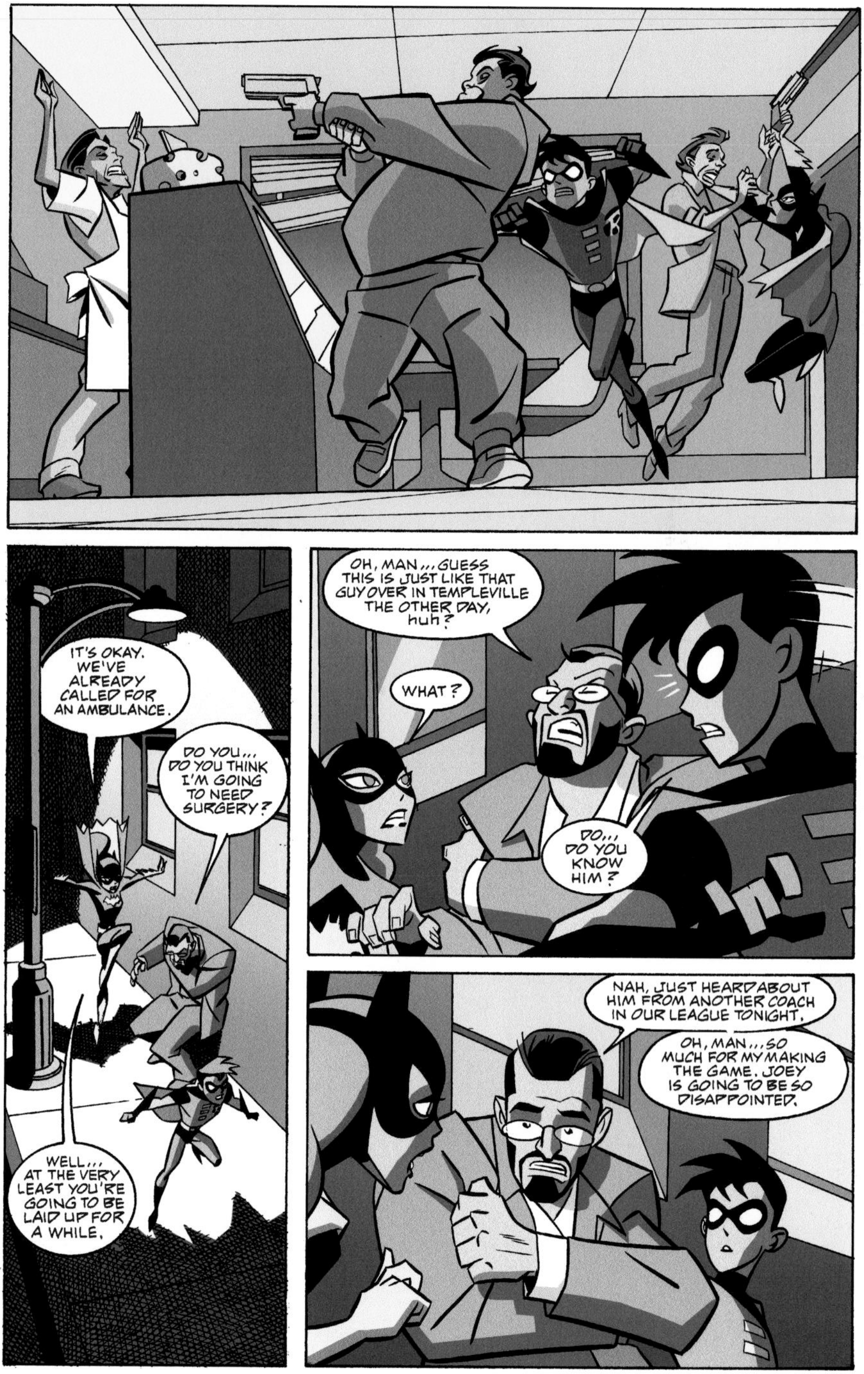
IT'S OKAY. WE'VE ALREADY CALLED FOR AN AMBULANCE.
DO YOU... DO YOU THINK I'M GOING TO NEED SURGERY?
WELL... AT THE VERY LEAST YOU'RE GOING TO BE LAID UP FOR A WHILE.
OH, MAN... GUESS THIS IS JUST LIKE THAT GUY OVER IN TEMPLEVILLE THE OTHER DAY, huh?
WHAT?
DO... DO YOU KNOW HIM?
NAH, JUST HEARD ABOUT HIM FROM ANOTHER COACH IN OUR LEAGUE TONIGHT.
OH, MAN... SO MUCH FOR MY MAKING THE GAME. JOEY IS GOING TO BE SO DISAPPOINTED.

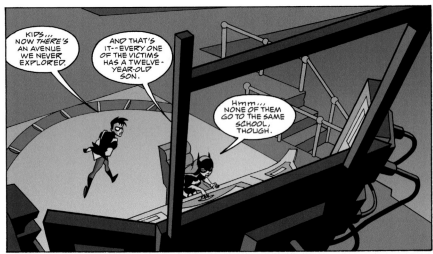

KIDS... NOW *THERE'S* AN AVENUE WE NEVER EXPLORED.

AND THAT'S IT-- EVERY ONE OF THE VICTIMS HAS A TWELVE-YEAR-OLD SON.

Hmm... NONE OF THEM GO TO THE SAME SCHOOL, THOUGH.

SO WHAT'S THE CONNECTION?

WELL... EACH OF THE SONS PLAYS HOCKEY.

AND THE VICTIMS ARE ALL COACHES.

BUT IT CAN'T BE THE SAME TEAM,

NOT EVEN CLOSE.

EACH KID PLAYS IN THE SAME LEAGUE, BUT THERE ARE SIXTEEN DIFFERENT DIVISIONS, AND EACH KID'S IN A DIFFERENT ONE.

THAT'S WHY NONE OF THE VICTIMS KNEW OF EACH OTHER, OR MADE THE CONNECTION SOONER.

THERE HASN'T BEEN MUCH PRESS AND THEY DON'T KNOW EACH OTHER THAT WELL. BESIDES, IT'S ONLY BEEN GOING ON FOR A FEW DAYS.

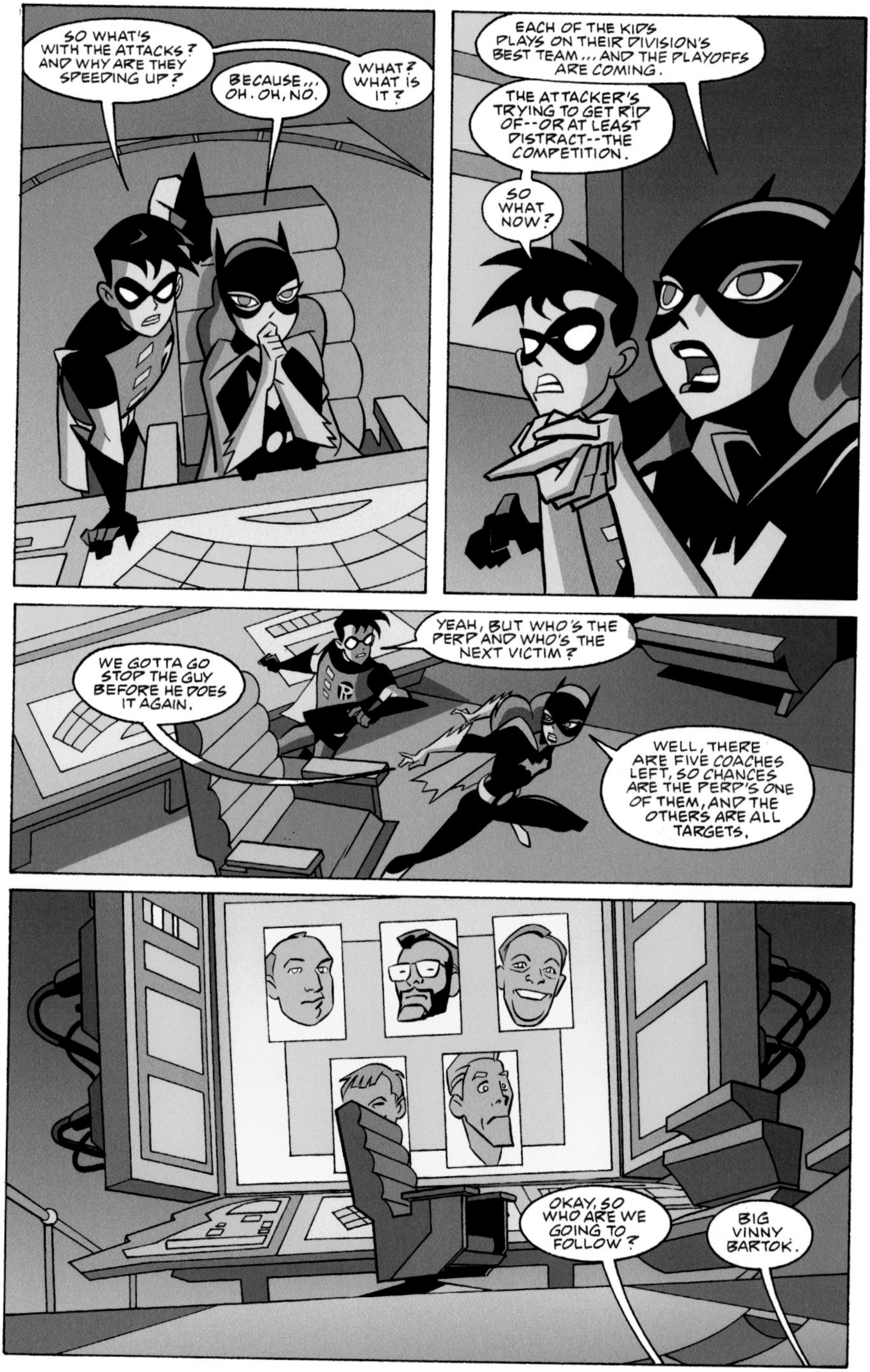

SO WHAT'S WITH THE ATTACKS? AND WHY ARE THEY SPEEDING UP?
BECAUSE... OH. OH, NO.
WHAT? WHAT IS IT?
EACH OF THE KIDS PLAYS ON THEIR DIVISION'S BEST TEAM... AND THE PLAYOFFS ARE COMING.
THE ATTACKER'S TRYING TO GET RID OF--OR AT LEAST DISTRACT--THE COMPETITION.
SO WHAT NOW?
WE GOTTA GO STOP THE GUY BEFORE HE DOES IT AGAIN.
YEAH, BUT WHO'S THE PERP AND WHO'S THE NEXT VICTIM?
WELL, THERE ARE FIVE COACHES LEFT, SO CHANCES ARE THE PERP'S ONE OF THEM, AND THE OTHERS ARE ALL TARGETS.
OKAY, SO WHO ARE WE GOING TO FOLLOW?
BIG VINNY BARTOK.

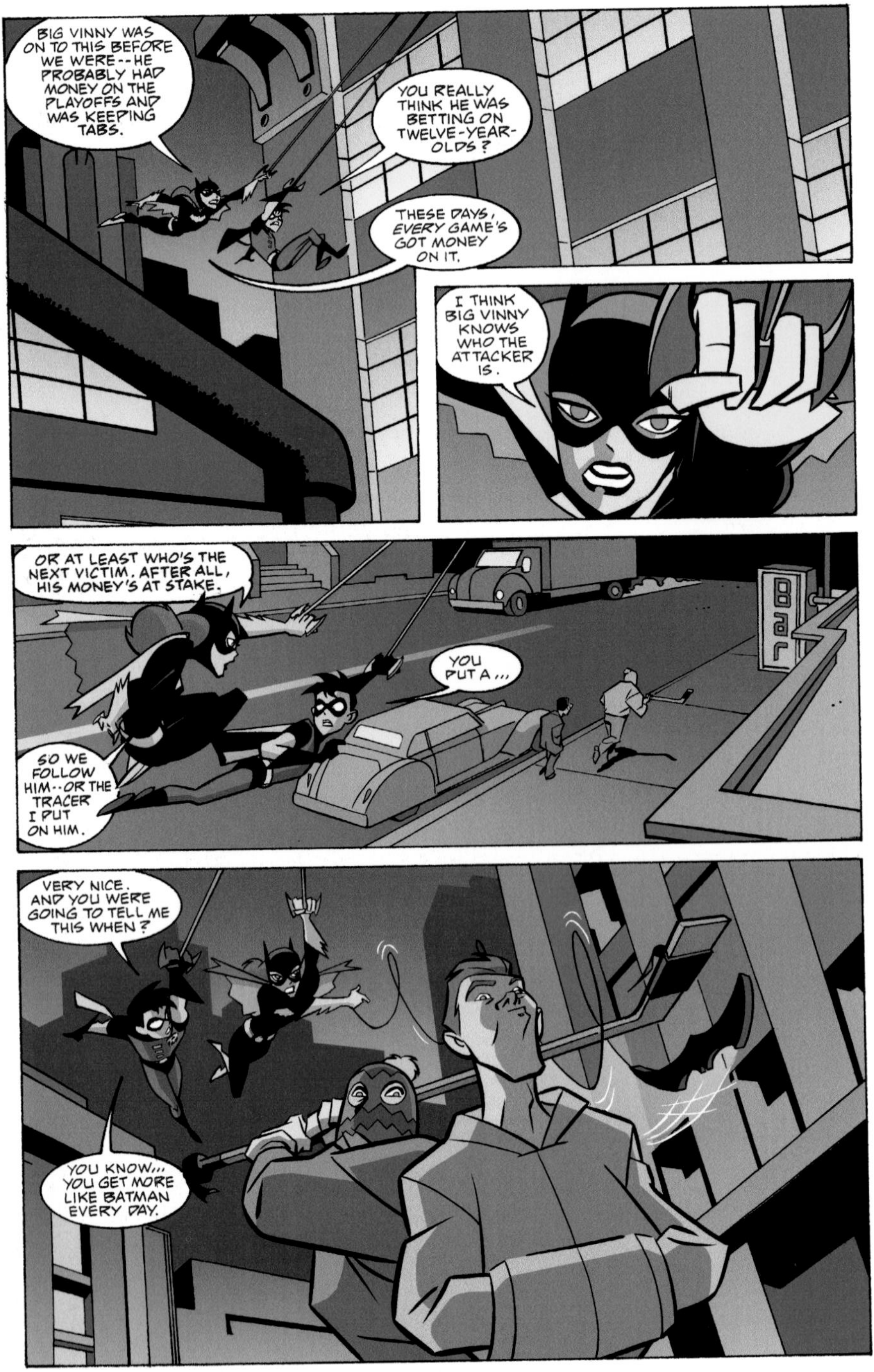
BIG VINNY WAS ON TO THIS BEFORE WE WERE--HE PROBABLY HAD MONEY ON THE PLAYOFFS AND WAS KEEPING TABS.
YOU REALLY THINK HE WAS BETTING ON TWELVE-YEAR-OLDS?
THESE DAYS, EVERY GAME'S GOT MONEY ON IT.
I THINK BIG VINNY KNOWS WHO THE ATTACKER IS.
OR AT LEAST WHO'S THE NEXT VICTIM. AFTER ALL, HIS MONEY'S AT STAKE.
YOU PUT A...
SO WE FOLLOW HIM--OR THE TRACER I PUT ON HIM.
BAR
VERY NICE. AND YOU WERE GOING TO TELL ME THIS WHEN?
YOU KNOW... YOU GET MORE LIKE BATMAN EVERY DAY.

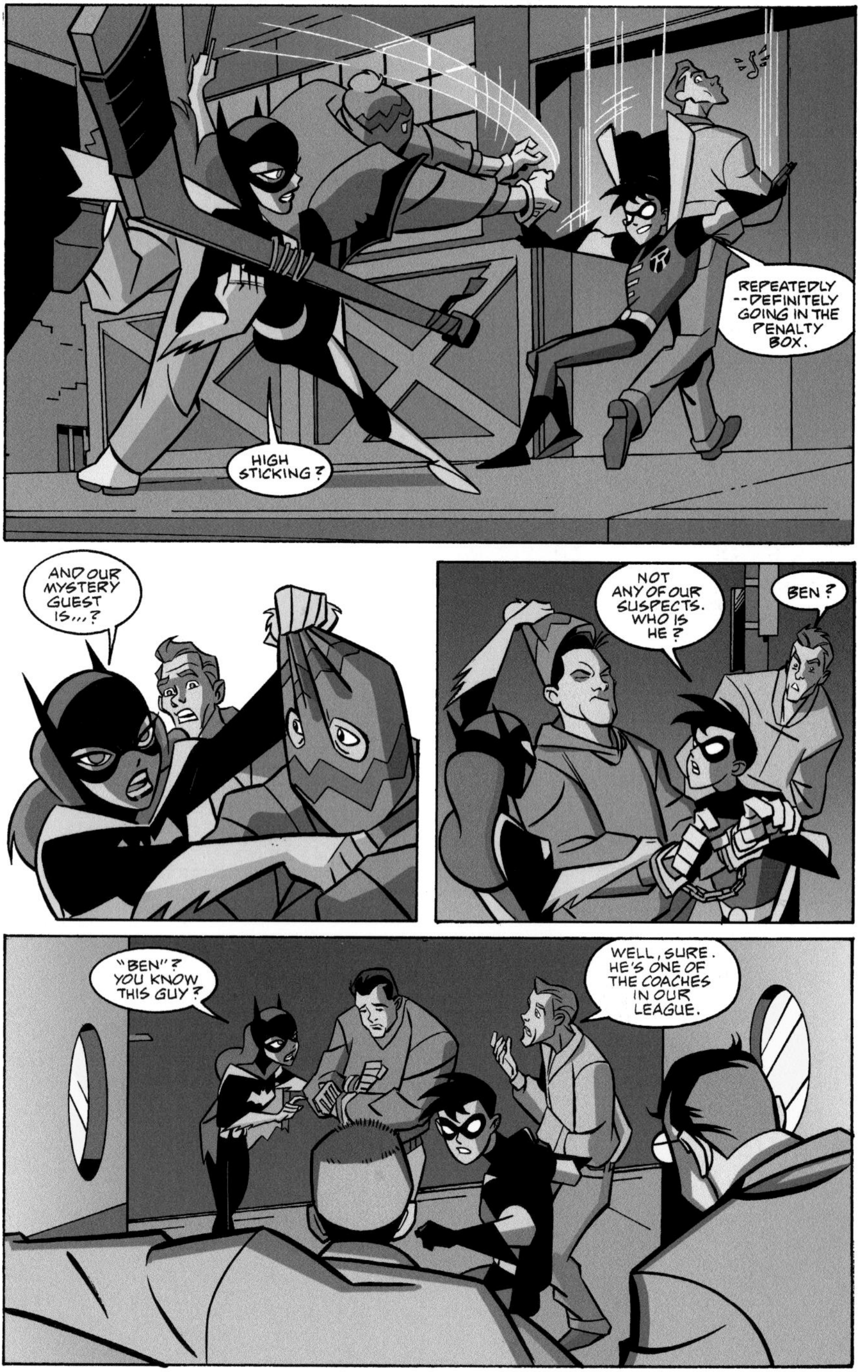
HIGH STICKING?
REPEATEDLY --DEFINITELY GOING IN THE PENALTY BOX.
AND OUR MYSTERY GUEST IS...?
NOT ANY OF OUR SUSPECTS. WHO IS HE?
BEN?
"BEN"? YOU KNOW THIS GUY?
WELL, SURE. HE'S ONE OF THE COACHES IN OUR LEAGUE.

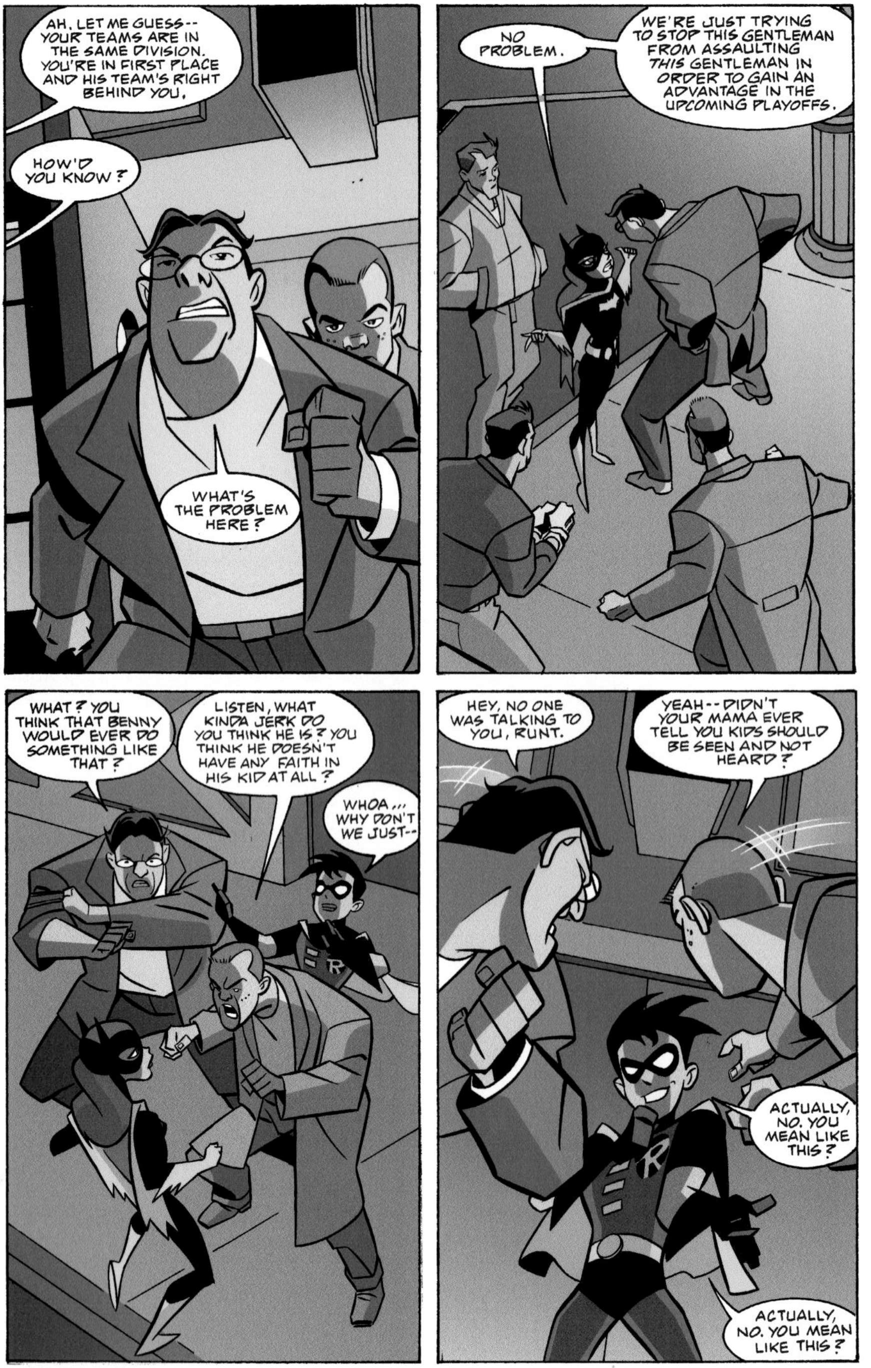
AH, LET ME GUESS-- YOUR TEAMS ARE IN THE SAME DIVISION. YOU'RE IN FIRST PLACE AND HIS TEAM'S RIGHT BEHIND YOU.
HOW'D YOU KNOW?
WHAT'S THE PROBLEM HERE?
NO PROBLEM.
WE'RE JUST TRYING TO STOP THIS GENTLEMAN FROM ASSAULTING *THIS* GENTLEMAN IN ORDER TO GAIN AN ADVANTAGE IN THE UPCOMING PLAYOFFS.
WHAT? YOU THINK THAT BENNY WOULD EVER DO SOMETHING LIKE THAT?
LISTEN, WHAT KINDA JERK DO YOU THINK HE IS? YOU THINK HE DOESN'T HAVE ANY FAITH IN HIS KID AT ALL?
WHOA... WHY DON'T WE JUST--
HEY, NO ONE WAS TALKING TO YOU, RUNT.
YEAH--DIDN'T YOUR MAMA EVER TELL YOU KIDS SHOULD BE SEEN AND NOT HEARD?
ACTUALLY, NO. YOU MEAN LIKE THIS?
ACTUALLY, NO. YOU MEAN LIKE THIS?

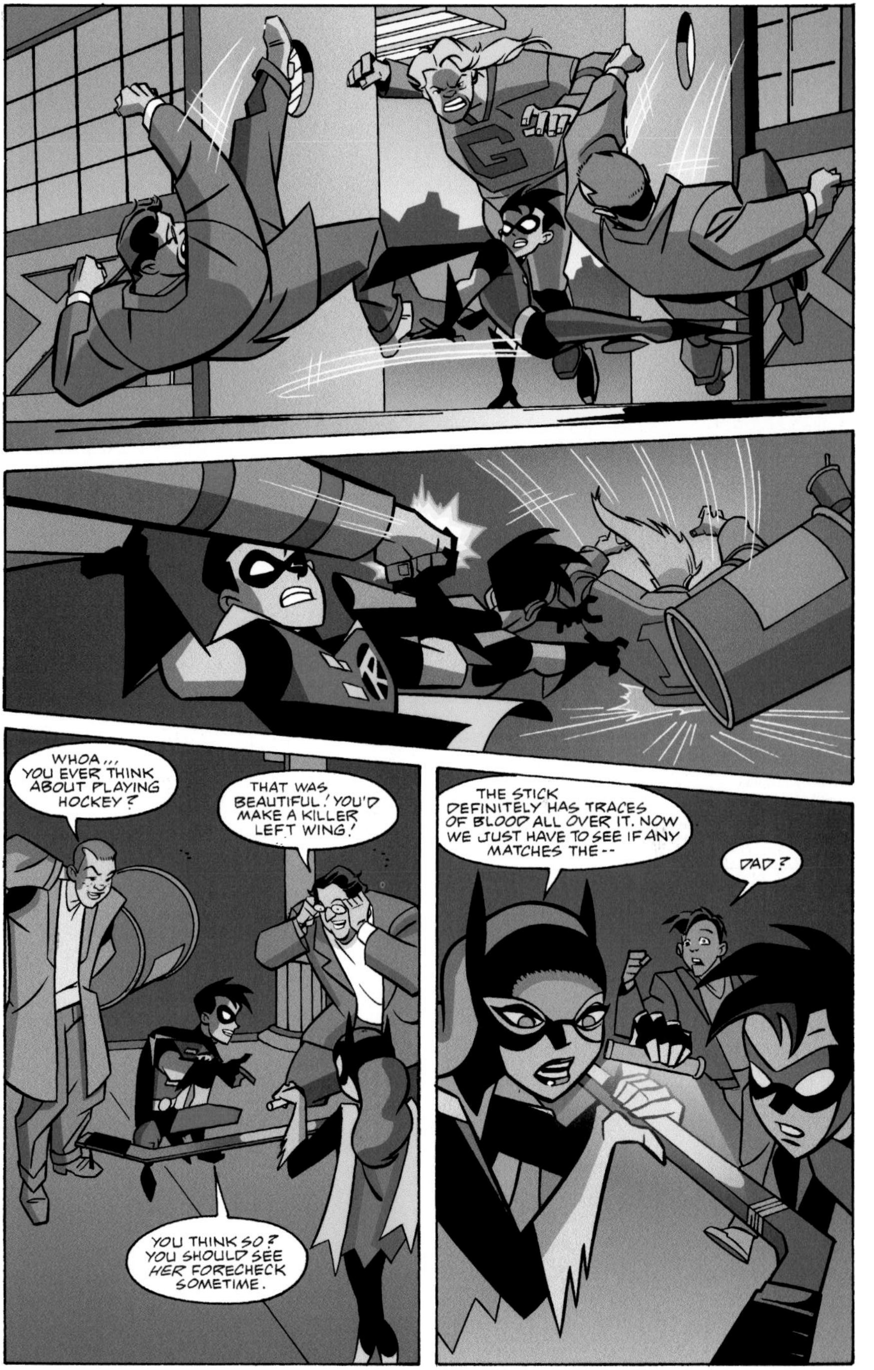
WHOA... YOU EVER THINK ABOUT PLAYING HOCKEY?
THAT WAS BEAUTIFUL! YOU'D MAKE A KILLER LEFT WING!
YOU THINK SO? YOU SHOULD SEE HER FORECHECK SOMETIME.
THE STICK DEFINITELY HAS TRACES OF BLOOD ALL OVER IT. NOW WE JUST HAVE TO SEE IF ANY MATCHES THE--
DAD?

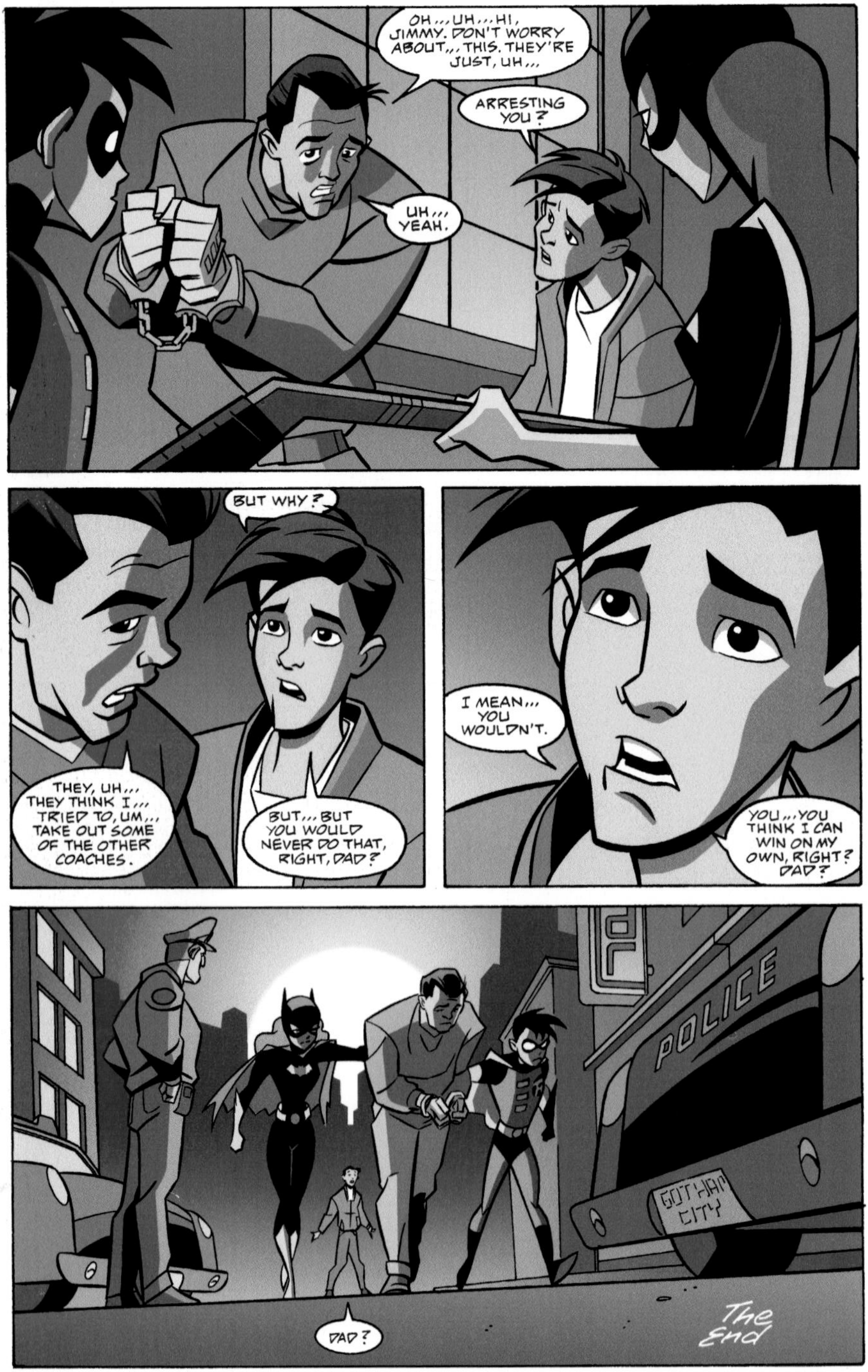
OH... UH... HI, JIMMY. DON'T WORRY ABOUT... THIS. THEY'RE JUST, UH...
ARRESTING YOU?
UH... YEAH.
BUT WHY?
THEY, UH... THEY THINK I... TRIED TO, UM... TAKE OUT SOME OF THE OTHER COACHES.
BUT... BUT YOU WOULD NEVER DO THAT, RIGHT, DAD?
I MEAN... YOU WOULDN'T.
YOU... YOU THINK I CAN WIN ON MY OWN, RIGHT? DAD?
POLICE
GOTHAM CITY
DAD?
The End

WANT MORE BATGIRL?

"The superhero book I've always wanted and needed—heartwarming, vibrantly alive, a loving portrayal of Cassandra Cain that will leave readers hungry for more."
—Marjorie Liu, *New York Times* bestselling author of *Monstress*

Shadow OF THE Batgirl™

SARAH KUHN
NICOLE GOUX

Don't miss out on another Batgirl...
Cassandra Cain, in *Shadow of the Batgirl*!
From writer SARAH KUHN and artist NICOLE GOUX comes a harrowing
of a girl who overcomes the odds to find her unique identity.

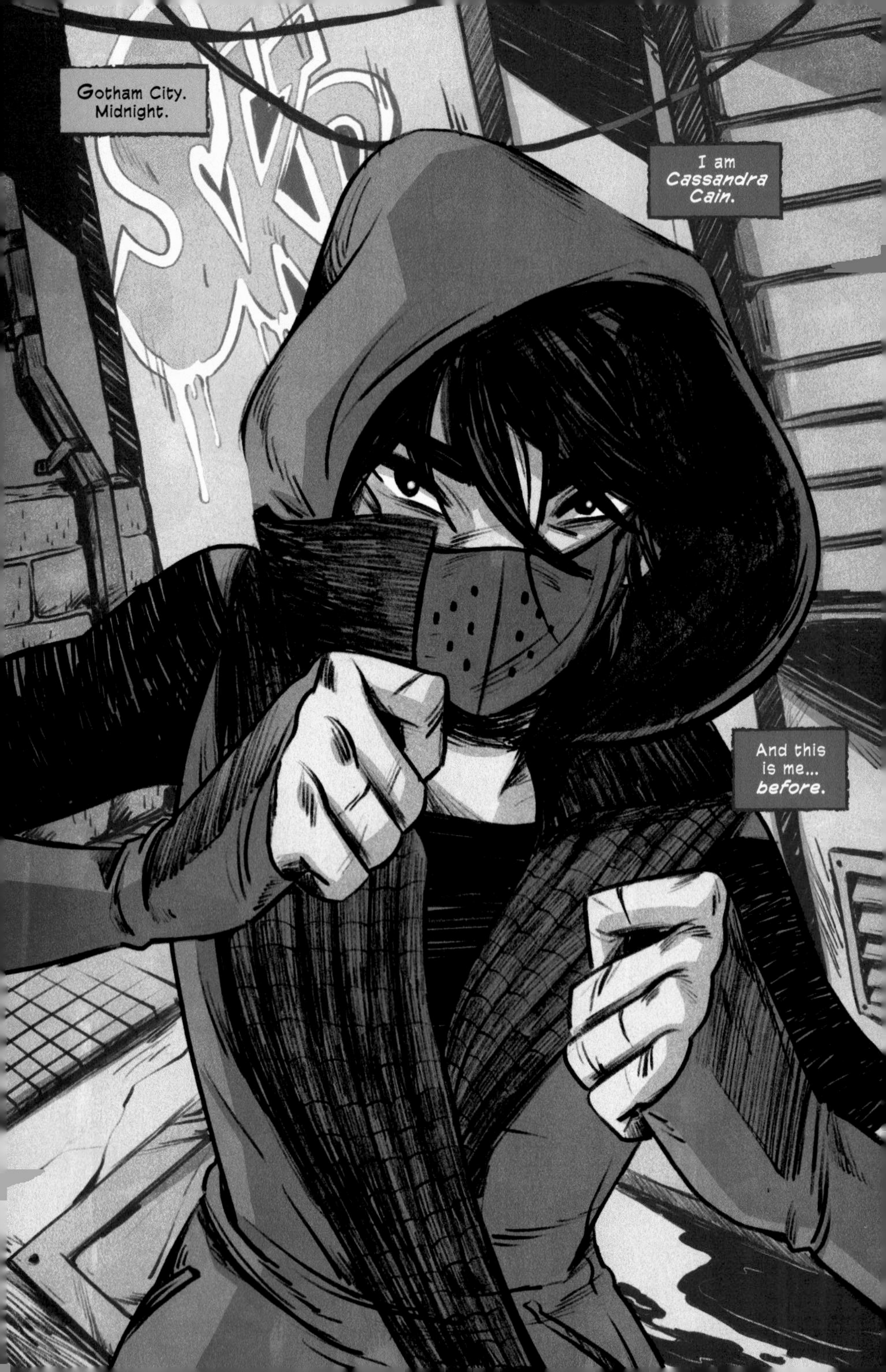
Gotham City.
Midnight.
I am *Cassandra Cain.*
And this is me... *before.*

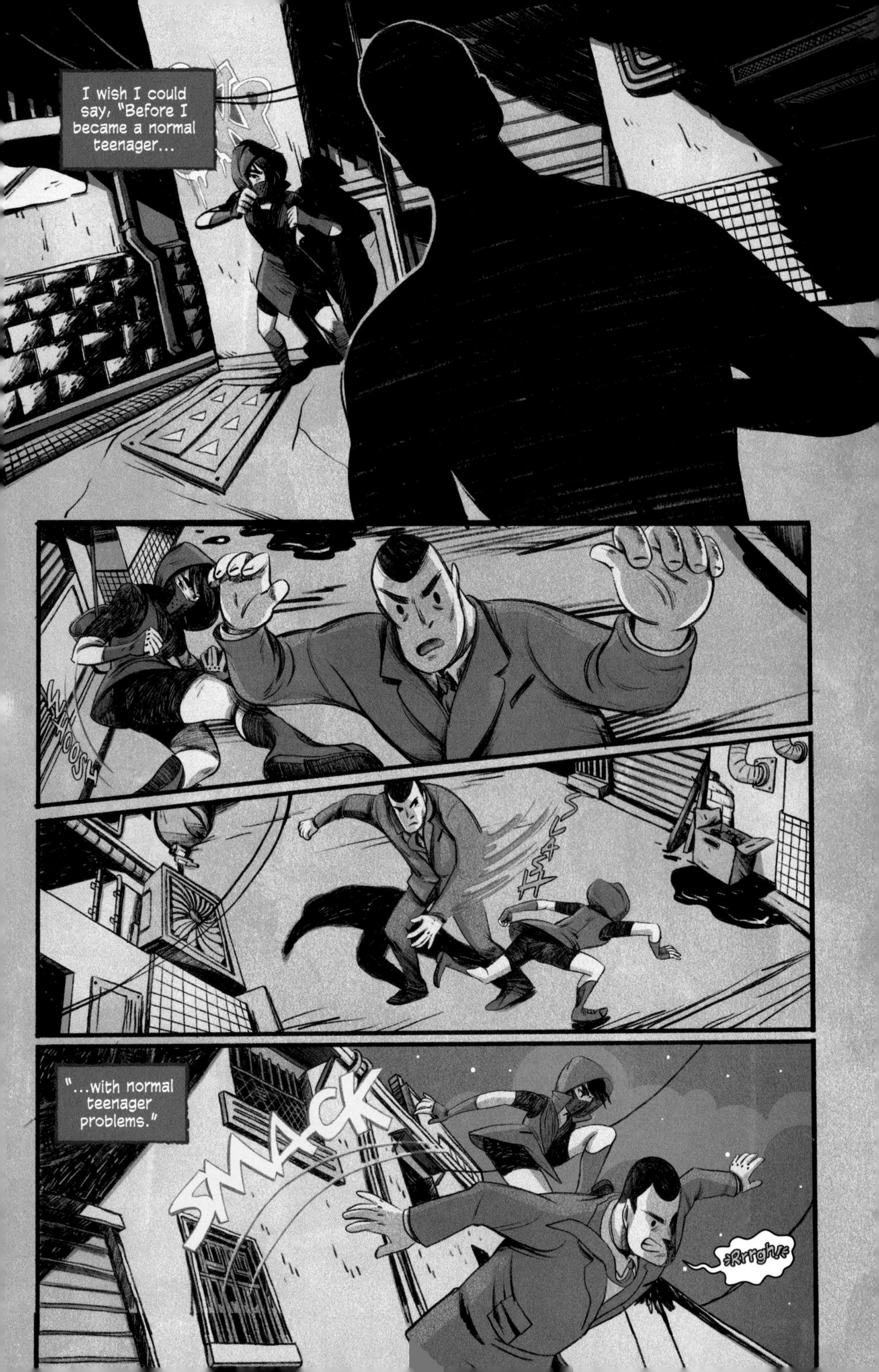
I wish I could say, "Before I became a normal teenager...
WHOOSH
SWISH
"...with normal teenager problems."
SMACK
Rrrgh!

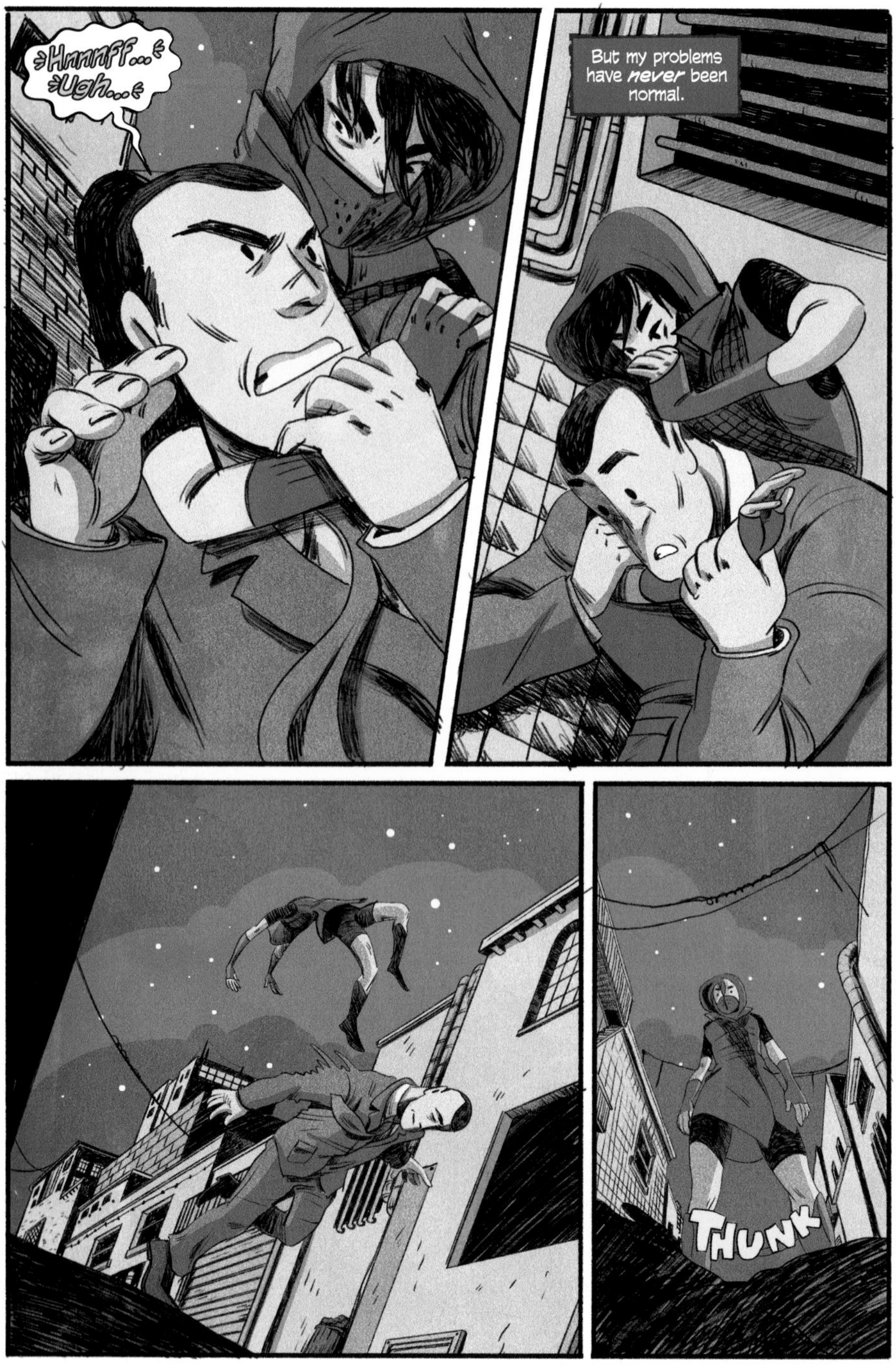
Hnnnff... Ugh...
But my problems have *never* been normal.
THUNK

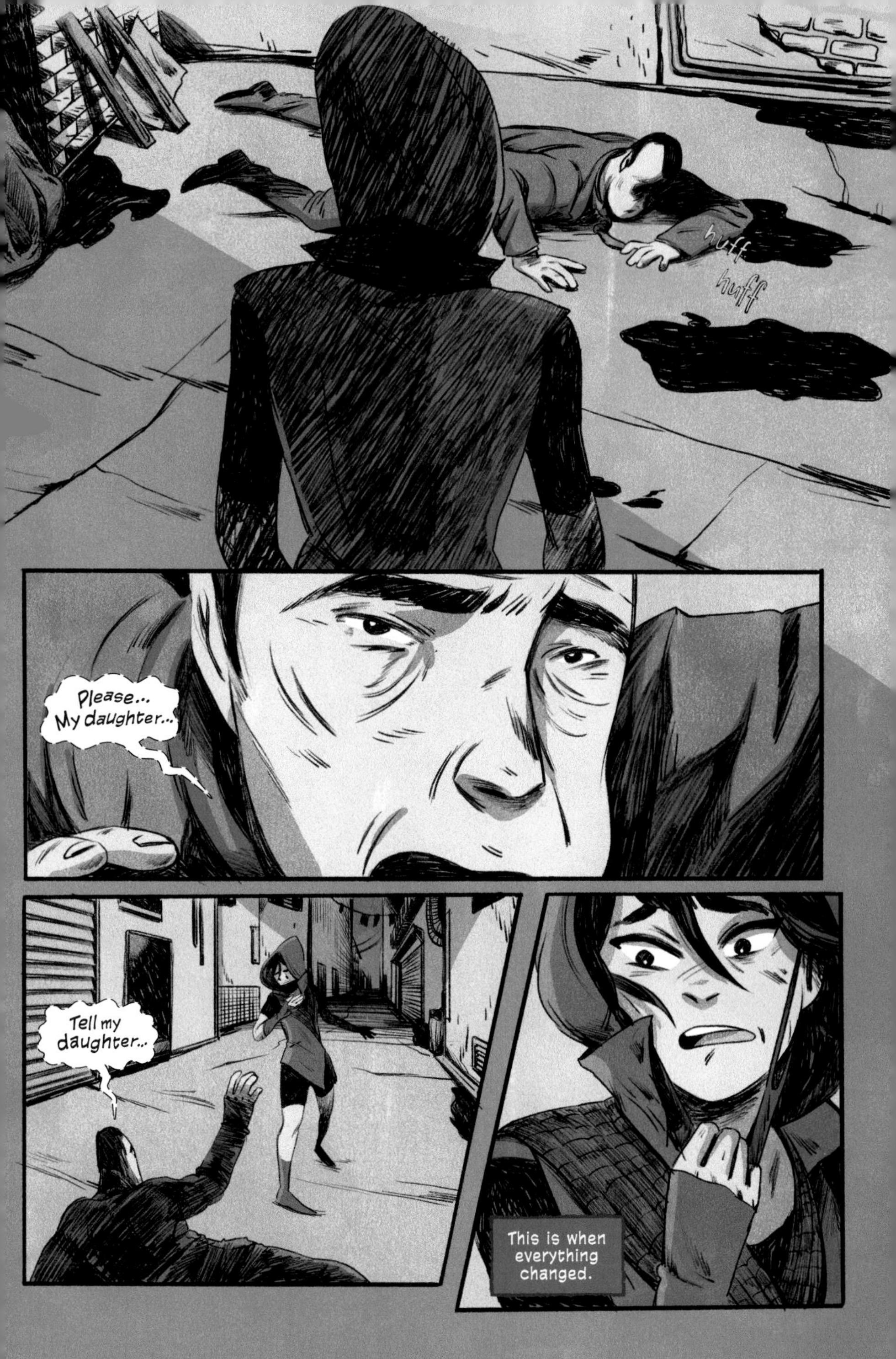
huff
huff
Please... My daughter...
Tell my daughter...
This is when everything changed.

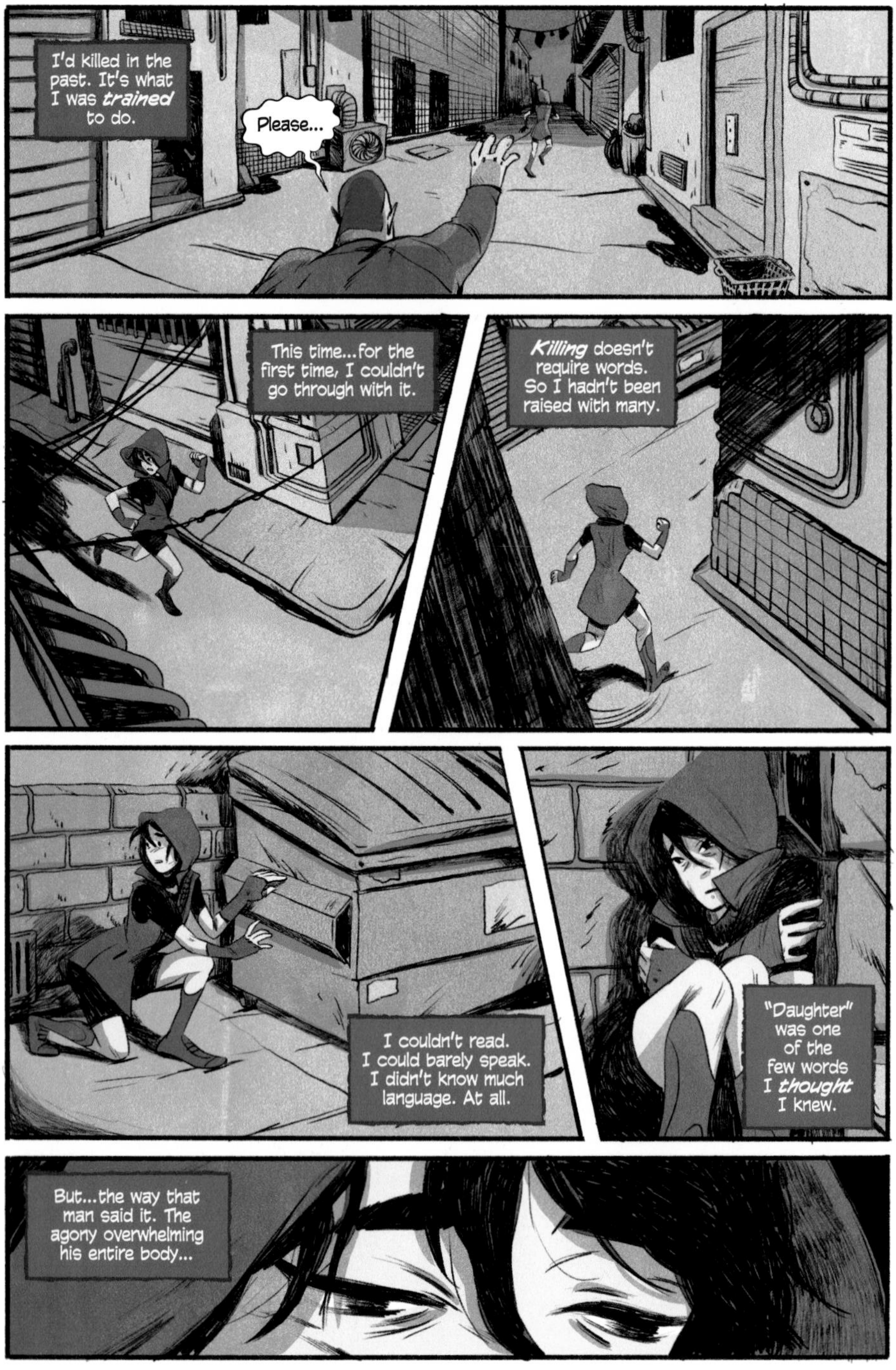
I'd killed in the past. It's what I was *trained* to do.
Please...
This time...for the first time, I couldn't go through with it.
Killing doesn't require words. So I hadn't been raised with many.
I couldn't read. I could barely speak. I didn't know much language. At all.
"Daughter" was one of the few words I *thought* I knew.
But...the way that man said it. The agony overwhelming his entire body...

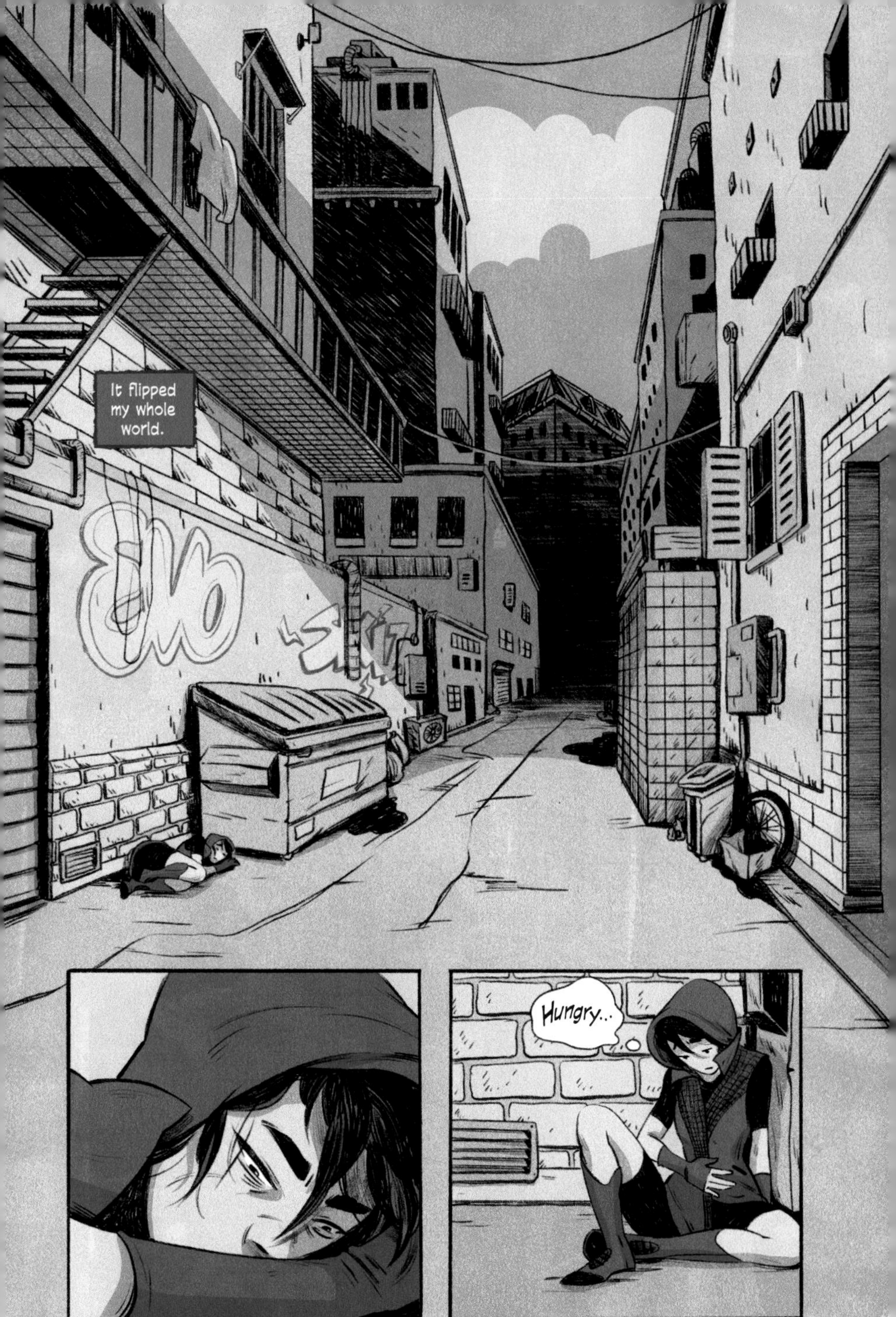
It flipped my whole world.
Hungry...

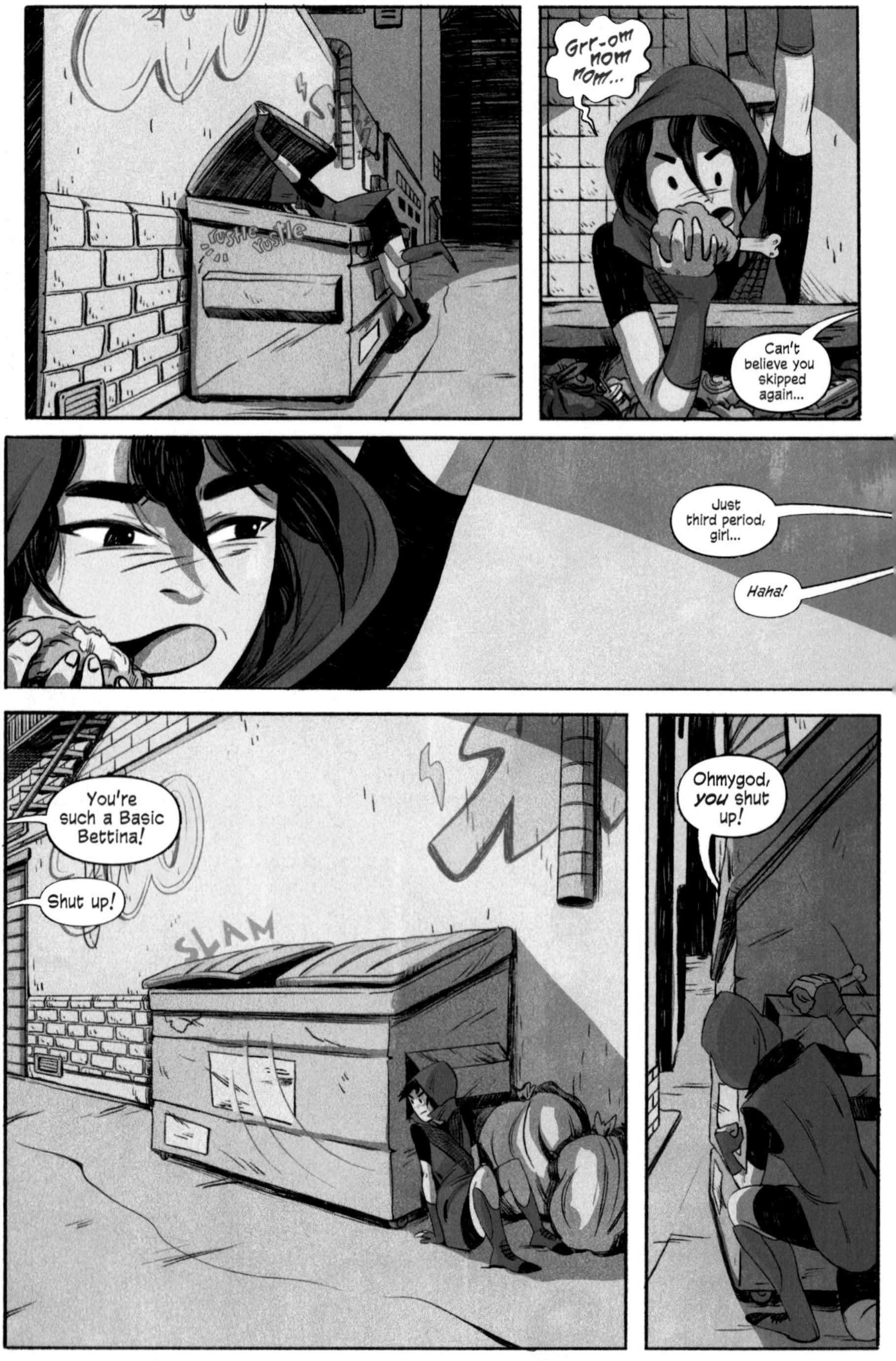
rustle rustle
Grr-om nom nom...
Can't believe you skipped again...
Just third period, girl...
Haha!
You're such a Basic Bettina!
Shut up!
SLAM
Ohmygod, *you* shut up!

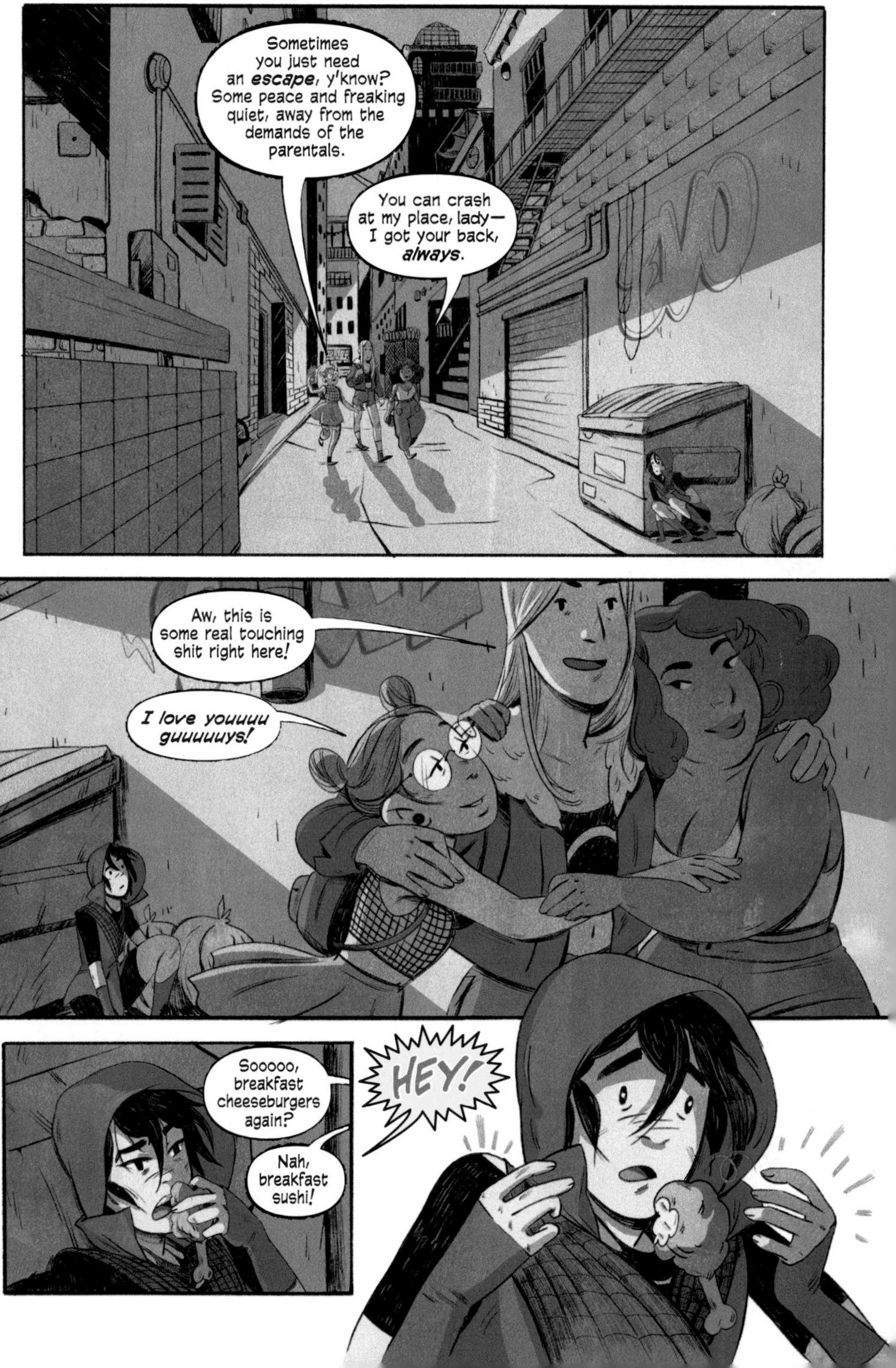

Sometimes you just need an *escape*, y'know? Some peace and freaking quiet, away from the demands of the parentals.
You can crash at my place, lady— I got your back, *always*.
Aw, this is some real touching shit right here!
I love youuuu guuuuuys!
Sooooo, breakfast cheeseburgers again?
Nah, breakfast sushi!
HEY!

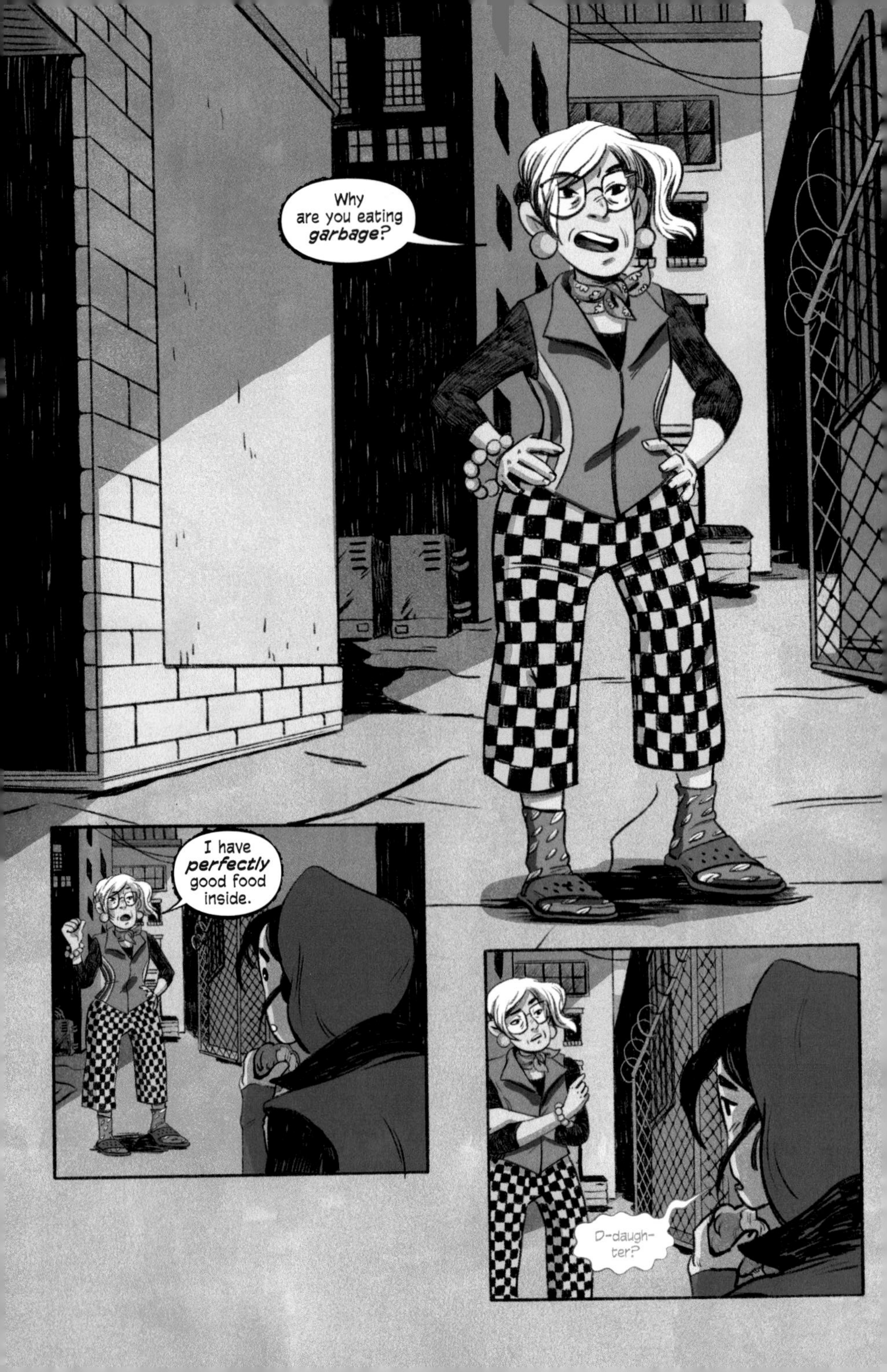
Why are you eating *garbage*?
I have *perfectly* good food inside.
D-daugh-ter?

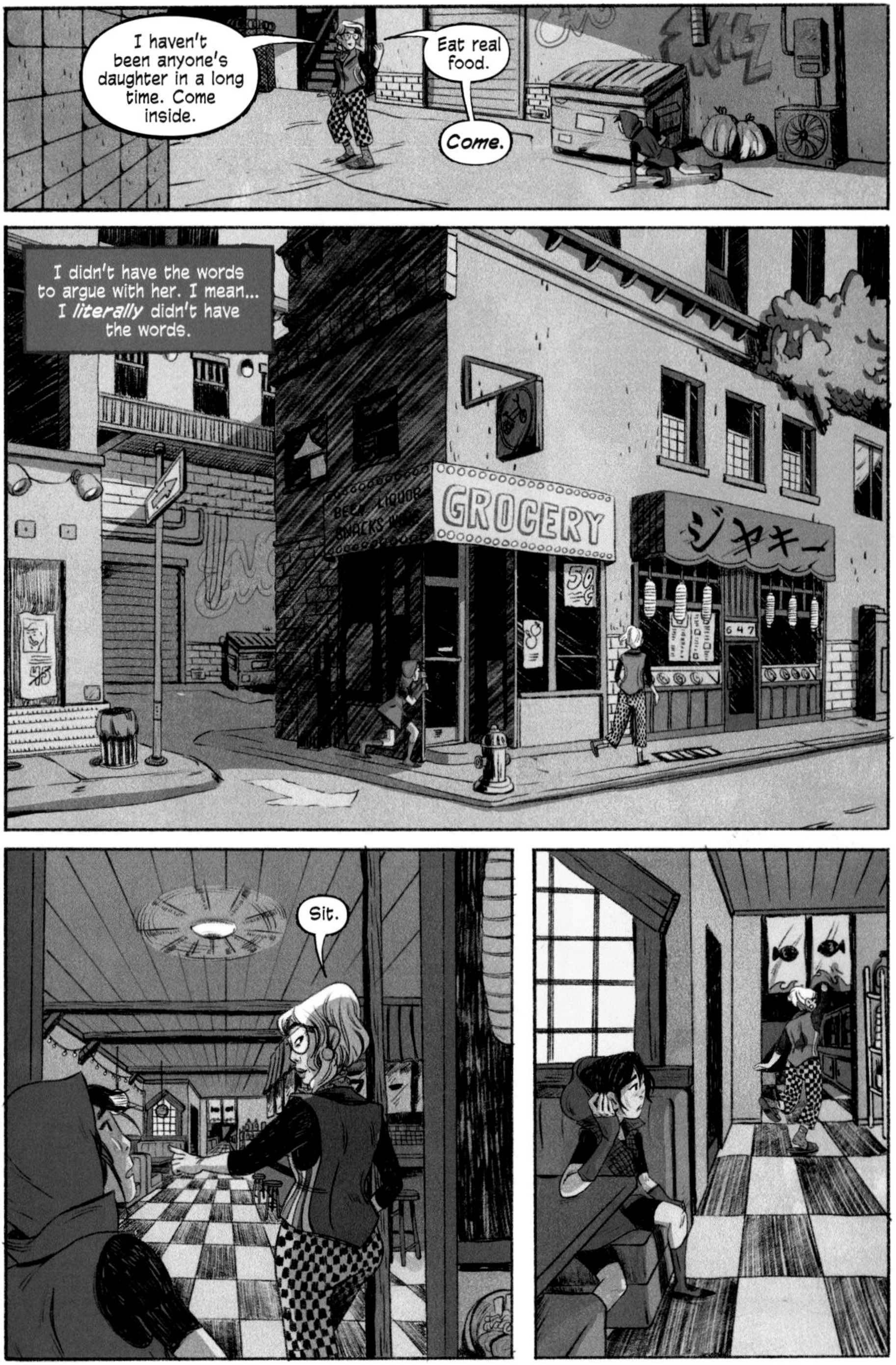

I haven't been anyone's daughter in a long time. Come inside.
Eat real food.
Come.
I didn't have the words to argue with her. I mean... I *literally* didn't have the words.
GROCERY
50¢
ジャキー
647
Sit.

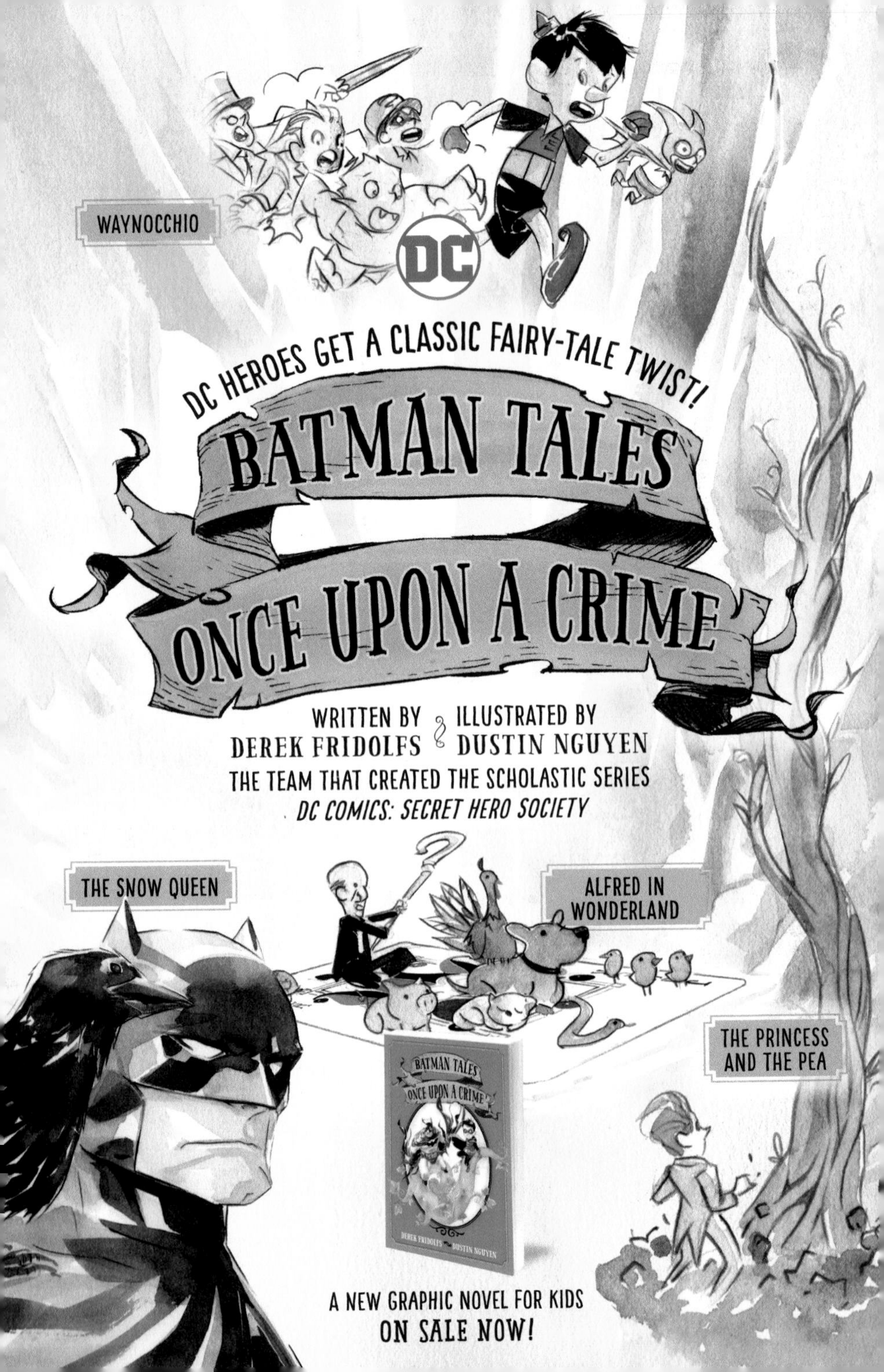
WAYNOCCHIO
DC
DC HEROES GET A CLASSIC FAIRY-TALE TWIST!
BATMAN TALES
ONCE UPON A CRIME
WRITTEN BY DEREK FRIDOLFS & ILLUSTRATED BY DUSTIN NGUYEN
THE TEAM THAT CREATED THE SCHOLASTIC SERIES
DC COMICS: SECRET HERO SOCIETY
THE SNOW QUEEN
ALFRED IN WONDERLAND
THE PRINCESS AND THE PEA
BATMAN TALES
ONCE UPON A CRIME
DEREK FRIDOLFS
DUSTIN NGUYEN
A NEW GRAPHIC NOVEL FOR KIDS
ON SALE NOW!